Teach English as a foreign language

For my mother and late father, Mary and Jim Riddell

Teach English as a foreign language

David Riddell

For UK order enquiries: please contact Bookpoint Ltd,
130 Milton Park, Abingdon, Oxon OX14 4SB.
Telephone: +44 (0) 1235 827720. *Fax:* +44 (0) 1235 400454.
Lines are open 09.00–17.00, Monday to Saturday, with a 24-hour
message answering service. Details about our titles and how to
order are available at www.teachyourself.com

For USA order enquiries: please contact McGraw-Hill Customer
Services, PO Box 545, Blacklick, OH 43004-0545, USA.
Telephone: 1-800-722-4726. *Fax:* 1-614-755-5645.

For Canada order enquiries: please contact McGraw-Hill Ryerson
Ltd, 300 Water St, Whitby, Ontario L1N 9B6, Canada.
Telephone: 905 430 5000. *Fax:* 905 430 5020.

Long renowned as the authoritative source for self-guided
learning – with more than 50 million copies sold worldwide –
the *Teach Yourself* series includes over 500 titles in the fields of
languages, crafts, hobbies, business, computing and education.

British Library Cataloguing in Publication Data: a catalogue record
for this title is available from the British Library.

Library of Congress Catalog Card Number: on file.

**First published in UK 2001 as Teach Yourself: *Teach English as
a Foreign Language* by Hodder Education**, part of Hachette UK,
338 Euston Road, London NW1 3BH.

First published in US 2001 by The McGraw-Hill Companies, Inc.

This edition published 2010.

The *Teach Yourself* name is a registered trade mark of
Hodder Headline.

Typeset by MPS Limited, A Macmillan Company.

Printed in Great Britain for Hodder Education, a Hachette UK
Company, 338 Euston Road, London NW1 3BH
by CPI Group (UK) Ltd., Croydon, CR0 4YY.

The publisher has used its best endeavours to ensure that the URLs
for external websites referred to in this book are correct and active
at the time of going to press. However, the publisher and the author
have no responsibility for the websites and can make no guarantee
that a site will remain live or that the content will remain relevant,
decent or appropriate.

Hachette UK's policy is to use papers that are natural, renewable
and recyclable and made from wood grown in sustainable
forests. The logging and manufacturing processes are expected to
conform to the environmental regulations of the country of origin.

Impression number	10 9 8 7 6 5
Year	2014 2013 2012

Contents

Acknowledgements

I would like to thank:

Jeff Mohamed and John Shepheard, for many years of personal and professional inspiration. And to Jeff and his wife Deanne for being the perfect employers in the perfect city of San Francisco!

Sue Hart, my Editor at Hodder, for her consistent support and encouragement, and for giving me the opportunity to write this book.

Meet the author

I grew up wanting to be a DJ, and I particularly wanted to have the breakfast show on Radio 1! Well, such are childhood dreams! Instead I ended up teaching English, and training others to do the same – not quite the same thing, but it is a job that has never been dull, and never been predictable.

I have met wonderful students from around the world in my classrooms, several of whom have become long-lasting and close friends. I have had some fantastic colleagues. I have worked in some great schools.

Of course, it's not all good! You never get rich teaching English, and some students can try your patience (and some colleagues, too!). But I have had so many happy times teaching, learnt so much from my students about different cultures, and seen so many success stories. At its best, it's a great job; full of variety and unpredictability.

And it has been so satisfying to train so many others to teach over the years. And this book is part of that process ... a chance for me to share some of the things that I believe help people to be good teachers, based on over 25 years' teaching experience. I hope it helps! But if a radio station comes calling for me ...

Only got a minute?

You may want to teach English as a Foreign Language as a career, often because you want to live and work abroad or perhaps you plan to travel and simply want to pick up some teaching work along the way.

You'll need to be a native English speaker or have a very high level of English in order to teach the language. Many people attend a TEFL training course which equips future teachers with a better understanding of the English language and how to teach it – the methodology. Standard intensive training courses are usually four weeks long and will include teaching practice to 'real' students. If you complete the course successfully you will receive a certificate that will then be your 'passport' to future work.

Not all teachers, however, attend this kind of course: some may do shorter, 'taster' courses or complete online courses, or not do any kind of course at all. And not all language schools require a certificate, though for many, especially schools in popular European destinations such as Spain or Italy, it is essential.

When you teach English as a foreign language you will teach vocabulary, pronunciation and grammar. You will also cover the four key skills which are Reading, Writing, Listening and Speaking. You will probably use course material which generally includes a Student's Book, a Workbook and a Teacher's Guide, as well as other audio and visual material. You may create your own resources too, or find others online.

The course material you use will help you teach the language and plan your lessons, but it is important to consider your students. Are you teaching one-to-one, small or large groups? How old are your students? What are their interests? What do they like doing or talking about? As your experience as a teacher grows you will adapt your lessons, and the materials you use, to suit your students.

Whatever the reasons for your interest in Teach English as a Foreign Language, you will find this book is packed full of useful information about methodology, class management and lesson planning; everything you need to develop your skills as a TEFL teacher.

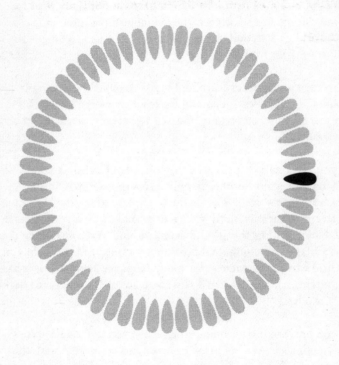

5 Only got five minutes?

English is a 'global' language, and is the most commonly used language of international business, science and technology. It is often referred to as the modern lingua franca, a language that is used for communication by people who do not share the same mother tongue. As such it is the language most often taught around the world as a second/foreign language, and its teaching is the subject matter of this book.

The huge demand for learning English around the world obviously results in a significant demand for teachers of English. But how do you become, or prepare yourself to become, a teacher of this language?

If you are a native speaker of English, then English is your first language or your 'mother tongue'. This in itself may mean you can teach English – you know instinctively *how* to speak the language correctly – but it is rarely sufficient to make you a good teacher of the language. For this it is advisable to undertake a training course and obtain a teaching qualification. Not only will this help you to find work as a teacher (for many language schools it is a basic requirement), but it will also give you an excellent base to develop as a teacher.

If you are looking for a teaching course you will come across a sometimes confusing array of acronyms connected with the profession. TEFL is the term for Teaching English as a Foreign Language and you will be looking for a TEFL course and a TEFL qualification. The terms EFL (English as Foreign Language) or ESL (English as a Second Language) are also commonly used but you will also come across ESOL (English for Speakers of Other Languages). To obtain a recognized qualification you will usually attend an intensive, four-week course that will include plenty of teaching practice. You will also learn a great deal about methodology (how to teach English) as well as classroom management and lesson planning.

Who you are teaching is an important consideration once you start teaching (with or without a teaching qualification). And this will probably depend on *where* you are teaching. Do you plan to travel and teach abroad? Or will you be teaching in an English-speaking country (the UK, the US, etc.), to students who have travelled there to learn? In the first case, you will be teaching *monolingual* groups: they share a common first language or mother tongue, Italian, for example, if you are teaching in Italy. In the second case you will be teaching *multilingual* groups. Your students will come from a variety of different countries and they will not share a common language (or culture).

In both of these situations it is most likely that you will be teaching adult learners (16+) (though you may find yourself teaching young learners, too). However, the age range of your students, the size of the group and their range of interests will vary dramatically. Part of your role as a teacher will include tailoring your lessons to reflect the age and interests of your students, although this is something that experience will teach you rather than a course or a book.

There is no single, 'correct' way to teach English as a foreign language, but there are many generally accepted methods and precepts. One of these is speaking only English with your students rather than their mother tongue (known in the profession as 'L1'.). Sometimes the use of L1 may be useful, to give a quick translation for example, especially for students at lower levels. However, it is best to be avoided on a regular basis and students themselves will expect you, as the teacher, to give your lesson in English. It is also important to encourage students to speak amongst themselves in English, though this is more difficult for monolingual groups, who will inevitably resort to speaking to each other in their mother tongue. For multilingual groups this will be more achievable; English is genuinely their *lingua franca* in the classroom.

Students have other expectations of their teachers, and your manner in the classroom is important to them. Every teacher's style and personality is different, but generally they will expect you to be encouraging, supportive and friendly. They would like the lessons to be interesting (and fun!). They expect you to know your subject well, but also to know them and show an interest in them, their likes and dislikes, their culture. The right classroom manner can really make a difference to learners.

Once you are in the classroom, what exactly will you be teaching, and how? What you teach depends on the level of the group you are teaching. You will likely be using course material, with a Student's Book, Workbook and Teacher's Guide. Published material is invaluable; it will guide your students through the language in a logical and progressive manner. However, because each teacher and each group are different, you will also rely on other materials, such as online resources or, indeed, your own resources.

Teaching a language can be roughly described as teaching vocabulary (words for things, concepts and actions) and grammar (how these words are put together to make meaningful units of communication). This book focuses on both of these areas, as well as pronunciation and the four skills (Reading, Writing, Listening and Speaking). In your course materials the language will usually be presented through a topic. An example may be the topic of 'shopping'. Your vocabulary component could include food – *to buy, apple, tomato, lettuce* – and your grammar could include *I would like to buy apple and tomatoes*. This brings us to a very important point: context. An important part of EFL methodology is teaching the language within a context. We cannot say what *would* means on its own; it is meaningless. It needs to be part of a sentence and that sentence needs a context. Who is speaking? What is the situation and what is the purpose of the conversation? Context helps students understand the language and engage with it.

We often teach English through a text: this can be a written text (a story, a newspaper article, etc.) or a recorded text (a news bulletin, a conversation in a shop, etc.) and this leads us to what are known as the four skills: Reading, Writing, Listening and Speaking. Reading and Listening are known as 'receptive' skills (students receive and understand the language). Writing and speaking are 'productive' skills (the student needs to produce the language). This books looks at each skill in detail.

Planning your lesson is extremely important and teachers need to have clear aims. It is also important to think from the students' point of view when considering your aims. What will they learn or practise in the lesson? Within a lesson you will plan different stages and will cover a variety of tasks, from board work and written tasks to listening and role plays. You will ideally have one main aim and other secondary aims when you plan your lesson. Writing a lesson plan is an extremely useful process and is also an important part of most training courses.

If you are starting, or planning to start, your teaching career, this book is full of practical help and tips. It will guide you through the key areas of teaching techniques, classroom management and lesson planning. You will also find useful sections on job hunting and career development. Teaching English can be an exciting and very rewarding experience and you'll find all you need here to prepare yourself for your future career.

10 Only got ten minutes?

English is spoken as a first language by over 350 million people, with the largest populations of speakers in the United States and the United Kingdom. However, it is as a second language that English becomes the most popular language of choice for many learners. This is due to the global nature of the language. It is used universally as the international language of business, science and technology. Knowledge of English is often a requirement in many occupations, such as medicine and computing. The demand, therefore, to learn English, and the need for English teachers, is high.

Many teachers of English are native speakers. English is their first language, their mother tongue, and they are therefore equipped with an instinctive knowledge of their subject. However, knowledge of a subject does not necessarily make a person a good teacher of that subject, and this is also true of English. Although there are teachers who haven't attained a qualification, and some may teach very well, a teaching qualification is essential to equip you with the knowledge and techniques you'll need to be a good – and successful – teacher. (If you are currently on a teacher training course, you will find that this book complements your course content.)

There is a wide range of courses and qualifications on offer for trainee teachers. The three internationally recognized qualifications are the Cambridge CELTA, the Trinity Certificate, TESOL and the SIT TESOL. The first two are awarded by Cambridge University and Trinity College, London, respectively, and the latter by the SIT Graduate Institute, Vermont, USA. The courses to obtain these certificates are usually intensive 4-week courses with at least 6 hours of teaching practice. You can attend these courses at centres around the world and many trainee teachers do choose to travel abroad for them, perhaps to the country where they would like to teach. The advantage of these particular qualifications is that they are often a stated requirement of many language centres for applying for jobs.

The acronyms associated with the world of English language teaching (ELT) can be confusing. TEFL refers to Teaching English as a Foreign Language, TESL means Teaching English as a Second Language and TESOL is Teaching English to Speakers of Other Languages. The latter two terms are more widely used in the USA, but you will probably come across all of them at some point.

Many teachers choose to teach English abroad, in a Language Centre, but there is also a great demand for teaching English in English-speaking countries such as the UK, the USA, Australia, Ireland, etc. Students may travel to that country to learn, or they may live there and study. Where you teach will be an important factor in the kinds of groups you will encounter and the needs of learners will differ accordingly. If you are teaching abroad you will teach monolingual groups who share the same mother tongue and, broadly speaking, culture. If you teach in an English-speaking country, your groups will be multilingual. The students will speak a variety of languages as their mother tongue and they will not share the same culture.

Your students will generally be adult learners (16+) (though you may find that you are required to teach younger learners, too). Some students will be attending the English course to complement their school or university studies. Other will be learning English for their own personal interests, as a hobby or to help them in their jobs. Some students are looking specifically for Business English, and may be financed by their companies to study. Or they may wish to take recognized English Language exams, such as the Cambridge First Certificate of English. If you are teaching in an English-speaking country you may find there is a bigger demand for intensive courses, with daily rather than weekly attendance.

Where and who you teach are important factors, but if you are about to embark on a teaching career, your current concern is probably how does a teacher teach English? Like many things, there is no single right way to teach the language, but is it accepted that immersing students in the language and teaching through context is essential. This book starts with a chapter on being a student and that is an important consideration. What do students expect from you as a teacher? How do they want to be taught? Some students enjoy English being explained to them, with lots of rules and practice exercises. Others prefer to just communicate, and would rather not have books or pens and paper. Every student has a different way of learning, and somewhere between these two extremes is the course to steer as a teacher. However, generally speaking, most students will prefer and see the advantage of a more communicative approach when it comes to learning a language.

It is generally accepted that it is important to speak English at all times to your students. If you are working abroad you may learn, or already speak, the students' mother tongue. This is referred to as L1, and using L1 in the classroom can be useful on occasions. However, it is best to be avoided if our aim is to immerse students in the language. This is particularly true of students learning in non-English-speaking countries, as they won't have the same opportunities to practise their English outside the classroom.

Many trainee or newly qualified teachers feel daunted by the question of 'grammar' and how to teach it. The example given in this book discusses 'should'. A key point is that if we want to cover certain language or structures in a lesson, we must first give a context. Without a context 'should' is meaningless. The context in this book is based on the sentence *You should wear a suit*. Immediately the language has more meaning and this meaning can be built up through situational presentations and texts or recordings.

As well as giving context we need to consider the three things that students need to know when learning new language: the meaning, the pronunciation and the form. As a teacher you need to ensure of course that your students understand the meaning in a given context, but also how to pronounce the language and how to write it (the form).

This is often referred to as MPF. Once students have covered these three elements they then need to use and practise the language.

When teaching new vocabulary the meaning of new words can be conveyed in a variety of ways and, although dictionaries are a useful tool, we must think about illustrating and clarifying the meaning, rather than just explaining it. New words can be illustrated and clarified through showing drawings or pictures, through realia (showing the actual object, an apple, for example), though mime, matching exercises (such as picture and words) and, with higher level students, activities which encourage deducing the meaning from the context.

Before moving on to pronunciation of new language, check that the students have understood the meaning through concept questions. Concept questions are formulated by defining the essential information we have. To give an example, let's use the word *library*. Teaching this new word we need to convey three points. 1. We can borrow books from a library. 2. We cannot buy books from a library. 3. We can sit and read in a library. So our concept questions would be *Can you borrow books from a library? Can you buy books from a library? Can you sit and read in a library?* Ideally, these concept questions should require 'yes' or 'no' answers or very short answers.

With regard to pronunciation, there are many different ways of speaking English and many different accents and dialects. Exposing students to as many of these as possible will equip them well for speaking in the real world, outside the classroom. Teaching pronunciation needs to cover sounds, stress (stress in a word and stress in a sentence), intonation (the rising and falling of our voice to convey meaning) and connected speech (how sounds and words change or disappear when linked). At times you may need to focus part of a lesson on pronunciation and at other times it may be an occasional feature of a lesson, perhaps through sporadic drilling (controlled repetition of words or sentences, guided by the teaching).

When teaching English we often teach through texts. These may be written texts (a magazine article, an extract from a book, an email, etc.) or recorded texts (a news bulletin, a weather report, a conversation). Understanding these texts requires two of the four skills which you will encounter in your EFL training: Reading and Listening. These two skills are often grouped together as they are known as passive or receptive language skills. They require understanding of the language, but they do not require a student to produce the language in written or spoken form. The latter are the remaining two skills: Writing and Speaking.

In a Reading or Listening skills lesson it is important to stage the lesson to establish interest and include a variety of tasks. The very first stage, however, needs to cover vocabulary that is needed to understand the text. Students must not worry about understanding every word, but there will be some words that are essential and you will need to 'pre-teach' these in advance. It is then important to get the students interested in the topic, you want them to *want* to read the text or listen to the recording. Personalized discussion of the topic is very useful. For example, if 'holidays' is your topic, low-level students can simply list places they have been to, while higher level students may describe a holiday. Your first skills task should be an easier task, where students listen or skim read for the gist of the text or recording: they are basically 'pulling-out' key information. Further tasks should require more careful listening or reading to demonstrate understanding

Speaking and Writing skills are both productive skills but do not have the same similarities when teaching. Broadly speaking, writing is more formal. It requires more accuracy, with the emphasis on spelling and punctuation. Speaking is about immediate communication, where mistakes and slips of the tongue occur naturally. Accuracy is important, but fluency is key: the ability to talk fairly freely, without stopping or hesitating too much. Speaking activities are often good follow-up activities at the end of Reading or Listening tasks, to give further practice of the language. Setting up a speaking activity needs careful planning and much will depend on your class size. Ideally, you need to step back from the group and discreetly monitor and encourage the students. Don't correct while they are in full flow but leave correction for when the activity has finished.

Students are naturally motivated to practise English through speaking, but often less so through writing, unless they are preparing for an exam. Motivation, then, and creating interest in the topic, is crucial. A writing task may be integrated with other skills activities, or it may be the focus of a whole lesson if an exam is involved. Students often feel under pressure when writing, so the lesson needs to be carefully staged and the teacher needs to give plenty of support and encouragement. Students need to be clear about the appropriate style of language required for the task (a formal letter of application, an informal email, etc.) and to be able to use the appropriate linking expressions, as well as the appropriate layout and structure of the piece.

While writing, and speaking, students will inevitably make mistakes and when and how you correct these is important. In fact, a whole unit in this book is dedicated to correction. The crucial issues are which mistakes to correct, when to correct them and, importantly, who corrects them. We may presume that the teacher does all the correcting, but in fact it is important to involve students. They can be encouraged to correct themselves (self-correction) or each other (student-to-student correction). This promotes learner independence and confidence. Pronunciation mistakes are often corrected immediately, but if your students are involved in a speaking activity you should usually leave correction for later, so as not to interrupt their attempts at fluency. Whether you feel all mistakes should be corrected is a question of personal judgement. It can be very demoralizing, so always praise and support as much as possible.

If you are on a training course you will be required to prepare detailed lesson plans each time you teach. And as a newly qualified teacher, you will probably continue to write lesson plans for some time. The starting point for your lesson plan should be your lesson aims. Try to approach these from the student's point of view, rather than your own. Instead of 'teach new vocabulary' your aim should be 'for students to learn new vocabulary'. However, this aim in itself is too vague. A clearer aim would specify 'for students to learn 10 new words connected with computers and practise these in a written gap-fill activity.' You should have one or two overall aims for your lesson, within which each stage of the lesson should have clear aims. Be sure your aims are achievable and realistic: this will depend on the students, their level and the time available. And always make sure your lessons include a good variety of activities and interaction.

An important part of your planning should be anticipating problems. These may be problems with the language, such as anticipating *false friends*. These are words which look familiar in a foreign language but actually have a very different meaning. (The English word *embarrassed* compared with the Spanish word *embarazada*, which means pregnant.) Also, you need to anticipate unexpected problems in the classroom. These might range from late arrivals and dominant students to missing materials or technology problems (your CD player doesn't work). As a teacher you need to be prepared for any eventuality, and as your teaching experience grows, so will your ability to deal with problems.

Finally, when you are teaching you are likely to be using published materials. As nice as the idea sounds, it would be impossible to prepare all your own materials, even if you wished too. Published course books are invaluable, but they need to be judged by you with your class in mind. You may not be able to choose the course material, but ideally it should contain interesting and useful topics with a suitable level and a logical progression for your students. No course book can be perfectly adapted to your groups, so approach your material as follows: **use** some of it, **reject** other parts, **adapt** some and **supplement** with other resources (your own perhaps, or online material, for example).

The topics we have touched on here, from teaching techniques to lesson planning, are all covered in detail in this book. There are also useful sections on teaching one-to-one and testing, as well as career prospects and professional development. Whether you are currently training to be a teacher or have just embarked on your teaching career, this book will offer you all the tips, ideas and practical help you need to continue your journey in the world of English language teaching.

Introduction

Despite the title of this book, I do not think it is possible for someone to 'teach' himself or herself how to teach, without actually doing it, just as you cannot learn from a book how to use a computer if you do not have a computer to use. However, I do know from my experience as a teacher trainer that there are EFL/ESL teachers who have no qualifications or training. This is not good for the profession, and it is certainly not good for the students. But it is a fact. I also know that even those people who do undertake a training course need as much practical help and support as they can get, not only during the course, but also – and maybe particularly – after the course, as they begin their first teaching assignment. So, you cannot teach yourself to be a teacher, but you can learn and improve your skills as you go along.

This book, therefore, is intended for these three types of reader:

▶ teachers teaching without having had any training
▶ teachers who have recently trained and who lack experience
▶ trainee teachers doing a training course

By 'teachers' I refer to those in any country, teaching to monolingual and multilingual classes, to students whose first language is not English, and to students who are classified as *adult learners* (generally defined as 16+). Since the book has such a broad focus it inevitably deals with the general, rather than the specific, teaching context. This is no bad thing. The book's purpose is to provide new teachers with the basic teaching skills, background knowledge and awareness that will subsequently enable them to develop and fine tune what they do in the classroom.

I have seen situations where too much is expected of new/trainee teachers. Many of my ex-trainees have complained about the lack of support and help from some first-time employers who sometimes seem to expect students to know everything from having done a four-week training course, or similar. This is unrealistic. Equally, tutors on training courses should not forget that most of their trainees have never been in front of a class before in their lives and that they need support and encouragement as well as expert training.

Fortunately, most employers and tutors do provide such support. However, they are not always available when needed by the new or trainee teacher. I hope this book will fill that space.

This book should not be seen as the be-all-and-end-all of EFL/ESL teaching. To many experienced teachers reading the book (a book not intended for such readership!) much of what I have written will be seen as prescriptive, just as the typical training course and most course books are prescriptive. But I will always argue, from long experience, that a level of prescriptiveness is needed (and welcomed by trainees) at the beginning of their teaching career. I make no apologies for being prescriptive in this book – once teachers have more experience and confidence, they can develop their awareness and methodology. The models of teaching that I outline here can be applied successfully in most contexts, giving new teachers a much-needed degree of security. Please note, when referring to teachers in general, I have used 'she'/'her' throughout; students are referred to as 'he', 'she' or 'they' (singular and plural).

This book is not intended for experienced teachers or for those teaching young learners. It is not intended to apply in all parts to all teaching contexts. It certainly does not cover all aspects of teaching. Instead, it aims to raise awareness of the role of teachers and students teaching and learning English, and to give practical ideas for teaching English as a foreign or second language to adults.

This is effectively, a teaching 'handbook' which can be referred to at short notice for suggestions, examples and reassurance. It is just the beginning of the long process of becoming an effective and successful teacher. It has been written to provide help and encouragement. I hope it does.

Good luck, and enjoy the ride! It won't be dull.

David Riddell (davi77@hotmail.com)

1

Being a student

My own memories of my schooldays and the teachers that taught me are very vivid. As a learner of French I experienced two very different styles of teaching – one where I was taught primarily in English, and one where I was taught mostly in French. I found the second much more intimidating, but also much more effective. The first was safe, comparatively easy, but did little to make me a competent user of the language. Just as it was no good for someone to *show* me how to change a spark plug (I had to *do* it to learn), so it was no good for me to learn a new language without getting more opportunity to use it. That is one reason why our students in EFL are mostly taught entirely in English, regardless of their level. Allow a couple of students to start using their own language and you will quickly hear loud complaints from the other students – they know that this is not helping their learning.

Teachers have differing views on the use of L1 (the student's mother tongue) in the classroom, and it depends to an extent on whether you are teaching a monolingual or a multilingual class. In a multilingual class, lessons are taught almost entirely in English, partly for the reason already given, and partly because this 'total immersion' approach encourages real communication as opposed to rule learning and the completion of exercises. Of course, there may be times when the occasional quick translation may be helpful, but if either the teacher or other students start using non-English to any extent beyond this, the students are very likely to become unhappy.

In a monolingual class it is inevitable that the students will speak their own language more, and perhaps the teacher will too (if she knows it!). But if the teacher starts teaching in that language rather than English, the *authenticity* of the target language will be lost.

Insight

L1 is your students' first language, their mother tongue. If you are teaching abroad (i.e. in Italy) it is inevitable that students will sometimes speak to each other in their own language (i.e. Italian). If you are teaching a multilingual group (i.e. foreign students in London), they won't have a common L1 to use in this way.

All teachers, especially of 'General English', know that different students prefer to learn in different ways. Let's be honest here – as much as teachers believe in the effectiveness of the 'communicative approach', there are still many students who prefer to listen to explanations of grammar, learn rules, and do practice exercises. It is *safer* – just as when my French teacher taught in English. On the other hand, there are those students who only want to 'talk', being more concerned with fluency than with accuracy. There are students who want learning to be 'fun', and those who perceive 'fun' as 'not learning'.

It is obvious, then, that 'being a student' is a complicated existence. We, as teachers, have to appreciate this and be as aware as we can of our students' different attitudes to learning.

Insight

Students have different learning styles. Some students prefer to be taught through exercises and grammar rules, whereas others seek a purely communicative approach. In either case, avoiding the use of L1 in the classroom will help students immerse themselves in English.

Task

Here are some questions I used in a survey done with some of my students. Before I report the findings, answer the questions yourself based on your own experience of new-language learning.

1 What makes a good student?
2 What helps you when you are learning a new language?
3 How important is learning grammar when you are learning a language?
4 Should learning be communicative, or should you learn from explanations, rules, and practice exercises?
5 How important is it for a student to have some responsibility for their own learning and not to rely exclusively on the teacher?
6 Is it a good thing to be in a class with students from your own country (of course, in non-English-speaking classes students will all be from the same country, so this question does have rather limited value!)?
7 Is it a good thing for the teacher to use your language?

STOP here and consider your answers before reading on!

The students I asked were from eleven different countries – Japan, Mexico, Brazil, Russia, Turkey, Italy, Israel, France, Korea, Algeria, and Spain. They were intermediate and upper intermediate level students studying in London with ages ranging from 18 to 45. Most had experience of learning another language besides English, and all had experienced more than one learning style.

I also put the same questions to Thomas Grossmann, a Swiss German teacher who passed his Proficiency in the month of December. Six months later, he was a qualified EFL teacher and was teaching shortly after that. This remarkably quick transformation made Thomas an ideal person to ask about both learning and teaching.

But first the student reactions:

1 What makes a good student?
'respect your teacher'
'know that you're not the only student in the class'
'you must have a desire to study'
'listen'
'respect other students'
'be interested'
'socialize with other students and teachers'
'speak in class'
'pay attention'
'do your homework'
'spend time outside class using English'
'go over what you have learnt in class'
'know why you are learning English'
'respect the culture of the country'
'be attentive, disciplined, active in class'

'Respect' is a word that came up several times, and some cultures are especially respectful of the role of the teacher. Others have had strained relationships with teachers from their own schooldays and are perhaps still a little suspicious of teachers in general. Most, however, have opinions about what the role of the teacher should be, something we will look at in the next unit.

Having a 'desire to study' – an 'interest' in what is being learnt – is crucial, in my view. The inquisitive student, the one who wants to know 'why?' and 'how?' and who asks lots of questions, may be the student that new and learning teachers dread the most, but in the long run these are the students who thrive and make visible progress and who keep the teacher challenged and rewarded.

'Pay attention' and 'listen' are very important points, too. 'Listen' should be followed by 'respond' because to listen is not enough. Think of any conversation you have had with a person who, you know full well, is not really listening to what you are saying. It is frustrating. Their thoughts are elsewhere and you do not have their attention. Students whose minds wander, or who are content only to listen (back to that 'safe' option!) suggest that their desire to study, to learn, is limited. This was certainly the view of the students I spoke to, some of whom were themselves 'guilty' of this at times!

'Go over what you've learnt', 'do your homework', 'use English outside class' are points which cannot be emphasized too much. I should add that all my students stressed the ideal of learning English in an English-speaking country, if possible. This obviously makes it much more possible to use English outside school, as well as making the learning process more authentic. But, of course, this is not always possible.

However, it is important for students not to perceive their lessons as the be-all-and-end-all of their learning. Yes, they should do their homework. Yes, they should revise what they have studied. But most of all they should take whatever opportunity they can to use their English – speaking, listening, reading, writing. As teachers we should not only encourage them to do so, but also tell them *how* to do it (e.g. suggesting English newspapers, both online and printed, as well as English radio and TV, which can also be accessed online, plus magazines, books, etc. to read). The student who limits his 'learning' to inside the classroom will make very little real progress.

Insight

Learning and practising English outside the classroom is just as important as classroom input for students. Students who don't live in an English-speaking country will need extra guidance and encouragement. Suggest English newspapers (printed or online), TV and radio (online) as well as books and magazines.

2 **What helps you when you are learning a language?**
'be in the country of the language'
'don't be shy'
'watch TV'
'a balance and variety'
'use only English when possible outside class'
'have a part-time job if possible'

Most of these have already been mentioned. The point made about the part-time job only applies to work in an English-speaking country, but this situation certainly plunges the student into using English authentically.

Watching TV (equally, watching films, listening to the radio, reading newspapers, etc.) underlines what has already been said about using English outside class.

3 How important is learning grammar when you are learning a language?

'grammar, grammar, grammar is very boring'

'quite important'

'very important'

'gives meaning to conversation'

'not too much'

'it is important because if you learn grammar you can speak properly' (whatever 'properly' means!)

Predictably, different views were expressed, reflecting, in part, students' own language-learning experiences from earlier education. The very word 'grammar' has negative connotations for most people, and can be a real turn-off in the classroom, much as the word 'homework' can. But it is a word with an undeserved reputation! Ask most people what they understand by 'grammar' and they will usually come up with 'rules', 'exercises', 'copying from the board', 'boring', 'not useful', etc. Say to a class 'Now we're going to do grammar' and you won't be greeted with a sea of smiling faces – though some students still view the learning of rules as 'real learning'. We will look at this issue in Unit 5.

4 Should learning be communicative, or should you learn from listening to explanations and making notes and doing practice exercises?

'beginners need more practice exercises, after that learning should be communicative'

'it should be more communicative because if French schools did that we would speak better English'

'communicative, otherwise it is boring'

This 'communicative' approach is partly the result of using only English in the classroom, but more than this, it is giving students the opportunity to use the language they are learning in authentic contexts. We will look at this much more later, but it is the overwhelming view of students I have taught that this communicative approach is more successful, more real than the approach of rule learning.

5 **How important is it for a student to have some responsibility for their own learning and not to rely on the teacher alone?**
'very important'
'teacher helps to show you the right way'
'trains you for "real life"'
'it is important to have some responsibility for your own learning'
'a good student has some responsibility outside the class, but they have to be guided'

The student who comes to class but never uses his English outside it (more likely when they are learning in their own country), or who never studies outside it, will make very little genuine progress. The classroom is not 'real life' (as mentioned above). It is *artificial*. Everything is controlled by the teacher and how she has planned the lesson.

We have to encourage our students to read English, speak English, hear English, write English. We also have to encourage learner independence *within* the classroom. Unit 5 will explore these issues.

6 **Is it a good thing to be in a class with students from another country?**
(this is mostly relevant to classes in English-speaking countries)
'more interesting'
'different cultures'
'yes, it makes you use English'
'it is good to open your mind, and we have to speak English'

7 Is it a good thing for your teacher to use your language some of the time when teaching?
'teacher must first try and explain in English'
'never, never'
'only with low-level students'
'it is not necessary'

These comments support the views expressed at the start of this unit and show how aware most students are of the need to immerse themselves in English in the classroom.

Insight

As a teacher working abroad, you may speak the language and you may occasionally use L1 in the classroom. This may be particularly true when teaching low-level groups, i.e. giving a quick translation. Most students, however, prefer to be immersed in English while in the classroom: your approach as the teacher is key.

Comments from Thomas Grossmann, from his perspective of a student who became a teacher, are also very relevant. His views on what helped him gain the Cambridge Proficiency of English in a relatively short time cover many of the points already mentioned, as well as one or two others:

'a positive attitude towards the language, the country where it is spoken, and its people'
'absorbing as much language as possible (especially vocabulary, phrasal verbs and idioms) by watching TV, talking with native speakers, listening to audiobooks'
'reading books, magazines, newspapers'
'discussions in class'
'being able to figure out a grammar rule for oneself' (described by Thomas as the 'aha' effect!)
'not being afraid of making mistakes'
'a good reference book'
'trying to get the "feel" and "rhythm" of the language'
'copying the pronunciation from native speakers and slightly exaggerating it'

'the iron will to learn the language (motivation)'
'keeping penfriends'

Thomas also says: 'I think an advantage I had was that I learnt English in England where I could use it every day. I imagine that if I had learnt it in Switzerland it would have been much harder and less close to my heart. My views on effective learning since becoming a teacher haven't altered much. Every person has his or her individual way and pace of learning and, whatever that is, it should be encouraged. Another point which I think is very important (especially if one doesn't learn English in a country where it is spoken), is to use as much *real* language as possible.'

Summary

- ▶ Our students usually have different favoured learning styles, influenced by their previous learning experiences.

- ▶ Most prefer, or accept the advantages of, a mostly communicative approach to their learning.

- ▶ Students have to accept some responsibility for their own learning and not rely only on the teacher.

- ▶ Learning has to include authentic practice, and has to continue outside the classroom.

- ▶ Students need motivation and commitment.

- ▶ Students prefer – and expect – English to be the only language spoken in the lessons, except with very low-level classes.

  Everything which has been mentioned in this unit inevitably affects the role of the teacher and how she plans her teaching, and this is what the next unit will look at.

2

Being a teacher

Most people remember at least some of their teachers from school-days, whether positively or negatively. Teachers make an impression. And students have expectations. If being a student is a 'complicated existence', then being a teacher is trying to meet the many varying expectations that students have, and that the teacher herself has, of the teacher's role. Perhaps we should say 'roles' because 'teaching' is only part of what the teacher has to do inside – and outside – the classroom.

Task

1 Think back to your own schooldays and the teachers you had. Which ones did you consider to be 'good' and which were 'bad'? Why?
2 If you studied a language at school, how did that teacher approach her lessons? What was effective and not effective and why? How did you learn? Was anything lacking in your lessons?
3 On the basis of your previous answers, what do you think constitutes an effective and popular teacher of English to speakers of other languages? Make a list of the most important qualities.

STOP – do this task before reading on

Many people have experienced the 'listen and take notes' approach to language learning, followed by doing practice exercises from a book, and with a strong emphasis on remembering what has been learnt, as opposed to using the language. It must be stated that some students do prefer this approach (which is not necessarily to say that it is an effective approach). This method implies a very limited responsibility for the teacher whereas, in reality, the effective and popular teacher has a multitude of responsibilities.

The survey I did with students highlighted not only this multitude of responsibilities, but also the expectations that students have of their teacher. Students, of any subject, are a critical and discerning audience, which can make a teacher's job hard. However, if teachers can respond to their students' personalities, attitudes, needs and backgrounds, they will become better teachers.

Insight

Another useful task is to imagine yourself now as a teacher. How would you like your students to see you? What do you think your students will expect of you? What qualities do you have that will help you succeed?

What makes a good teacher?

I asked the same students featured in Unit 1 'What makes a good teacher?' Of all the questions I asked, it was this one that produced the most opinions. In no particular order, these are some of the qualities mentioned in their replies:

'they must be passionate about teaching, and patient, adapting to the level of the students'
'a good teacher must be strict, friendly, interesting'
'should be passionate and intelligent'
'should teach grammar clearly'
'should not rely on the course book only'
'must know students' individual needs'
'help students make progress'
'give interesting lessons'

'be kind'
'not show a distance'
'be funny'
'have an original teaching style'
'have energy'
'have lots of patience'
'adapt the course book'
'treat students as individuals'
'be stimulating'
'know the students' names'
'you must know your students'
'must care'
'it is not enough to know your subject'

'Knowing your subject is not enough'

Just from these comments it is obvious that a teacher has to be more than a 'teacher'. That last comment – 'it is not enough to know your subject' – underlines the point that it is not enough for a teacher to go into a classroom and effectively 'give a lecture' while students make notes. Of course, the teacher has to know her subject – this is essential – but it is not enough.

For new or trainee teachers, however, 'knowing your subject' feels more than enough! What strikes terror into new teachers' hearts is the 'G-word' – grammar. The most common cry I hear is 'I don't know grammar – I never did it at school.' Or, if grammar was learnt at school, it was in the form of so-called rules of language, and terminology that has all been forgotten. Well, 'grammar' is, or should be, much much more than this. We will see in a later unit what is involved in learning 'grammar', and how it can be 'taught'. However, that is the 'teaching' not the 'knowing'. Yes, as teachers we *do* have to know how the present perfect simple is formed and how it is used. We need to know what a phrasal verb is and the different kinds that exist. We need to know why we can say 'if I *left* now' rather than 'if I *will* leave now', and we need to know why *may* has different meanings in the sentences 'You *may* leave now if you want' and 'Luc's late, he *may* have missed the bus'. The 'mistake' new or trainee teachers sometimes make is to think that they have to know everything straight away. Well, relax. First, no teacher knows everything about the language they are teaching and never will.

Second, teachers starting out are students themselves, students of the language they are teaching. You learn as you go along and you build up your knowledge. This is how it has to be. So don't read a grammar book from cover to cover. Instead, concentrate on understanding the language that you are going to be focusing on next in the classroom. Little by little your confidence will grow.

Insight

A lot of new teachers feel afraid of 'grammar'. Remember, as a new teacher you can't know everything about the language you are teaching and you will learn a lot as you go along. Concentrate on the next lesson you have to teach, and prepare carefully. This will give you more confidence.

The teacher also has to know *how* to teach. She has to have an awareness of effective and successful methodology. The comments about the teacher not relying on the course book, giving interesting lessons, having an original teaching style, and being stimulating, all confirm that students want – expect – their teacher to teach in a much more challenging and interesting way than simply setting them work from the course book. The main part of this book deals with this very area – the methodology.

'Give interesting lessons'

Students get bored easily! They expect the teacher to plan her lessons so that learning becomes interesting, challenging and varied. They expect the teacher to teach in a way that is appropriate to the level being taught, and to the individuals in the class. They expect the teacher to adapt and supplement the course book being used and definitely not to rely on it as the sole resource. In short, they expect the teacher to know *how* to teach effectively, and for the teacher to 'be stimulating'.

We saw in Unit 1 that students generally respond better, and benefit most from a communicative approach to learning, and it is this approach that we will focus on here. Very frequently, people who have undertaken training courses in teaching English in the communicative way have told me they wish they had learnt a language in the same way. I certainly wish I had.

'Know your students'

But still that is not enough. A teacher may know her subject. She may know how to teach it, but she has to know the people that she is teaching – and I don't just mean 'know their names', though that is important, too! So, find out about the students – the people – that you are teaching: what they like and are interested in; and what they don't like and are not interested in. Find out about their previous learning experiences. Find out what their expectations are of the course you are going to be teaching. Find out what their aims are. Ask them about themselves: their country, their culture, their interests. Speak to them outside class. Speak to them inside class! *Listen* to them. Show an interest in what they are saying. Show an interest in them as human beings. Be approachable. Help and support them. Be friendly. *Respond* to their needs. Be tolerant. Be patient.

In my opinion, no teacher is complete if they do not go beyond 'teaching the lesson'. The personal qualities required by the teacher described here can be summed up in the phrase 'show an interest'. If you do not want to show an interest in students as human beings, you will only have limited success as a teacher.

'Be passionate and patient'

Thomas Grossmann, remember, can look at the roles of the teacher from both perspectives. When he gave me his views on being an English teacher he had only recently started his first job, and only a short time before that had passed his Cambridge Proficiency of English exam. He trained in England and went on to teach in his home country, Switzerland. This is what he says:

> I think to be a successful teacher you have to like the job. One should be able to motivate the students and make lessons fun. A dash of humour would be good, too. The ability to explain something complicated in a clear way is important. Having patience, creativity, and good communication skills are an advantage, too.

> I started teaching and it's great fun. I was really nervous before the first lesson but everything went smoothly. The worst thing that has happened to me as a teacher was that I wanted to teach them too much – I had three fifty-minute lessons and prepared a lesson plan for each lesson. But after two lessons I was still doing material which I had prepared for the first and in the end I hurried them just to get through everything. Looking back, I think that was a mistake.

You have to 'like the job'. Yes, you do. Of course, at times all teachers want to scream and do *anything* but go and teach their 25th hour of the week. But there are few jobs, if any, which are always positive. With this job, you meet people from all over the world; you have the scope for creativity (mentioned by Thomas), and can have a very good time. As one of my students said, a teacher needs to have energy – you have to always appear enthusiastic about what you are doing, even at 9 am on Monday. If the teacher appears uninterested, the students will become that way themselves.

But, as Thomas says, you *do* need enormous patience at times. And
when, inevitably, the time comes when you do want to scream, just
think back to how difficult you found it to learn a new language,
or to remember it the next day. In other words, keep thinking of
how the student is feeling – maybe tired, maybe frustrated, maybe
stressed – and if you then show impatience, how will that affect
them thereafter?

Thomas also mentions humour. This doesn't mean the teacher has
to be an entertainer, but that they should inject some fun, some
light relief from time to time. Most humour arises naturally from
the different situations that occur with the various students in your
class. The sound of students laughing is (usually!) a very welcome
sound, so encourage it when appropriate.

'Help students make progress'

Teachers must know how to plan their lessons appropriately
(see Units 17–20), and how to assess objectively the strengths and
weaknesses of their own teaching in general, and of specific lessons.
This is all part of professional development (Unit 25).

If there is not this critical self-evaluation, there will be no
development or progress. New or trainee teachers have a tendency
to dismiss most of their lessons as 'disasters', but this usually
revolves around something terribly minor like 'I forgot to give the
instructions before handing out the papers'. As we shall see later,
one of the first questions the teacher should ask herself is 'Did I
achieve my aims?' The better the planning, the more likely the
lesson will be effective.

Summary

▶ Teachers have many different roles inside and outside the classroom.

▶ They need to know their subject.

▶ They need to use appropriate teaching methodology.

▶ They need to find out about their students; know them; respond to them.

▶ They need to demonstrate various personal qualities.

▶ They need to show interest in their work and their students, and they must have limitless energy!

▶ They need to plan lessons according to the needs of their class.

▶ They need to know how to properly evaluate the success of a lesson, and evaluate their own strengths and weaknesses.

As this whole book is about 'being a teacher', this chapter has been no more than an introduction. One point not mentioned in this unit – but another vital aspect of the teacher's role – is classroom manner and management. This is what we will focus on in the next unit.

3

Classroom management and manner

We saw in the previous unit that a teacher has many roles, including managing her classroom and students. We shall look at how she does this, and at the manner she adopts when teaching. Effective classroom management is an essential ingredient in successful teaching. For the purposes of this unit we will focus on the following:

Teacher talk	the grading of the teacher's language and the amount spoken, instruction-giving, directions
Gestures	how gestures can help to clarify what a teacher wants her students to do
Interaction and management	factors to consider, depending on who is interacting with whom in the classroom and in the teacher's management of the class
Manner	the importance of an appropriate teaching manner

Teacher talk

The teacher has to use a level of language which will be understood by the students in the class. This level will be influenced, of course, by the level of the students. This does not mean speaking at an unnaturally slow pace, or raising your voice – do not patronize your students. If a student has a poor level of English this does not mean they lack intelligence, so never give that impression to them. Instead, *simplify* the language being used. For example, rather than saying 'work in pairs', to a very low-level class, say 'work in twos' (accompanied by a gesture pairing students off). There is no point in saying 'work in pairs' when they might not know what 'pairs' means.

Rather than just saying 'underline' (e.g. 'underline the correct answer'), *demonstrate* visually or by a gesture what you mean.

The same applies to the teacher's language in general conversation. Rather than saying 'What did you get up to last weekend?', say 'What did you do…?' And rather than saying 'Do you want me to go through your job application with you?', say 'Do you want me to look at…?' So, *simplify* your language.

When teaching, this *grading* of language needs to be accompanied by an appropriate level of *teacher talk time* (TTT). This does not mean 'try not to talk' (I have seen new teachers struggling desperately to avoid speaking at all having been told to keep their TTT low!). It means 'don't use too much *unnecessary* language, because the more you say, the more likely you are to be misunderstood. There are times when the teacher has to do a lot of talking. There are times when lessons need to be teacher-centred. But what we should be aiming for is *economy* of language coupled with appropriate grading. It's a little like the advice for packing a suitcase. First pack it, then reduce the contents by half to what you *really* need. As a teacher, it is easy to start saying far more than you have to, and to run the risk of confusing your students. This is especially the case the lower the level of the class. Clearly, a class of advanced students will understand most of what you say, and you can be less careful with your language. But if you are teaching an elementary class, for example, you need to think about everything you say.

Task 1

Look at the following examples of teacher talk. They are a combination of instructions, directions, and general chat (either as part of the lesson or before or after it) given to an intermediate level class. Try to simplify the language, and reduce the TTT to an appropriate amount. In some cases you might also want to question how the teacher's choice of words may impact on the students' motivation level. When you're done, check the key on page 28.

Look at the following examples of teacher talk and identify the problem:

1 'I want you to do this exercise in which you have to answer ten questions. You can do it by yourself if you prefer, or work with your partner. When you finish I'll put you in larger groups for you to check your answers.'
2 'I want you to do a mingling activity now, which I'm sure you're going to hate!'
3 'No, erm, make that threes ... wait a minute, there's thirteen of you, better make it threes and one four. Javier, do you want to work in a "3" or a "4"?'
4 'That's a jolly nice scarf. It must have cost you a bomb.'
5 'I'm handing out a piece of paper...'
6 'This is going to be boring but it has to be done.'
7 'This is going to be easy...'
8 'Did you enjoy that?'
9 'I want you to go through Exercise 1 and work out the answers. You must also justify your answers.'
10 'Would you like to stand up, please?'

Tips for successful instruction-giving

1 Plan your instructions – even script them at first if you feel it will help you.
2 Having planned them, review them and edit as necessary.
3 Only say what you have to.
4 Use simplified language, but do not over-simplify for the level.
5 Don't patronize (e.g. talking unnaturally slowly or loudly).
6 If you are getting blank faces, it probably means they are not understanding. So adjust your language as you speak, if necessary.
7 When giving instructions, make sure the students are looking at you and listening to you.
8 Don't give out papers before your instructions unless you have to – you will lose the students' attention.
9 Stand front and centre. Keep still.
10 Project your voice *slightly* so your instructions stand out.
11 Maintain eye contact.
12 Break up the instructions: 'Do questions 1–5. Say if the sentences are true or false. Give reasons for your answers. Work together. You have five minutes. Go.'
13 Only give instructions for what they have to do at that time, not later.
14 Give an example of what they have to do / do Question 1 with them.
15 Give a rough idea of how long they have.
16 Make it clear if you want them to work individually, in pairs, or in groups.
17 Don't ask lower-level students 'So, what do you have to do?' – they haven't got the language for this, and confusion will result. Once your instructions are over, tell them to begin, then check everyone is doing the activity correctly and deal with individual problems.
18 If one person says 'I don't understand', help that person individually. Don't hold up the rest of the class, and the lesson.
19 Don't *invite* the students to do something; politely *tell* them. So, don't say 'Would you like to stand up?', say 'Stand up, please'.

20 Students like – and expect – the teacher to be polite but direct in her language. They need to be told clearly what they have to do and how you want them to do it. Don't be afraid to do this! But don't tell the students they are going to find the activity boring, or difficult, or interesting, or easy!

Gestures

Everyone uses their hands and face to express or clarify meaning. Teachers do it more than most because they quickly realize how much meaning their body language can add to the words they are using. At the beginning, you may have to remind yourself to do a 'writing' gesture with your hand when you say 'I want you to write...' to a low-level class; but after a while you will use gestures all the time quite automatically. You can work out for yourself what appropriate gestures you can use to clarify meaning – but make sure your choice is clear, appropriate, and consistent. You will find that your students' understanding will be greater as a result. You will also find yourself gesticulating more than you need to when you are outside the teaching context!

Task 2

Consider what gestures you could use to indicate the following. There are no 'right' answers; the aim of this task is to get you thinking what gestures *you* might use in the classroom.

1 'Work in pairs / threes.'
2 'Get in a circle / straight line.'
3 'Stand up / sit down.'
4 'Listen / Read / Write / Speak.'
5 'Tick the right answer.'
6 'Think about...'
7 'Look at me.'
8 What gesture could you use to indicate the student is wrong in his answer? Only partly right?

9 'Past tense' / 'Now' / 'In the future'.
10 What type of gesture could you use to clarify the meaning of word/sentence stress?

Tips

1 Be clear/unambiguous.
2 Be consistent.
3 Don't over-exaggerate to the extent that you appear patronizing.
4 Don't use inappropriate gestures (e.g. pointing is considered rude by most people).

Insight

Gestures help clarify meaning and are very useful for giving instructions. Plan some key gestures, such as for 'Listen, Read, Write' and use them consistently. Observe students' expressions to see if they have understood – often they may not like to admit that they haven't!

Interaction

There is a huge variety of different teaching contexts worldwide. Whether you are teaching a class of six sitting together in a semi-circle ('horseshoe') formation in a multilingual class, or a monolingual class of fifty students sitting behind rows of desks, you must consider how best to manage your classroom and the people in it. Because there is a huge range of possibilities, there are very few 'rights and wrongs', but lots of questions for the teacher to consider.

Here is a selection of questions to think about. The answers sometimes depend upon the situation! With some questions, you may have no choice (e.g. seating arrangements). With other questions, it is possible to give general answers.

- Where do you want the students to sit for a particular activity?
- Do you want them to work individually? In pairs? In groups?
- If you need them to work in pairs, what will you do if there is an odd number of students?
- If you are teaching a multilingual class, do you want to separate students who speak the same language?
- Where are you going to place yourself? What does it depend on?
- Will you always stand?
- How can you try to be sure all the students can hear you?
- Where will you stand when you use the board?
- How does your distance and position affect your 'relationship' with the class?
- How important is eye contact and why?
- How important is it to use your students' names?
- What will you be doing when the students are working individually/together?
- Should every activity last until all students have finished it?
- How can you attract the class's attention at the end of an activity?
- How can you politely stop two students from talking when they should be listening to you?

What should you check in your classroom before the lesson begins?

Tips

1 Plan in advance what type of interaction you want for each stage of the lesson (teacher to class / pairs / groups etc.).
2 If you need even numbers (A working with B) and you get an odd number of students, two students can work together as 'one' (A, A and B). Don't participate yourself because then you will not be able to monitor other students.
3 In a multilingual class try, if possible, to have students from different nationalities working together to encourage only English in the lesson. In any case, vary who works with whom from time to time.

4 If you are doing 'teacher to class' work, stand where you can be seen by everyone (usually front and centre). If students are working together, go around and monitor their work, helping individuals as necessary and generally just 'keeping an eye' on how everyone is doing. If someone finishes an activity quickly, give them something else to do. You should aim to keep everyone busy all of the time, otherwise pace drops and students get bored (especially at higher levels).

5 Sometimes it might seem more appropriate to sit – if you have a smallish class and are just 'chatting', for example. This would not be appropriate, though, if you have a class where students are forced to sit in rows.

6 When using the board, try not to block students' view. Stand to one side. If you are still blocking someone's view, move out of their way as often as you can so they can see what you are writing.

7 Writing on the board is not easy … it needs practice. Make sure your board looks neat, well organized and clear. Students copy what you write so it needs to be a proper 'record' for them to copy and refer to in the future.

8 Maintain eye contact with your class. This will keep you aware of how students are reacting to each part of your lesson (for example, you can usually tell if someone is not understanding what you are saying just from their facial expression). This will help you to remain in control of the lesson. Also, as in any conversation, it is polite to look at the person you are talking to!

9 Learn your students' names as quickly as you can and use them! Again, this is just polite. But it is very difficult to attract a student's attention in class if you do not know their name. 'Excuse me, you…' (or equivalent) is simply not acceptable. Students will expect you to know who they are and show an interest in them. For the first two or three lessons it is perfectly understandable if you cannot remember all the names, but after that it gets embarrassing. Do a 'name-game' activity on the first day, perhaps. If the class is all new, they too will want to learn names.

10 If students are working together or individually on an activity for which you have given them 'ten minutes', this does not mean *literally* ten minutes. It is just a rough idea of how long they have. Maybe they only need five minutes, or maybe you realize they are having unexpected difficulty and need a few extra minutes. So be flexible. Do not feel that you have to wait for every single person to finish what they are doing before you stop the activity – very rarely does everyone have time to finish. Otherwise, you are running the risk of bored students sitting twiddling their thumbs, waiting for the lesson to continue. Do not be afraid, then, to say 'OK, stop there. Don't worry if you haven't finished; we'll go through the answers together.'

11 Devise a way, which works for you, to attract the attention of the class when you want them to stop working together and listen to you again. Projecting your voice (not shouting!) may be enough; tapping the board with a pen works for some; perhaps raising your hand. The bigger the class, the more important this will be.

12 If two students are chatting to each other when they should be listening (to you or another student), stop them, otherwise it becomes very distracting. If you are teaching adults, treat them as adults – so just a gentle and polite request for them to listen.

13 Before the lesson begins, check you have everything you need – board pens/chalk, books/photocopies, audio material. Check you have any technology that is required – CD player, overhead projector etc. – and that you know how to use it. Do not wait for the lesson to begin to check all this since if you hit a problem you will appear unprofessional.

Manner

In my opinion, however good you might be at teaching, however well you might know your subject, however popular you might be with you colleagues, if you do not treat your students with personal respect then you are not a good teacher. I have seen and heard teachers shouting at adult students before (for being late to class, for example). I have seen teachers tell students to go away and not disturb them during their tea break. I have seen teachers treating students with remarkable rudeness. And I always shudder when I witness this (only very occasionally, thank goodness). I would rather employ an 'average teacher' who is friendly and kind to students, than a highly skilled teacher who shouts at students or has no patience with them. Yes, it can be a very frustrating job. Yes, some students will want to make you scream at times. Yes, you will teach students with very different cultures from your own. But if you have limited patience or tolerance levels, then this isn't the job for you. If you are not friendly and patient with your students then they will not respect you, whatever the standard of your teaching.

So, be friendly. Show an interest in the students as people. Be patient. Be tolerant. Be understanding. Have a joke with them. Never shout at an adult student. Talk to your students outside class. If you can actually like them, all the better. Think of how you want to be treated by a teacher if you were learning a language in a foreign country, and of how you expect others to behave towards you in daily life.

Insight

Students are dedicating their time (and money!) to be taught by you. Treat each student with respect, patience and encouragement and you will create a positive learning environment for everyone.

1 *'Answer the ten questions. Work together.'*
Avoid unnecessary talk ('in a moment'), unnecessary instructions ('when you've finished') which can be saved for later, complex words ('avoid').

2 *'Stand up and walk around...'* (accompanied by a gesture).
'Mingling' is teacher language, avoid it. If you say 'you're going to hate it' then they probably will!

3 *'Work in twos* (plus gesture)'.
These were clearly unplanned instructions from a teacher who hadn't thought about how the activity was going to work!

4 This is the teacher chatting outside class. Poor grading ('jolly'), inappropriate and overly-colloquial language ('cost you a bomb') even for a high-level class.

5 Don't give a running commentary! You don't need to tell them that you are handing out paper. Also, never give instructions while doing something else at the same time.

6 Again, don't be negative when setting up an activity!

7 If you tell them it's going to be easy and it isn't, how will they feel? If it is easy they may wonder why you gave it to them in the first place.

8 And if they say 'No'?

9 Avoid phrasal verbs ('go through'). Say 'do'. And 'justify' is too difficult. Say 'give reasons'.

10 *'Stand up, please.'*
If you ask them if they want to stand up and they say 'No', then what?

Summary

▶ Teachers need to adjust their language to suit the level of the class they are teaching.

▶ This is done not by talking loudly or unnaturally slowly, but by simplifying the language they use.

- ▶ With lower levels especially, teachers should restrict the amount of language they use.

- ▶ Meaning can be clarified by the use of gestures and other body language.

- ▶ Instructions should be clear, relevant and precise – planned in advance if necessary.

- ▶ Class management is an important part of the teacher's responsibility and it needs to be thought about before and during the lesson.

- ▶ Teachers should adopt a supportive, friendly and encouraging manner.

4

....

Teaching grammar via a situational presentation

What is grammar?

> **'An abstract system of rules whereby a person's mastery of their native language can be explained'**
>
> (Adapted dictionary definition)

Different dictionaries define 'grammar' in different ways, but they all effectively talk about the 'rules of the language'. I don't think it really matters what definition we give the word, anyway, as we all have an idea in our minds of what the word means to us. However, do not assume, as many do, that 'grammar' equals only 'tenses' or verb forms (e.g. present perfect, past continuous/progressive). Grammar is language and how we use it; tenses are just a fraction of our language.

Personally, I don't like the word 'grammar' as it has too many negative connotations. For many it implies the rather dry learning of rules and then controlled practice of these rules with little or no communicative practice. Grammar doesn't have to be like this, and it shouldn't be. Despite my own dislike of the word, I will continue to refer to 'grammar' lessons, or components of lessons, because it is not a word English teachers can avoid!

What is much more important than a definition of the word 'grammar' is knowing what students need to know when they are learning language. We also need to know different ways to 'teach' grammar. And there's another awkward word: 'teach'. 'Teach', like 'grammar', has connotations. It implies a lot of teacher talk and explanations, initial student ignorance of what is being covered, a beginning and an end (they didn't 'know' it before, they did after), and it implies a completeness (they now know everything there is to know about this). You don't hear a teacher going into class saying 'I'm going to teach them relative clauses today', but teachers do know what their aims are in any lesson. I prefer 'clarification' of language to 'teaching' of language, but like 'grammar', 'teach' is a useful, all-embracing word that has to be used, and will continue to be used here. But do not think that language is just a series of unrelated items that can be dealt with one by one!

There are other words and terms that are, let us say, controversial in the profession, but at this stage of your career it is more important to concentrate on how to 'teach' than to be concerned with terminology.

What do students need to know?

They need to understand **meaning** within the given context.

They need to know the natural **pronunciation** of the language.

They need to know how to form the language (how it is constructed).

This is often referred to as **MPF**. As well as knowing the MPF, students need to use the language – **practice**.

This is a simplistic answer to the question, but for new and training teachers it is a very helpful one, especially when it comes to assessing if the lesson you have just taught was successful in terms of your language aims. We will look at each of the MPF areas in the remaining part of this and later units.

Situational presentations

'Presentation' is another controversial word! For many it implies, as does 'teach', that language can be broken up into convenient chunks which can be taught in isolation and built upon brick by brick until students 'know English'. Of course, it does not work this way. Experienced teachers know how best to develop a student's awareness of the language without falling into the 'Today we're going to do conditional sentences' approach. But until experience has been gained, it is very difficult to avoid dealing with language in chunks. Too much should not be expected of a trainee teacher, but it often is! Certainly, no person can become a teacher in four weeks – but they can develop their teaching skills and awareness sufficiently to be able to go in and deliver a reasonably successful lesson. That is where the real training begins.

So I make no apologies for talking about 'situational presentations', or 'a lesson on the 2nd conditional', or whatever. Rightly or wrongly this is what trainees are exposed to on training courses, and this is how the majority of course books deal with teaching and language. Once you gain real experience, you will be able to re-evaluate your approach.

Language needs context because context provides meaning. One way to illustrate meaning is via a situation. This can be done in a number of ways, including pictures. This situational presentation tends to be quite controlled by the teacher, at least initially, but with the students involved at all times. Let's take the word *should* – a modal auxiliary verb which, like other modals, can have different meanings depending on the context. If a student asks 'What does *should* mean?' you cannot usefully answer them. In isolation it is meaningless. If we put the word into a sentence – *You should wear a suit* – this is better because the word now fits in grammatically to a sentence – the form is illustrated. But meaning is still very limited. We don't know who is speaking, who they are speaking to, and why they are speaking. In short, there is no situation, thus no context, thus no meaning.

Insight

Context is crucial to understanding the meaning of language. You can't teach the meaning of the word *should* on its own. It needs to be part of a sentence: *You should wear a suit*. But we need to know who is talking, why and to whom. Giving this context will give real meaning to the language.

One way to provide context whilst maintaining student involvement is as follows. This is for an elementary/ pre-intermediate class.

Stage 1

Spend a few minutes on a class discussion about unemployment in the students' countries, how people go about finding work, the stages of applying for a job – leading to tips for a successful interview. The teacher asks questions and maximizes student talking time.

Stage 2

The teacher says she has a friend, Jason who is going for an interview tomorrow for a job at the bank. She elicits from the students how Jason should appear when he goes for the interview (appropriate clothes, shaved, hair combed, etc.). She then shows a picture of how Jason typically appears and asks if this would be appropriate for his interview. She highlights his dirty shoes, uncombed hair, unshaven face, and casual clothes.

Stage 3

The teacher says she saw Jason earlier. She emphasizes that Jason is her friend and she really wants him to get this job but is not confident because the interviewer is likely to expect interviewees to be dressed in a certain way. So, pointing to Jason's casual clothes the teacher asks if the students think it would be a good idea for Jason to go to the interview dressed in this way. Having established that it wouldn't, and still pointing to Jason's clothes, the teacher

says 'So what did I say to Jason when I saw him?' If possible, the teacher could also have a picture of someone wearing a suit to make the contrast with Jason's clothes and to make it clearer to the students what she is thinking. At this point, the teacher is testing to see if any students are familiar with the language being presented, wondering if anyone will reply *'You should wear a suit'*. This is the teacher's model/marker sentence containing the language being targeted. Maybe someone will know it, or may say the sentence with mistakes. Or maybe no-one has any idea. This is not important, you are just seeing if anyone knows it. If no-one does, the teacher says the sentence to the class, making sure everyone is listening!

At this stage of the lesson the main focus has been on meaning. The model sentence *You should wear a suit* now has a context, and the 'function' of 'giving friendly advice'. The function is basically the reason for speaking – other examples being 'inviting', 'apologizing', 'refusing', 'expressing surprise', etc. What the teacher has therefore done is to *illustrate* meaning by means of a pictorial situation and introduced a *model sentence* containing the *target language* (subject + *should* + base verb – this is the form). The function of giving friendly advice has been established via the situation. Depending upon the precise level of the class and what you have taught them before, you may need to have begun this lesson by checking they understood essential vocabulary (*suit, polish, shave, comb, suggest*) so as not to have the lesson 'stall' at a critical point. See Unit 7 for ways of presenting vocabulary.

Insight

In the example above, the teacher has personalized the context (it's her *friend* that forms the basis of the context). This is always a good idea if possible, as it helps students engage with the language – and remember it better too.

So far in this lesson the only aim that has been achieved is that meaning has been illustrated. However, it is essential that the teacher checks that the students really have understood the meaning. The fact that one student, maybe, has given you your model sentence does not mean that everyone has understood its meaning in the given context. Before you go any further in this unit, therefore, you should read Unit 8, then return to complete this unit.

Read Unit 8 now!

Now you have read about how to check students' understanding of new language, the **meaning** of MPF has been covered for this example lesson. As for the **pronunciation**, you should later read

Unit 9, but for now it is enough to say that the students must hear you say the model sentence several times naturally and then be given the chance to say it themselves. This is not as straightforward as it may sound, as we shall see later. But if we are teaching language for active use then the students need to know how to say it!

The **form** of the language has already been implicitly established via the giving and repetition of the model sentence. But this needs to be checked, just as the meaning needed to be checked. In the 'Jason' lesson it is easy to elicit further examples of *should*: *You should polish your shoes*, *You should comb your hair*, *You should shave*. These sentences can then be put onto the board (keeping the students participating by getting them to tell you what to write). Form can be highlighted by using different colour pens, if possible, and/or a substitution table:

		wear a suit
		polish your shoes
You	**should**	comb your hair
		shave
	shouldn't	wear those clothes

You is not unnecessarily repeated, nor is *should*. This way the form is further highlighted. Notice the same subject is used – the sentence *He should wear a suit*, for example, is not giving advice and therefore has a different meaning.

You could, if you feel it appropriate, label the respective parts of the sentence (subject/*should(n't)*/base verb). You could include your concept questions and answers. You could also mark sentence stress and intonation. Whatever degree of detail you decide is necessary, students need to have some 'take-away' record of the form that is being covered in the lesson – the above illustration is probably the minimum requirement.

Insight

Students need a clear written record of the form of the language once they have understood the meaning and mastered the pronunciation. You can involve them in this by inviting volunteers to tell you what to write or to come up to the board and write it themselves.

We will come back to form and pronunciation elsewhere, but the initial 'presentation' via pictures is an approach which is very commonly used, especially at lower levels.

Because it is primarily 'teacher-led' it is a method more suitable for students whose level of English is not high rather than for more advanced students, who need a greater learning challenge (see next two units).

Tips

1   If you are using pictures, make sure they are clear, simple and appropriate.
2   If necessary, check essential vocabulary at the start of the lesson.
3   Build the context slowly, carefully and clearly – *guide* the students and keep them involved throughout. Don't tell them what they can tell you. By continually asking them questions you are also checking they understand.
4   Have an obvious 'target' – a model sentence which will be a logical conclusion to your context build. In my example, *You should wear a suit* was a logical 'conclusion' to the storyline.
5   Try to elicit the sentence if you can; otherwise just tell them. If they have never come across this language before, it just tells you the extent of your task. It does not mean your context wasn't clear!
6   If possible, show your context to a colleague or friend beforehand to see if they think it is clear and appropriate.

You should also research the language yourself so you know everything you need to know about it. You need to anticipate possible problems your students might have with this language. These could include:

- confusion about the time reference
- a desire to refer to it as a tense (e.g. present simple – which it isn't!)
- incorrectly adding a *to* – You should to wear a suit
- thinking that by changing the person (e.g. from *you* to *I*) the function remains the same – it doesn't.

See Unit 19 for more on anticipating language problems.

Task

For each of the sentences below:

a Try to work out the form. In simple terms, what is the fixed structure that never changes? Refer to the *should* example earlier. Another example is '*I wish I hadn't done it*' = subject + *wish* + *subject* + *had/hadn't* + past participle. It sounds a bit complicated and 'grammatical' but it helps you, and students, know how a sentence is built.
b Think of a possible **context** and establish the **function** (e.g. 'giving advice') and meaning, including the time reference.
c Think about, or even prepare, a possible picture(s) to illustrate your meaning.

Do not worry about the level of the class these sentences might be aimed at, but none would be for a very low-level class, so assume that your students have a reasonable level of English.

1 I shouldn't have done it.
2 I'm going to France next week.
3 Would you mind helping me?
4 Let's go to a concert.
5 I've worked here for ten years.

Do this now, and check it later!

Key to task

1 I shouldn't have done it.

Form: subject + to be + *ing* form of verb (= present continuous progressive)

Function: maybe 'expressing regret about past action'

Context: student copies from another student in an exam, tells a friend about it the next day and expresses regret.

2 I'm going to France next week.

Form: to be (present form) + *going* + base verb (NOT the present continuous/progressive!)

Function: maybe 'giving information about future schedule'

Context: two busy friends with diaries trying to arrange to go out, one explains that the next week is impossible.

3 Would you mind helping me?

Form: *would you mind* + -*ing* form of verb

Function: maybe 'polite request for help' – asking now, but for help in near future.

Context: person at airport struggling with heavy cases, asks a passer-by for help.

4 Let's go to a concert.

Form *let's* + base verb (NOT 'let us' as this is unnatural in spoken English).

Function: maybe 'making a suggestion' – suggesting now what you could do later.

Context: two friends wanting to go out later, not sure where to go. One looks in the entertainment guide to see what's on, notices a concert and suggests that.

5 I've worked here for ten years.

Form: subject + *to have* (present) + past participle (present perfect simple)

Function: maybe 'giving reason for wanting to find a new job'. Time reference is past to present (from ten years ago to now) and maybe continuing into the future, at least for a while.

Context: employee to employer explaining why they have decided to leave the company – wanting a new challenge.

For each of the above **contexts**, meaning can be illustrated either with visuals or some other way (e.g. a recorded dialogue). But in each case there is a situation which illustrates the **meaning**. How much detail you give the students about the **form** will depend on their level. Higher-level students are normally comfortable and confident using terminology, lower-level ones much less so – it is pointless referring to 'subject' if they do not know what a 'subject' is!

Summary

▶ The meaning, form and pronunciation of new language needs to be covered, and communicative practice should be given, too.

▶ Situational presentations are controlled and effective ways to introduce language at certain levels.

▶ They can be done via visuals as long as these are clear and appropriate.

▶ Teachers need to be clear in their own minds of the meaning of the target language, how it is formed, and how it is spoken.

- This type of presentation is usually teacher-led, but with student involvement throughout. Let them do as much of the 'storytelling' as possible.

- Have a model sentence to work towards – elicit it if you can; give it if you can't.

- Check they really have understood the meaning (Unit 8).

This approach makes language more real than just a series of rules and explanations. The students see the language in a situation that is real and that provides the meaning. The teacher, therefore, starts with meaning and then introduces the language. In a sense, it is grammar in disguise, useful if you have students who are demotivated by thinking they are about to do a grammar lesson. If it works well, the presentation is interesting, even enjoyable. Above all, it is much better than giving an 'explanation' of a language point.

Some other ways to approach language teaching will be covered in the next three units.

5

Teaching grammar via a text or recording

The 'presentation' approach featured in the previous unit involved the teacher supplying a situation, possibly using visuals, in order to build a context with her students and eventually leading to a 'model sentence' containing the target language. It was very teacher controlled, though with full student participation, and rather contrived. It is a method which is effective, especially with lower levels, but no one method can, or should, be used exclusively or else it becomes predictable and boring. In addition, the method described is not especially challenging for higher-level groups. What we will look at in this unit, then, is another approach which provides variety from the previous one, a greater challenge, more learner autonomy, and a more realistic context.

Task 1

Look at the reading texts below and answer the following questions:

  a Does the language seem relatively simple, or high level for an intermediate class?
  b Does the text seem authentic ('real') or 'made-up'?
  c What specific language point appears to be potentially the most difficult/useful to focus on in class?

1 Bertrand's San Francisco experience

Bertrand is French and he lives and works in the north of France. His English is very good because he studied it at school and uses it in his job. A few months ago, he went to San Francisco for the first time to visit some friends he met in France a few years ago. He stayed for a week and in that time Bertrand and his friends had a very busy time – they visited Fisherman's Wharf, rode in the cable cars, saw the sea lions by Pier 39, ate in a different restaurant every day, walked up the steep hills, and did lots of shopping in the fantastic department stores. And, of course, they took lots of photographs.

At dinner one evening Bertrand and his friends – Marie, Myrianne and Norbert – were having dinner when the fire alarm sounded, but the waiters didn't seem to be worried, they just carried on working. Everyone around them carried on eating. They thought it was so weird, everyone carrying on with their meals even though the fire alarm was sounding. Bertrand and his friends decided to get out quickly, but just as they went out of the door they saw a sign by the entrance warning customers that there was going to be a fire alarm test that evening and they should ignore it. Bertrand and his friends quietly sat back down again to continue their meal feeling a bit embarrassed.

The friends continued to tour San Francisco and sample the different food at all the many restaurants in the city, and not listening to any more fire alarms! They had a wonderful time and had a lot of fun. They didn't know when they might meet again but this had been a great experience for them all. Bertrand was sad to leave his friends, especially as he knew he had to go back to work three days later.

2 A special offer

Abibus have been producing top-class cars with unbeatable value for 12 years. We have been talking to you, our customers, a lot recently to find out if there was any way of making our cars even better than before and you told us that our product is as good as it gets. The only way to make *Abibus* cars even more attractive would be to reduce the price, but that can't be done … or can it? Well, yes it can! From the beginning of next year, for a period of six months, we are cutting the cost of all our *Abibus* cars by 10% – yes, 10%! So from January 1 next year, *Abibus* cars will be 10% cheaper, but still top class. We have been doing business with you for 12 years. Now for the next 12!

3 Living in France

When I left my country a few months ago to work in France, I was very excited – I still am! But it hasn't been easy! For a start, there's the language. I used to study French at school, but that was a long time ago, so when I moved to Paris I knew it would be difficult because I had forgotten most of what I'd learnt. And I knew that driving would be a problem because I'm used to driving on the left, but in France they drive on the right! So, the first few times I drove here, it was really strange and difficult. It's still not easy, but I'm getting used to it – slowly! I really like the life here, though, – it's fast and exciting. The food is very different – it's generally great, but I'll never get used to eating frogs' legs. I was told that it tastes like chicken, but I don't agree! But the wine is great, and there are so many different types of cheese, I love it!

There are so many places to visit, and things to do, but a lot of people who visit France only come to Paris. Paris is great, but France is a fantastic country – the south of France is beautiful, and with great weather. And the north of France has some great places to visit – Lille is really pretty and is a friendly area. Yes, I'm really glad I live in this country now!

Key to task 1

1 Bertrand's San Francisco Experience

<u>Level of language</u>

Although this is the longest of the texts, the language is quite simple for intermediate students. *Steep* hills, *sample*, *embarrassed*, and maybe *department stores* are the only items of vocabulary that could cause problems, and the grammatical forms should mostly be familiar.

Insight

Familiarize yourself with the text you want to use and think about its suitability in terms of level for your group. Identify in advance any vocabulary that might cause problems or be unfamiliar. Plan how you can clarify or elicit meaning.

Authenticity

Definitely made up! It has the feel of having been specially written and graded (in terms of language). And the 'fire alarm' situation is somewhat contrived. This contrasts with authentic or near authentic texts. An authentic text is a 'real' one, e.g. a newspaper article. A near authentic text is one which is not real, but appears real – maybe something adapted from its original form, or an authentic-sounding made up text. The 'Bertrand' text is neither authentic nor near authentic. This does not mean that it is not valid to use, as we will see. What is important about this text, which makes it okay to use, is that the use of the target language is authentic. There is only one example of the target language, and it is surrounded by other language. So the text, while sounding a little contrived, is valid for classroom use.

Language to focus on

They were having dinner when the fire alarm sounded.

In this example from the text, we are using two verb forms – the past progressive (continuous), and the past simple. The progressive is *were having* and the simple is *sounded*. In the sentence, they started dinner **before** the fire alarm sounded, and may or may not have continued after. Thus, the simple **interrupts** the progressive.

This language point is a very useful one to focus on, and appropriate for the level.

How this can be done, we will see later.

2 A Special Offer

<u>Level of language</u>

Higher than in the previous text, though not significantly (*top class*, *unbeatable value*, *cutting the cost*, *to do business*) – certainly not so high that meaning is unclear.

<u>Authenticity</u>

Again, this is not an authentic text. However, it is near authentic because it was adapted from a real text and it sounds more real.

<u>Language to focus on</u>

Present perfect progressive, e.g. *Abibus* have been producing cars for 12 years. This describes an activity which started at a definite point in the past and continues to the present, with the likelihood of it continuing into the future. The present perfect tense, both simple and progressive, is a particularly difficult one for students, and there are differences between British and American use.

3 Living in France

<u>Level of language</u>

The vocabulary would be reasonably straightforward for intermediate students, but there is a variety of verb forms used with some complex time references (see below).

<u>Authenticity</u>

Not authentic, but adapted from an article about people working in different countries, so near authentic.

Language to focus on

Different uses of *used to*:   *I used to study French at school.*
                                   I'm used to driving on the left.
                                   I'm getting used to it (driving on the right).
                                   I'll never get used to eating frogs' legs.

You may not focus on all four uses at the same time, but with a higher-level class you could. Consider for yourselves how these differ in meaning and time reference!

Insight

Texts should ideally be authentic (real newspaper articles) or near authentic (adaptations or edited versions). This will mean that the target language is surrounded by plenty of other language. This is more challenging for higher level groups and gives a more realistic context.

Using texts to illustrate meaning

Before we look at the advantages of using texts to illustrate the meaning of language that you want to focus on, we need to consider possible methodology. If we refer to the 'Bertrand' text above and assume we are teaching an intermediate group of multilingual adults, we could follow the stages below:

1 Ask the class if anyone has been to / would like to go to San Francisco. If anyone has, they can tell the others about it. If no-one has then they can tell you what they imagine San Francisco. to be like. Alternatively, show pictures of San Francicso (steep hills, cable cars, Fisherman's Wharf, etc.) to get the class talking about it.

2 Tell students they are going to read about Bertrand, who visited San Francisco. They will have to read the text quickly and answer the questions:

Why did Bertrand visit San Francisco?

How many people was he with?

Why did they stop eating?

Did they finish their meal later?

Students read the text, and then work together to answer the questions. You then check the answers.

3 Highlight the sentence from the text *They were having dinner when the alarm sounded* and focus on the language (MPF). From this point on, you could follow the procedure described in the previous unit (concept questions, pronunciation work, highlighting the form on the board, eliciting further examples). This is a crucial part of the lesson as it is where you need to focus on the target language and check understanding.

4 Provide students with varied activities such as practice of the progressive / simple 'interrupted' action. See Unit 10 for more on practice activities.

Stage 3 above might appear a 'quick check' which almost gets in the way of everything else, but it is, in fact, the most important part of the lesson because this is where you are checking meaning, form and pronunciation. This is not a 'reading' but a 'grammar' lesson, so Stage 3 must not be a 'rush job' to get on to some fun practice activity that you have planned; students cannot have practice of something which they do not first understand.

So what is the purpose of the Reading part of the lesson? The text does what the picture of Jason in the previous unit did (*you should wear a suit*) – it provides a context, and the context illustrates meaning. However, it is important that the Reading text/tasks are not so demanding that students end up spending much more time trying to understand the text than working on the grammar. The tasks that you provide, therefore, need to be relatively straightforward (as above in Stage 2). They should serve to check basic understanding of the context, as well as directing students towards the specific language that you will focus on later. The lesson effectively starts as a Reading, but the text is there primarily to provide a later language focus (compare this with a Reading comprehension lesson – see Unit 11).

There are, of course, many variations to the stages listed above. But what we have looked at here is one way of dealing with grammar via a text, keeping a basic approach similar to that of the previous unit, but adapting the way meaning is illustrated.

Task 2

Look at Texts 2 and 3 above and the language focus suggested. How might you stage each lesson (following a similar pattern to the first text)? There is no key for this task, but it will help you to come up with possible ideas for yourself.

The three texts above are all 'made-up', though two are adapted from authentic sources. Sometimes it is easier and more convenient to devise your own texts to suit your requirements, but if you do, ensure that the level is appropriate for the students you are teaching, and that there is enough 'other language' in the text, not just a very unnatural over-use of the target language. Even with the 'Bertrand' example above, un-authentic as it is, there is plenty of 'other language' – with only one example of the target language.

Ideally, however, it is better to use authentic texts if possible. Course books (and you are likely to be using one) will usually 'present' language via authentic / near authentic material, but sometimes you may find, for example, **a newspaper article** which contains a piece of language that you want to focus on in class. Similarly, you might introduce language via **a recording**. Have a look at this conversation from a cassette. What piece of language do you think the teacher wanted to focus on later?

Jill	Hello.
Guy	Hello, er, Jill?
Jill	Yes, speaking.
Guy	It's Guy here.
Jill	Oh, hello Guy. How are you?

(Contd)

Guy	Fine, thanks. Er, I was wondering if you could, er, babysit for us tonight?
Jill	Yeah, sure, what time?
Guy	Er, we're going out at about 7.30.
Jill	7.30? Yeah, fine, what time do you want me to come round?
Guy	About seven?
Jill	Fine.
Guy	We'll leave some food for you.
Jill	Great. That would be lovely.
Guy	And some wine, if you like.
Jill	Cool.
Guy	See you later, then … and thanks again.
Jill	No problem, see you later. Bye.

Despite the 'script', this is an authentic recording – what you have above is merely the transcript. The two teachers were given a situation ('Guy – you want Jill to babysit tonight / Jill – you are available to babysit tonight / Guy – call Jill') and from that they improvised a telephone call. This was recorded, and the transcript written up afterwards for the teacher's benefit. So on the recording it sounded like a natural conversation. Most of the time, however, teachers don't need to go to all this trouble because the course book you will be using will have many recordings to introduce language, just as they have many texts. But sometimes you might prefer to prepare your own. If you do, don't script it, and make sure the recording is clear to use in class. And, as with the texts, make sure it is, at the very least, near authentic in sound and containing 'other language'.

Insight

Course books supply plenty of authentic recordings and usually supply an audio script for reference. Creating your own recordings, however, can also be very rewarding.

The piece of language that the teacher wanted to focus on from the recording was the very hesitant and polite request *I was wondering if you could* + base verb, as a means of introducing other forms of request. The possible procedure could be the same as with the text. For more on Listening comprehension lessons, see Unit 12.

It is important to stress, though, that you will rarely want to make up your own texts or recordings when course books use this approach so much, and when there is so much authentic material available to use.

Advantages of this approach

The previously described situational presentation using pictures is a largely teacher-centred approach, albeit with student involvement. It is, as we saw, an approach particularly effective with lower levels, primarily because there is very little 'other language' for them to deal with. With the approach described in this unit, however, there is a great deal of 'other language'. How much, and at what level, will be influenced by who you are teaching (you can, for example, edit a newspaper article if you feel it is too long and the reading part of the lesson would take up too much time). Also you shouldn't allow students to get concerned by unknown vocabulary in the text/recording if they don't actually need to know it for this lesson. As we saw before, the principal aim in such a lesson is language-related, not skills-related.

With the right level, therefore, this approach has a number of advantages, if executed properly:

▶ It is more challenging.
▶ Various skills are required.
▶ There is generally greater variety/stimulation.
▶ It is less teacher-centred.
▶ Students are exposed to the target language in an authentic/ near authentic setting.
▶ Consequently, they see/hear the target language before having to focus on it.

- The target language is surrounded by 'other language'.
- Students should be encouraged to read/listen in English in their everyday lives, to be exposed to 'real English' – using this approach in the classroom encourages them to do so.
- The whole approach becomes more natural, less contrived.
- Course books use this approach a lot, making preparation easier for the teacher!

Possible dangers

- The text/recording part of the lesson may go on too long, leaving inadequate time for the language focus/practice (unintentional language neglect).
- It is sometimes tempting for new teachers to devote too little time to the language focus part of the lesson (intentional language neglect).
- The text/recording may be inappropriate in terms of level.
- The tasks provided may be inappropriate in terms of level, or just too time consuming.
- If the text/recording is made up, it may contain too unnatural use/over-use of the target language.

Overall, the approach is very realistic and stimulating.

Summary

- Texts and recordings can be a very effective way of illustrating meaning of particular language.

- The approach involves a greater challenge for higher-level students.

- Skills work and language focus are integrated.

- Target language is surrounded by other language, which is more 'real'.

- Students are exposed to the target language before having to focus on it.

- There is greater variety and interest.

- The teacher should ensure that the language focus part of the lesson is given adequate time.

- Texts/recordings can come from course books, authentic sources, or be made up.

- Made-up texts/recordings need to be 'near authentic' (e.g. recordings should not be scripted).

6

Teaching grammar via 'test teach test'

We have looked at two different ways of focusing on grammar in the classroom; via a situational presentation, and via a text or recording – the latter usually from a set course book. Another approach is what is often referred to as **Test Teach Test**. In very simple terms, this approach begins with the teacher giving the students some kind of task relating to a particular piece of language with the basic aim of seeing how much the students already know, or do not know, about this language. So let's do it! Have a go at this:

Task

Complete these sentences using *the/a/an*:

1 I really like _____ actor who plays Johnny Redway.
2 I'm just calling to say how much I enjoyed _____ concert.
3 I hope you'll give her _____ gift on her birthday.
4 _____ unemployed receive money from the government.
5 Last week I went to buy _____ book for my trip, but when I got to the end of _____ book I discovered some pages were missing!

Why did you choose these answers? Can you think of any rules?

Now complete these sentences with *the*, or add nothing:

6 The bus can carry _____ 45 passengers.

7 I wasn't born in _____ England. I was born in _____ United States.

8 _____ politicians are not generally respected by society.

9 I spent the evening in _____ bar drinking _____ beer.

10 On _____ last evening of his vacation, Zsigmond and his girlfriend went on _____ beach. They looked at _____ moon and talked about _____ love! He thinks he's so romantic!

Why did you choose these answers?

The object of this exercise, given to the students at the start of the lesson, is to discover how much they know or don't know about articles (*a/an/the*), and to allow the students to discover the same facts for themselves! It gives the students some immediate responsibility for their own learning, especially if they can work on this task together in pairs or groups sharing their knowledge. Assuming you are giving this task to, say, an intermediate class, then your students are likely to get most of the answers correct. What they might have more trouble with is the 'why?'

This part of the lesson is the first **Test** in 'Test Teach Test'. But 'test' (or 'quiz' in American English) is a somewhat misleading and intimidating word as it gives the impression that students are under pressure and need to provide correct answers. In fact, it is a *discovery* task – but somehow 'Discovery Teach Test' doesn't have the same ring to it!

By having the students work together on the task, the Test element is reduced. If they are told to work in silence and not to compare answers afterwards, then they will feel pressure. Of course, it is perfectly valid for them to work individually at first, as long as they then get a chance to compare their answers before the teacher goes through it with them.

The teacher, having set up the task, should now be monitoring and evaluating as she observes how much / how little the students seem to know, and what the particular problems are that will need to be clarified later. Also, she may be able to deal with some individual problems while the class is working.

> ## Insight
> This is a student-centred approach. Encourage students to work together to complete the task, although they can also work individually as long as they have time to compare their answers at the end. Listen and observe each group. You will soon identify which elements need clarification.

It is important, too, not to think that this first **Test** must be 'grammatical' in its presentation, such as the above one on articles. It can also be communicative and unstructured, supposing some prior exposure to the language you are to focus on.

For example, for a lesson on prepositions of place and position (*in the corner*, *on the shelf*, *under the table,* etc.) you might begin by asking students to describe to each other a room in their accommodation, or the classroom you are teaching in. Or you might provide a picture of a room and give them the same task. As they work, you listen to see how accurately or inaccurately they use prepositions in their descriptions.

Another example: for a lesson on the second conditional sentence (e.g. *If I won the lottery, I'd buy a house*), you might ask your students to tell each other what they would do if they won a huge amount of money. Better still, give them a greater variety of 'What if?' type questions to discuss.

For experienced teachers and high-level classes, you can also throw open the lesson and ask the students to tell each other everything they know, or think they know, about the language in question. But this really should not be tried by newer teachers, and certainly not by those on training courses!

Having done this first **Test** the teacher now has to do the Teach part of the lesson. To be honest, this is a tricky stage in this kind of lesson for a new or trainee teacher, for the simple reason that you do not know, until the lesson is underway, exactly what

you are going to have to spend most time on. If your students
have completed the first task very well (going back to our task
on articles); or if they have used the target language reasonably
accurately in communication (e.g. the prepositions), then your own
task at this stage will be less demanding. However, if they have
been very inaccurate and confused in their use of the language,
then you are going to have to do a lot of clarification. But if they
have done a conventional grammar exercise, your first job in the
Teach is to check the correct answers. So let's do that by going
back to the task on articles.

Key to task

1 *The actor*, because there's only one and you know who is
   being referred to – it is definite.
2 *The concert*, for the same reason (compare this with *I'd love
   to go to a concert some time* – one concert, any concert).
3 *a gift*, because you don't know what gift, so it is *any* gift,
   but just one.
4 *The unemployed* (The jobless, The disadvantaged...) – referring
   to particular groups in society.
5 *a* book / *the* book – going from any book to the specific book
   that I bought.
6 No article (*the bus can carry 45 passengers*) – there is no article
   before a number except when referring to a particular group
   (e.g. *the 45 passengers on the bus had a lucky escape when...*).
7 *In England, in the United States*. No articles before most
   countries, except when the country includes a plural, e.g.
   The Netherlands.
8 No article before *politicians* because you are talking about a
   general group in society (compare with question 4).
9 *a bar* (unless there's only one where you live, or you are
   referring to your 'usual' bar). No article before names of
   drinks when you are talking generally. Compare this with
   I'd like a beer (meaning a *glass* of beer), and *the beer in this
   bar is particularly good*.
10 *the last evening* (referring to a specific evening); *the beach* –
   only one; the *moon* – only one. No article before *love* –
   referring to a general and uncountable noun.

As you go through the answers and reasons it is absolutely essential that you do not assume that because one student has given you the correct answer and reason, everybody else in the class agrees or has understood. So you need to ask concept questions and elicit further examples as you go along. This is partly why this approach is harder for new teachers. Unlike previous approaches, and especially the situational presentation, where the teacher has more control over how the lesson flows, this approach may require you to deal with a lot more student questions!

Insight

Remember to continually check understanding as you go through the answers. Ask students some concept questions or get them to give further examples to be sure. You might worry that students will ask lots of questions at this stage. Plan your lesson carefully so that you are thoroughly prepared.

But if you have planned and researched your lesson, as you should have done, this should not be too much of an ordeal! Remember, students ask questions not to trap you, but because they are inquisitive about the language. You may not always have a grammatical answer to give, but more often than not you can answer based on what you instinctively know is correct.

New teachers might feel safer giving students a more communicative first task (such as the two examples above) because this way they won't have to cope with explaining why certain answers are right or wrong. But, of course, they will still have to clarify meaning, form and pronunciation, as in any other kind of language lesson. In this **Teach** stage you are doing the essential tasks we mentioned earlier – you are clarifying meaning (concept questions, more examples etc.), form, and pronunciation. You may wonder about pronunciation of articles, but the weak pronunciation of 'a' (/ə/) is important. Having said that, there will be much less pronunciation work on articles than on a grammatical structure.

You might possibly think that articles are quite straightforward – they are not, especially when you consider their different usage in other languages. The task on page 54 did not even get into areas such as those nouns which sometimes have an article and sometimes don't (*I'll see you at school* vs. *I'll see you at the school*)! So, as with any piece of language – research it, anticipate problems, be prepared.

The final stage in this approach is the second Test. If the first Test is really *discovery*, then the second test is really *practice*. And the example task on page 54 could also be used as 'practice'. You may, then, ask 'What's the difference?' The difference is the *aim*. With the Test 1, the aim is to find out how much the students know about the language before the teacher focuses on it. The aim of Test 2 is to have practice of the language *after* the teacher has focused on it. So the nature of the activity may be very similar, but the aim – the reason for doing it – is quite different. Test 2 could involve one, or more than one, practice activity, perhaps one that is an 'exercise' and one that is communicative. See Unit 10 for more on practice activities.

It should be noted that all the approaches to teaching grammar that we have looked at can be used with teaching vocabulary as well, and you need to bear this in mind when you read the next unit (Teaching vocabulary).

Tips

1 If the first Test is an accuracy-based exercise (like the one on articles here), make sure it only deals with those aspects of the target language that you want to focus on in your lesson.
2 Monitor carefully this first Test in order to assess how much or how little the students know, and what specific problems you might have to deal with later.
3 Help with individual problems as they come up at this stage.
4 Make sure that the task you choose for the first Test is appropriate for the level.

5 Have varied tasks for the respective Test stages of the lesson.

6 Make sure you know what the correct answers are and the reasons for them.

If you are unsure, refer to the previous two units.

Advantages of this approach

As with the text/recording method described in the previous unit, Test Teach Test is more student-centred in its approach. Indeed, of the three approaches, this is the one which immediately has the students working together and not responding to the teacher. Even with the text/recording approach, the teacher still has to establish interest and maybe teach some vocabulary. This method, however, presents the task (Test 1) straight away and only requires instructions. For this reason it is particularly effective with higher levels, but it can be used with lower levels (for example, having students categorize nouns represented in pictures into 'countable' and 'uncountable'). Another positive point is that you are assuming some prior exposure to the language and are allowing the students the opportunity to show you, and remind themselves of, what they know. By getting students to work things out for themselves, you are encouraging learner autonomy and reducing over-reliance on the teacher. What's more, this can be a challenging approach – just how challenging will depend on the level and the class. But, unlike the text/recording approach, the focus is very much on the language. Consequently it is clearer to the students what the point of the lesson is, and what the teacher's aims are. As mentioned before, another advantage is that the teacher can discover just how well the students know the language before focusing on it – thinking time!

Just as course books frequently introduce a language focus via a text or recording, so too they frequently introduce language via an activity ('Test'). This is a good way of having students think for themselves. It also helps the busy teacher as it is far easier to use an activity provided in the course book than to have to create one for yourself.

Possible dangers

Picking up on the last advantage, if you are relying on an activity in the book then you will be asking for trouble if you don't do the activity yourself beforehand. You need to check that it covers what you want to cover in the lesson and no more, and that you know what the answers are and why. It can be embarrassing if you confirm the answer given in the Teacher's Book but cannot give a reason for it if asked – or worse, if it is not the answer you would have given!

Insight

You may often be working from a course book, but don't rely too much on the Teacher's Book for answers. *Always* do the activities yourself, so that you know what the answers are and, importantly, why.

As mentioned before, the unpredictability of the approach can un-nerve new and trainee teachers – you just can't be sure how well the students will do that first activity! But if you have researched and planned properly, you'll be okay; and if you have monitored the students during the task, you will have an idea of what problems you will have to sort out in the **Teach**.

With high-level classes there is the possibility that they will complete the first activity successfully and with no difficulties, and they might wonder why they are doing something which is 'easy'. In truth, this might suggest that the teacher has simply chosen something at too low a level. Or maybe the students don't know as much as they think they do, so don't be afraid to challenge them with lots of questions. However, even if they do know it all, there's no harm in reviewing the language and giving them more practice of it. In fact, reviewing familiar language is a very important thing for them to do, so tell them so!

Summary

We have looked at three different approaches to the teaching of language – a situational presentation, via a text or recording, and now Test Teach Test. Let's again review the main points.

▶ The approach used should be varied and appropriate for the level, students and language being taught.

▶ The essential ingredients of language learning are **Meaning**, **Pronunciation**, and **Form** with plenty of varied practice, and whatever the approach, **MPF** should be covered.

▶ Text/recording or **Test Teach Test** approaches are more initially student-centred and challenging – therefore more appropriate for higher levels.

▶ Teachers should always research carefully the language they are teaching and anticipate possible student problems.

▶ Students should always be kept fully involved in the learning process and be encouraged to tell you what they already know.

▶ Students should be allowed and encouraged to ask questions and raise issues for discussion in relation to what is being taught.

▶ 'Grammar' should include communicative practice, but the more conventional exercise is good for focusing on accuracy; such exercises are often popular with students who perceive this as 'real' learning!

▶ Language learning should be varied, interesting, and challenging.

All three of these approaches can be adapted for the teaching of vocabulary, and the next unit looks at other approaches used specifically for the teaching of new words or review of previously taught ones.

7

Teaching vocabulary

We saw in earlier units that **context** is essential if language is to have real meaning that students can relate to. Students learning vocabulary sometimes make the mistake of relying too heavily on dictionaries which give no more than a definition – and this often contains words unknown to the student.

Teachers, too, sometimes resort to 'lazy' ways of clarifying.

Task 1

What is wrong with the following approaches to dealing with meaning in the classroom? The students are pre-intermediate.

1 Teacher asks class 'What does *scared* mean?'
2 Teacher asks class 'Does anyone know what *scared* means?'
3 Teacher asks student 'Tell the rest of the class what *scared* means'.
4 Teacher asks class 'Do you all know what scared means?'
5 Teacher tells class '*Scared* means *frightened*'.
6 Teacher tells class 'Check the meaning of *scared* in your dictionary'.
7 Teacher tells class '*Scared* is when you are in a situation and you feel really worried and think there might be some danger'.
8 Teacher tells class 'For example, you get *scared* before an exam'.

New teachers, especially, often use the above approaches because they are easy and safe and don't require much thought or planning.

But in terms of clarifying meaning, they are practically worthless. Here's why.

Key to task 1

1/2/3   Even if someone does know, they are unlikely to have enough language to clearly tell the rest of the class. And how do you know if the other students can understand?

4   They might think they do, but don't. Maybe they'll say 'Yes' just to escape the teacher's attention! And if someone does say 'Yes', will the teacher then assume that everybody else knows?

5   If they don't know what *scared* means, they are unlikely to know what *frightened* means.

6   Very lazy! And just how helpful will the definition be? One dictionary definition is '*to be filled with fear or alarm*'. Whereupon the students look up *fear* and *alarm*!

7   A wordy explanation – and misleading, as *worried* is not the same as *scared*.

8   *Scared* before an exam? Or *worried*? Or *nervous*? If you say that *scared* means *worried* then students will think a person is *scared* about a friend's health rather than *worried*.

We will look later at a variety of more effective ways of clarifying the meaning of vocabulary. But first, consider your own experiences of learning new words in a new language.

Problems when learning new words

Meaning

▸ A word may have more than one meaning (e.g. *odd*, *cut*, *patient*).
▸ First language (L1) interference such as 'false friends' – words with a similar appearance or sound to words in their L1 but with different meanings. For example, compare *sympathetic*

with the French *sympathique*, meaning a 'nice' person. In German *bekommen* means 'to receive', sometimes resulting in a German speaker saying what sounds like 'I'll become a glass of beer' when they mean to say *I'll have a glass of beer*.

▶ Words may have different connotations, i.e. the meaning can be interpreted in different ways (e.g. *slim/thin/skinny*).

▶ A student may understand the meaning of a word, but not the appropriate context in which to use it. This is particularly true of language which is especially formal or informal.

Form

▶ The spelling may be very different from the sound (e.g. *cough*).

▶ Students may be competent speakers of the language but poor writers.

▶ A word may be more than one part of speech (e.g. it may be a verb and a noun).

▶ If you teach a word like *to rely*, you also need to teach that it is followed by *on*.

▶ Some words are irregular (e.g. the plural of *person* is *people*, the plural of *sheep* is *sheep*).

▶ Different varieties of English have different spellings e.g. *color/colour*.

▶ Spelling patterns are not obvious, e.g. *happy/happier … hit/hitting*).

Pronunciation

▶ The sound may not correspond to the spelling, as **Form** above (another example being *sign*).

▶ Students may have difficulty knowing how many syllables the word is broken up into (a typical mistake being *clothes* pronounced with two syllables).

▶ It is hard to know which syllable is stressed.

▶ Some words have shifting stress, e.g. his *conduct/to conduct*.

▶ A group of consonants together – a consonant cluster – can be difficult, e.g. *crisps*.

- ▶ A speaker of a particular language might have difficulty with certain sounds, e.g. the Japanese with / l / and the French with / h /.
- ▶ Some words with different spellings and meanings are pronounced the same, e.g. *bear/bare*.

Issues of pronunciation are looked at in Unit 9 but in this unit we will concentrate on how teachers can clarify meaning to a class. However, as with any language, and as with any lesson, teachers need to anticipate possible problems students might have and why they might have them. This way the teacher will be better equipped to help the students. With vocabulary, it is all too easy – as we saw at the start of this unit – to give a quick dictionary-type definition of a word rather than properly to illustrate meaning.

Insight

As you get to know your students – their level, any particular L1 interference, or sounds which are particularly difficult for them – you'll be able to more easily anticipate the problems they may have with new vocabulary. This will help you prepare how to illustrate and clarify meaning, form and pronunciation for them.

The pros and cons of students using dictionaries

We need first to distinguish between different types of dictionary. A Spanish student, for example, may want to use his English/Spanish dictionary. Or a standard English/English dictionary. Or an English/English dictionary produced for English students (and available at different levels). Of course, this student will need his Spanish/English dictionary out of class. However, in my view, teachers should greatly limit the use of the bilingual dictionary in the classroom, especially at higher levels, because literal translation is not always helpful or accurate. But I believe it is unreasonable for students to be prevented from referring to dictionaries in the classroom. Why buy a dictionary and bring it to class only for a teacher to say 'No dictionaries'? Dictionaries, after all, have many advantages. They provide:

- ▶ meaning (but see disadvantages below!)
- ▶ spelling
- ▶ a pronunciation guide (syllables, stress, sounds)
- ▶ information about the part of speech (e.g. *v* for *verb*)
- ▶ and sometimes, example sentences.

However, for students to benefit from all this, they have to know how to use a dictionary, what the symbols mean, how to locate an entry, etc. As teachers, we have to help them with this, maybe even spending a lesson or part of a lesson on dictionary training.

We also need to make students aware of the potential disadvantages of using dictionaries, including:

- ▶ All meanings will be given, not just the one your students need – so they can be confusing.
- ▶ In an ungraded dictionary, the definitions may be too complex (remember the example earlier with *scared*).
- ▶ Students may not know how to find the information they need (thus the need for dictionary training).
- ▶ If they are using a bilingual dictionary, the definition given may not be 'correct' (false friend).
- ▶ Students may become too reliant on dictionaries.

Insight

Ask students to bring in a dictionary if they have one. Encourage them to think about the advantages and disadvantages of using one. They will almost certainly know how to locate a word, but may not be familiar with the different symbols and abbreviations. Look at examples which clarify these.

So the teacher needs to encourage use of English/English dictionaries in the classroom. She needs to provide some training on how to use them. She needs to allow use of the dictionaries, but not at any time. She needs to be realistic in allowing students occasional use of their own dictionary – sometimes it saves a bit of time! But she has to make sure that the student doesn't rely on the dictionary as a substitute teacher, or as a constant 'check' on what the teacher has said!

When do we teach vocabulary?

▶ You may be doing a vocabulary-based lesson (e.g. words associated with weather).
▶ You may need to teach words required for the reading or listening coming up later – but only the essential words that the students will need to complete the task(s). Unit 11 deals with the 'selection of vocabulary' for a skills lesson.
▶ You may be asked a question about what a particular word means.

We saw in Unit 4 that language teaching should cover **MPF** (**Meaning, Pronunciation and Form**), as well as providing Use (practice). This applies to vocabulary as much as it does to grammar. However, if you are teaching a word that is only going to be read or heard and not spoken (i.e. vocabulary for passive use – recognition only), pronunciation is less important. But if you are teaching it for active use (it will be spoken), then pronunciation will be very important.

How can we illustrate meaning effectively?

If explanations are to be kept to a minimum, especially at lower levels, then teachers need to employ other more effective methods which serve to *illustrate* and *clarify* meaning.

Task 2

Try to think of a way to illustrate the meanings of the following words, avoiding any wordy explanations. As with the grammar, we want to try and see if any students already know the word, so we try to elicit the word if we can. Therefore, do not write up or say the word and then ask 'What does this mean?'! Start with meaning.

If no-one knows the word, tell them, but by this time the meaning should be clear.

elementary
1 to jump (e.g. *He was so happy he jumped up and down*)
2 tired (e.g. *She was very tired because she had worked all day*)
3 credit card
4 rich (e.g. *Bill Gates is very rich*)
5 heavy (e.g. *The bag is very heavy*)
intermediate
6 greedy (e.g. *Don't be greedy, you've eaten enough*)
7 patient (e.g. *The hospital has 75 patients at the moment*)
8 similar (e.g. *These houses are very similar*)
advanced
9 to take after (e.g. *She takes after her mother; they look so similar*)
10 to be hard up (e.g. *Teachers are usually hard up*)

Tips

1 Use pictures or drawings. For example, rather than explaining what *lorry/truck* is, show them a picture of one.
2 Use realia (the actual object). For example, rather than explaining what a *credit card* is, show them one.
3 Use mime. For example, rather than explaining what *tired* or *jump* is, mime it. Also, with *heavy*... try to pick up something in the class and exaggerate the fact that is is heavy to lift.
4 Use contrasts. For example, with *heavy* you could also pick up something which is not heavy to emphasize the point.
5 Use synonyms of a lower level. For example, for *exhausted* you could say 'a word meaning *very tired*'. If you are teaching them *exhausted*, then they should know *tired*. But if the synonym is not of a lower level, you are wasting your time. The same approach can be used with antonyms.

6 Use spoken gap-fill sentences. For example: *I ate four pieces of cake… I was very* _____. If the students know *greedy*, they will complete the sentence. If they don't, you tell them – they now know the meaning. Much better than 'What does *greedy* mean?'! You could treat *patient* in a similar way – *Sick people in a hospital are called* _____. This combines the gap-fill with a simplified definition. With *similar* you could combine the gap-fill approach with two drawings on the board of, say, two houses which are similar, but not the same.

7 With higher levels, try to use more student-centred approaches to increase learner independence. This respects the fact that your students already have a good level of English. Higher levels need to be challenged more, and they quickly get bored if there is too much coming directly from the teacher. One way is to provide contextualized sentences – a sentence containing the word and making the meaning clear. Rather like the gap-fill sentence, but with no gap! Students work together, and if they don't know the word, they can deduce it from the context. For example, 'I am so *hard up* I can't even afford a newspaper.' You could use a similar approach with *take after*, maybe combined with pictures. Obviously, you have to check afterwards that the students really have understood the meanings (refer again to Unit 8).

8 Matching exercises can combine some of the above approaches. For example, match words with pictures, words with synonyms, words with simplified definitions, words in sentences with simplified definitions.

9 Following a reading task, students can look at given words in the text and match them with, or deduce, their meaning.

10 Course books usually have an excellent and varied selection of vocabulary tasks including all of the above. In general, teachers should avoid too much of a teacher-centred approach and instead encourage students to work more independently.

This idea of *illustrating* meaning rather than explaining it, and of starting with meaning rather than the written or spoken word, makes the learning of meaning more effective. But the point made in Unit 4 remains valid here. If you successfully elicit a word or correct answer from one student, it does not mean that everyone else has understood. You need to check understanding (e.g. with concept questions).

Insight

Plan ahead for illustrating the meaning of new vocabulary. Prepare any realia or pictures in advance. Think about any particularly difficult words that will need careful clarification and prepare your spoken gap-fill sentences (or synonyms, etc.) for these. Remember, variety in the way you illustrate meaning will keep your students interested and motivated.

Task 3

How could you check understanding of the words in the previous task? When you're finished, check the suggestions in the **Key** at the end of the unit.

How will the students remember what they have learnt?

Students have different ways of remembering. Some prefer to write up their own personalized dictionary with translations into their language, for example. Some try to learn and remember a certain number of words a day/week. Others keep a record of what they have learnt, but in a disorganized, random way. So what can the teacher do to help the longer-term learning process?

Tips

1 Show students how they might keep an organized record of their work (not just vocabulary) – there is no 'right way', but there are plenty of 'wrong ways'! One possibility is according to themes or topics.
2 The record should include a guide to meaning, form and pronunciation. The word should appear in a contextualized sentence.

3 Students should be encouraged to be selective in choosing the words they really feel are useful to them longer-term. They should disregard the others. They also need to know the difference between 'active' and 'passive' vocabulary.

4 Students need to be encouraged to personally review what they have learnt in whatever way they find helpful.

5 Teachers should do review activities in class from time to time – you can't just teach something in one lesson and never return to it!

....

Insight

At the beginning of a lesson, give a quick review of new vocabulary from the *previous* session. Alternatively, ask students which words they remember – then check understanding! At the end of a term, prepare a quiz to review key vocabulary, with matching exercises, pictures, etc.

....

Key to tasks 2 and 3

1 *Jump*	You could do a mime contrast, e.g. hop and ask 'Is this the same as jump?'
2 *Tired*	'I work all day with no break. Am I tired?' 'I slept for twelve hours. Am I tired?'
3 *Credit card*	Show examples of credit cards/travel cards/ID cards and each time ask 'Is this a credit card?' 'Can I buy something with a credit card? Do I need real money?'
4 *Rich*	'I have a million pounds/dollars – Am I rich?' 'I have ten dollars/pounds in the bank – Am I rich?'
5 *Heavy*	A series of contrasts with objects in the room.
6 *Greedy*	'I eat eight pieces of bread – Am I greedy?' 'I share my food with you – Am I greedy?' 'Is greedy positive or negative?'
7 *Patient*	'Is a patient usually sick?' 'Is everyone in a hospital a patient?' 'Do patients need to see a doctor?'

8 *Similar*	Use of pictures and realia would be effective (e.g. the clothes different students are wearing).
9 *Take after*	Again, pictures would be best.
	'My brother and I look completely different. Do I take after him?'
10 *Hard up*	'I'm rich. Am I hard up?'
	'I have very little money. Am I hard up?'

Notice with the last item that I did NOT say *If I'm rich, am I hard up?* This is a conditional sentence and may be too complex to understand. Keep your check questions simple!

Summary

▶ You should avoid the 'What does this mean?' approach.

▶ It is usually more effective to start with meaning and then elicit or give the word.

▶ Avoid giving non-simplified definitions or explanations of words.

▶ Train students how to use their dictionaries effectively. Limit, but do not put a ban on their use in the classroom.

▶ Be aware of some of the problems students have learning vocabulary as this will help you in your planning.

▶ Use a variety of ways to illustrate meaning depending upon the level of the class.

▶ With higher levels especially, but not exclusively, encourage learner independence – student-centred learning.

▶ Check that meaning really has been understood.

- ▶ If appropriate for the lesson, check pronunciation (Unit 9).

- ▶ Check that students are clear about the form of the word and sentence-fit.

- ▶ Make sure the words are being taught for a reason – that they will be used in the lesson!

- ▶ Help students to keep effective records of what they have learnt.

- ▶ Review what has been learnt from time to time.

8

Checking understanding of meaning

We saw in earlier units the importance of *illustrating/conveying* meaning of language, rather than *explaining* it. By providing meaning in context, teachers are providing their students with real language rather than abstract rules. But this is not enough. We have to *make sure* they have understood. If, as in the example in Unit 4, the teacher has used a situational presentation to illustrate the meaning of *should* for giving advice (*You should wear a suit*), the meaning may have been clearly *illustrated*. However, this does not guarantee that it has been understood. Teachers, therefore, must employ effective and efficient methods for checking the students' understanding of the meaning which has been illustrated. So how can this be done? And how should it not be done?

✗ **a** 'Do you understand?', 'Okay?', 'All right?' etc.
✗ **b** 'So, Gabriel, what does *should* mean?', 'Do you know what this means?'

Insight

It may appear that students have understood the meaning of language, and they themselves may believe they have, but we need to check this.

It is easy to ask these obvious questions. But when, as is usually the case, the students give the answer we are hoping for ('Yes'), it does not mean that we can safely move on to the next part of the lesson.

'Do you understand?' – 'Yes' proves absolutely nothing. Quite possibly, the student just wants to get the attention of the teacher placed elsewhere and saying 'Yes' is a quick way of doing this. Maybe the student thinks she does understand, but doesn't really – 'Yes' doesn't tell the teacher this. Maybe the student does indeed understand, but still the teacher has no evidence – and besides, what of the other students?

Asking a student to repeat or give the meaning is flawed for different reasons. Principally, does the student – even if he has understood – possess a sufficient range and level of language to express himself? Would other students understand him? Would the 'explanation' be correct? This approach can only really succeed with very high-level students, and when the teacher knows her class very well. In such circumstances, it is more effective with vocabulary than with grammar.

Concept questions

It is necessary, then, to use other methods of checking understanding, of which the most effective is **concept questions**. Let us consider again the model sentence featured in Unit 4 – *You should wear a suit* (advice to casually dressed friend about to go to a job interview). In order for the teacher to first illustrate the meaning of *should* in this context, and then check it has been understood, she needs to have recognized the essential meaning of the language in this context:

- ▶ we are talking about a possible future action (wearing the suit)
- ▶ the person we are talking to does not have to wear a suit (no obligation)
- ▶ it would be a good idea if he did – I want him to (friendly advice)

We can now turn these statements into simple questions:

1 Are we talking about the past, the present, or the future? **future**

2 Does this person *have* to wear a suit? / *Must* he wear a suit? **no**

3 Do I think it would be good for him to wear a suit? **yes**

If students give any answers different from the above, the assumption must be that they have not understood and some further clarification will be required.

| ✗ *Should he wear a suit?* | Avoid using the grammatical form being tested in the question. If they haven't understood it before, they won't understand it now! |
| ✗ *Will he wear a suit?* | Irrelevant, and impossible to answer, anyway! Avoid questions which focus on the **context** rather than the **concept**. |

Let's look at another example – *She's been to Hungary* – and consider the **essential information** of this present perfect simple statement:

▶ it happened in the past
▶ the listener doesn't know when, according to the sentence alone
▶ the listener doesn't know how many times the person went
▶ she's not there now (compare with *She's gone to Hungary*)

Again we can turn these into **concept questions** as follows:

1 Are we talking about the past, present, or future? **past**
2 Do we know exactly when she went? **no**
3 Do we know how many times she went? **no**
4 Is she there now? **no**

✗ *Has she been to Hungary?/Have you been to Hungary?* etc.

The second question is asking for information, not checking meaning. Both questions use the tense that is being tested – compare with question 3 above, which uses a simple tense instead.

We can use the same method with vocabulary. The **essential meaning** of *library* is:

- ▶ we can borrow books from a library (we assume here that our students understand *borrow)*
- ▶ we cannot buy books from a library
- ▶ we can sit and read in a library

Increasingly, libraries also contain other facilities such as video and music loans, but for the sake of this example we will focus on books!

The **concept questions,** therefore, become as follows:

1	Can you borrow books from a library?	**yes**
2	Can you buy books from a library?	**no**
3	Can you sit and read in a library?	**yes**

For *engaged* (as in *Marc and Laura have got engaged*) the **essential meaning** is:

- ▶ they are not married now
- ▶ they plan to marry
- ▶ they have promised each other / it is a definite plan

1	Are they married now?	**no**
2	Will they marry in the future?	**yes**
3	Is this definite / sure?	**yes**
4	Have they made a promise to marry?	**yes**

Insight

Plan your concept questions in advance. First consider the essential information in a statement. Then define this in simple sentences. Now turn these into simple questions. A useful question to start with may be: *Are we talking about the past, present or future?*

Tips to formulate concept questions

1 First analyse the language and its meaning within the given context.
2 Define the essential meaning in simple statements.
3 Turn these statements into questions.
4 Keep the questions simple in terms of both language and length.
5 Avoid questions which are not relevant to the *meaning* of the language.
6 Avoid using the same grammatical forms in the questions that you are testing.
7 Ask questions which do not require a lot of language in the answer.
8 Make sure the answers are clear and unambiguous.
9 Plan them in advance – until you have more experience and confidence, they will not be easy to think of on the spot.
10 Avoid the 'absurd' (e.g. *honeymoon* – 'Can you find honey on the moon'?)

Task 1

Now you try. For each of the following language items (given in bold), think of a context, define the meaning, and devise concept questions and expected answers.

1 **I wish I had** a car. (subject + *wish* + subject + past simple form)
2 **You shouldn't have taken** that book. (subject + *should(n't) have* + past participle)
3 **I'm looking forward to** my holiday. (subject + *to be* + *looking forward to...*)
4 **I had** my suit cleaned. (subject + *had* + object + past participle)
5 They're going on their **honeymoon**.
6 That watch is really **expensive**.

When you have finished, look in the **Key** on p. 83 and see if you're on the right lines.

It is also good, when appropriate, to use examples, realia, mime, pictures, etc., to check understanding.

Examples   For *difficult* you could contrast 3 + 3 with 37 × 37 and for each sum ask if it is difficult.

Realia   For *mug* (mug of tea) you could show a plastic cup, and a cup and saucer and ask if they are mugs.

Mime   For *slowly* you could mime walking quickly and then slowly and check that students have understood which is which.

Pictures   For *lorry/truck* show pictures of other vehicles and ask for each 'Is this a lorry/truck?'

As we saw in Unit 7, any of these methods can also be used for the initial illustration of meaning. In other words, you could convey the meaning of *diffi*cult by using the sums above, then check understanding via a similar example.

Insight

Concept questions can be used to check understanding of vocabulary items as well as more complicated language or grammatical structures. Try to keep your questions really simple, ideally so that just 'yes' or 'no' answers are required from the students.

Timelines

Time can be represented using many different verb forms. This can be confusing for a student when, for example, we use the present simple tense to refer to future time (e.g. *The train goes at 3.30 this afternoon.*) Concept questions can be used to check understanding of tenses and time, but there is another way which is particularly effective and that is using **timelines**.

Looking at the sentence *I was watching TV at 10 pm last night* we can identify the **form** as past continuous (progressive) – subject + *to be* / *was* or *were* + *-ing*. The **time** reference is an action which started **before** 10 pm and may have continued after 10 pm, but the action was already in progress at 10 pm. This can be represented on a timeline thus:

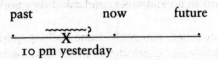

The x here represents the moment of 10 pm. The wavy line represents the ongoing action / state of watching TV. The wavy line begins before 10 pm and goes right up to the moment of 10 pm. The subsequent question mark beyond 10 pm represents the fact that we do not know if the person continued to watch TV after 10 pm, though they may have done. The wavy line is clearly set in past time only, consistent with this use of the past progressive.

Another example. *I had been waiting for the bus for 10 minutes before it came.* The first clause is in the past perfect progressive (subject + *had been* + *-ing*) and the second is in the past simple (*came* being the past simple form of *come*). This sentence is also set entirely in the past with one action going on for a period of time (waiting) before being stopped by an event (the arrival of the bus). In the timeline below, the wavy line again represents an ongoing action/state whilst the cross represents an event which effectively interrupts or ends the ongoing action.

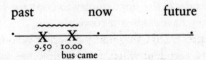

Timelines can be used to help illustrate meaning, and they can be used to check students have understood what has gone before. And here's an important point. If the teacher is using a timeline to check her students have understood the concept, then she must involve the students in the process of drawing the timeline. Students, then, need to know what a timeline is, and what the symbols the teacher uses actually mean (e.g. the wavy line). The teacher needs to be consistent in the way she draws timelines. The students can then effectively tell the teacher how to construct the timeline, or even draw it themselves. Timelines can be used in conjunction with concept questions. For example, a teacher may ask 'Where do I put the cross? Here? Or here?'

Insight

Understanding the relationship between tenses and time can be challenging for students. Timelines provide a visual representation of time and they are an excellent way of illustrating and checking understanding. Involving the students themselves in constructing the timeline is also very effective.

Tips for using timelines

1 Plan how to do them.
2 Practise drawing them.
3 Make sure the line can be clearly seen on the board.
4 Use different colours for effect and clarity.
5 Make sure students know what everything on the line represents.
6 Involve the students.
7 Use them in conjunction with concept questions.
8 Be consistent in how you draw them.
9 Make sure they accurately reflect the essential meaning.
10 Give the students the opportunity to copy the line, and check to see if they have copied it correctly.

Task 2

Now you try. Draw timelines for the following, then check the **Key**.

Start by analysing the language and defining the essential meaning, then draw the timelines.

1 I've lived here for 10 years.
2 This time next week I'll be on the plane.
3 I'll have finished by 3 pm tomorrow.
4 I've been to Ghana.
5 I saw *Titanic* yesterday, but I had seen it before.

Key to tasks 1 and 2

Task 1: Concept questions
1 Do I have a car now? **no**
  Do I want a car? **yes**
  Is it likely I will get one soon? **no**
2 Did you take the book? **yes**
  Do I think you were right to take it? **no**
3 Are we talking about the past, the present,
  or the future? **future**
  Will I have a holiday? **yes**
  Am I excited about my holiday? **yes**
4 Was my suit dirty? **yes**
  Is it clean now? **yes**
  Did I clean it? **no**
  Did another person clean it? **yes**
5 Are we talking about the past, the present,
  or the future? **future**
  Is a honeymoon a kind of holiday? **yes**
  When you go on holiday with your friends, is that a
  honeymoon? **no**
  Do you go on honeymoon straight after getting
  married? **yes**
6 In my opinion does the watch cost a lot of money? **yes**
  This watch (pointing) cost me £10 ($15). Was it
  expensive? **no**
  That watch (pointing) cost my friend £300 ($450).
  Was it expensive? **yes**

Note: These are only sample questions. You may have written
different ones which are still relevant.

Task 2: Timelines

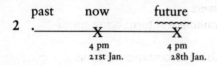

```
     past        now        future
1  ._____?_____.
      X          X
    1991       2001
```

```
     past        now        future
2  ._____.
                 X                  X
              4 pm               4 pm
            21st Jan.          28th Jan.
```

```
     past        now    ?   future
3  ._____.
               Wed.    X
                      3 pm
                      Thurs.
```

```
     past    ?    now        future
4  ._____.
              X
```

```
     past  ?    ?   now       future
5  ._____.
           X    X
        before yesterday
```

Summary

In this unit we have established the following main points:

▶ Teachers have to **check** that students have understood what they have learnt.

▶ Questions such as 'Do you understand?' are ineffective.

▶ Asking a student to explain meaning is, with few exceptions, unrealistic and can do more harm than good.

- ▶ Concept questions are an effective and efficient way to genuinely check understanding. They should:
  - focus on the essential meaning of the language in the context being provided
  - be short and simple in nature
  - avoid ambiguity
  - require very short answers
  - avoid the use of the grammatical form being tested

- ▶ Timelines provide a visual representation of time.

- ▶ Students need to be involved in the drawing of a timeline.

- ▶ Timelines need to be clear, simple, and accurate.

The process of checking understanding may take up a tiny percentage of your lesson, but it is a crucial stage. If the students remain unsure of meaning now, then they will struggle for the rest of the lesson, and will be unable to use the language naturally or correctly after the lesson. Checking understanding effectively is a difficult teaching skill, but it becomes easier with practice. After a while, you will find that you can do this 'on the spot' because your own confidence with language and its meaning and use will have grown with experience. To begin with, though, analyse the language carefully and plan how you will check understanding.

9

Pronunciation

What is **phonology**? In general terms we can say that it includes:

sounds the individual sounds of the language
stress both *word* stress and *sentence* stress
intonation the rising and falling of our voice to convey different meaning
connected speech including how sounds and words relate to each other in natural speech; how sounds alter or disappear, how words link etc.

Phonology is the subject of many books. This unit is more of a guide to how pronunciation can be incorporated into lessons rather than a unit about phonology.

Whether you are a Californian or a Texan, a Londoner or a Glaswegian, the Queen of England or a bus driver, there is no *right* and *wrong* way to speak. Just *different* ways. People have different accents and maybe dialects. There are numerous varieties of English spoken around the world – and they are all English. Of course there are differences. Between American and British English, for example, there are many differences, not least in pronunciation. Sometimes it really does seem as if they are different languages, and one is sometimes referred to as 'correct' English, and the other not. But I disagree with this. Indeed, I believe strongly that students should be exposed to as many different accents, dialects and varieties of English as possible and that we are doing students a disservice if we expose them only to what in Britain is sometimes referred to as 'the Queen's English', or 'BBC English'. 'BBC

English' refers to the days when all announcers and newsreaders seemed to possess standard south of England pronunciation. These days it is different, but not everybody is happy. When a popular news programme in England was presented for the first time by a Welshman, there were some complaints that a Welshman should be allowed to read the BBC news! As for the 'Queen's English' – well, no comment is required!

As a teacher, I try to play recordings that represent different British accents, and different varieties of English. At first, students find these difficult to understand. And that's the point. A student studying in London who visits Glasgow, or a student studying in San Francisco who visits Georgia, is going to find it difficult at first to understand what is the same language. I also strongly emphasize to my students that there is no right and wrong way to speak English (in terms of varieties of pronunciation), and that it is important for them not to be restricted to 'standard' English, whatever that is. And it is sad, in my opinion, when TV programmes in either Britain or the United States feature a character from the other side of the Atlantic who speaks in an extremely unrealistic way, unrelated to any variety of English.

Spelling and pronunciation

There is no clear relationship between spelling and pronunciation in English. Look at the following words:

cough – *tough* – *though* – *through* – they all end -*ough* but the pronunciation is different each time.

How can a student seeing the word *laugh* for the first time have any chance of knowing that *ugh* is pronounced /f/?

heard and *beard* both end -*eard*, but the sound is quite different!

How about *both* and *brother*? Both contain the letters *oth*, but they are pronounced differently.

Wednesday – so is that 'wed – nes – day'? No, it's /wen/ – a silent *d*.

Convinced now? This is a very strange language.

The sounds of English

What students need, then, is some representation of the sounds of English so that when they look up a word in a dictionary and see its phonetic transcription, they can work out the standard pronunciation of that word. This is not to say that we are trying to make our students speak in a certain way, just that they need a guide. Such guides will have alternative versions depending on the variety of English, so please do not consider the following example to be representative of the only 'correct' way to say these sounds; many readers will have additional sounds in their own speech, and may not recognize some of these examples!

> **Insight**
> The spelling of words in English, such as *cough* or *though*, does not indicate how they are pronounced. A phonetic transcription can help students pronounce new or unfamiliar words. cough = / kɒf / though = / ðəʊ /

The underlined part of each word represents the given sound (phoneme).

Vowels

b<u>ea</u>d	/ iː /
b<u>i</u>d	/ ɪ /
g<u>oo</u>d	/ ʊ /
f<u>oo</u>d	/ uː /
b<u>e</u>d	/ e /
th<u>e</u>*	/ ə /
b<u>ir</u>d	/ ɜː /
d<u>oo</u>r	/ ɔː /
c<u>a</u>t	/ æ /

c<u>u</u>t	/ ʌ /
c<u>a</u>rd	/ a: /
c<u>o</u>d	/ ɐ /

*known as the 'schwa' – the most common sound in English. In a word like *potato*, the first *o* is pronounced with a schwa (weak form); also the *e* in *terrific*.

Consonants

<u>p</u>i<u>p</u>	/ p /
<u>b</u>ul<u>b</u>	/ b /
<u>t</u>ac<u>t</u>	/ t /
<u>d</u>are<u>d</u>	/ d /
<u>ch</u>ur<u>ch</u>	/ tʃ /
<u>j</u>u<u>dg</u>e	/ dʒ /
<u>c</u>a<u>k</u>e	/ k /
<u>g</u>ar<u>g</u>le	/ g /
<u>f</u>ear<u>f</u>ul	/ f /
<u>v</u>i<u>v</u>id	/ v /
<u>th</u>ir<u>th</u>ieth	/ θ /
<u>th</u>is	/ ð /
<u>c</u>ea<u>s</u>e	/ s /
<u>z</u>one<u>s</u>	/ z /
<u>sh</u>eepi<u>sh</u>	/ ʃ /
trea<u>s</u>ure	/ ʒ /
<u>m</u>ur<u>m</u>ur	/ m /
<u>n</u>a<u>nn</u>y	/ n /
thi<u>ng</u>	/ ŋ /
<u>h</u>ope	/ h /
<u>l</u>u<u>ll</u>	/ l /
<u>r</u>ed	/ r /
<u>w</u>ent	/ w /
<u>y</u>acht	/ j /

Diphthongs

<u>rea</u>r	/ ɪə /
m<u>ay</u>	/ eɪ /

pure	/ ʊə /
boy	/ ɔɪ /
go	/ əʊ /
rare	/ eə /
buy	/ aɪ /
now	/ aʊ /

Why use such a transcription? Well, it helps give students a record of pronunciation. It helps them to use a dictionary more effectively, and it can aid the teacher doing correction work. Students need to get the chance to hear a sound within a word before being expected to try and repeat it – in other words, teachers should raise students' awareness. How to do this we will look at later.

Task 1

In Unit 19 you will see how important it is for teachers to anticipate problems students might have with the meaning, form, and pronunciation of any language being taught. With this in mind, look at the following, and consider what peculiarities of pronunciation exist in terms of sounds and their relationship with one another.

Example:

> *a pint of beer* the *a* is a schwa, 'of' is pronounced / əv / and
> *a pint of* sounds like one word.

1   asked
2   'Can you help me?' 'Yes, I can'
3   Do you want some?
4   Do you have to go?
5   I used to drive
6   Fish and chips
7   Peas
8   Goodbye
9   Shall we go?
10 I was working at home

Before checking your answers, let's consider one way of raising students' awareness and improving their own pronunciation skills, not just regarding sounds, but all aspects of pronunciation: **drilling**.

Repetition drills involve students repeating what they have heard. Consider the sentence *She's worked here for two years*. The teacher is covering the present perfect simple in her lesson for unfinished state and has illustrated meaning using the context of a teacher who... *has worked here for two years*. The given sentence has been elicited by the teacher and it contains the target language. Students, however, need to keep the language in context – it's no good their repeating *has worked* in isolation; they need to say the whole sentence. A good approach to drilling is as follows:

Having elicited the sentence *She's worked here for two years* the teacher repeats the sentence naturally, two or three times so the students can hear it. Then, the teacher should 'break up' the sentence using her fingers as representations of each word.

'She – has – worked – here – for – two – years'

Then, she repeats 'She – has' and joins her first and second fingers and say 'She's', and repeats the remainder of the sentence.

Finally, she repeats the whole sentence again naturally, perhaps demonstrating rhythm. This first stage is *giving a model pronunciation*.

Then, giving a clear direction to the students (spoken and gesture), the teacher tells the class to repeat what she has said. At this stage she says 'Repeat', and avoids vague instructions such as 'would you like to say that?' Students repeat the sentence together first (*choral repetition*) to give them confidence. Then, the teacher gestures to students in turn to say the sentence individually, eliciting correction as required.

With this sentence, the teacher's model needs to include the /iːz/ in *she's*; the /t/ sound of *-ed*; and the weak form with schwa of *for*.

> ## Insight
>
> **Drilling** is controlled repetition of words or sentences, guided by the teacher. First say the word or sentence naturally a few times. Then break up sentences or words and repeat them in 'chunks'. Students can repeat after you as a group and then individually.

Drilling applies equally to vocabulary, and the aim is for students to hear and give the correct and natural pronunciation of a piece of language. There are teachers who don't like drilling, or don't believe in it. But in my experience, students who are not confident about pronunciation welcome the controlled opportunity to have practice saying a new piece of language. They need to have confidence in their pronunciation, and this is one way to give it to them. Of course, you shouldn't overdo it at any stage, but done properly and appropriately, drilling is valuable and effective.

Key to task 1

1 a is pronounced /a:/ and d is pronounced /t/.
2 The first *can* is pronounced weakly /kən/, but the second is not – /kæn/.
3 *do you* is normally pronounced / djə / or /djʊ/.
4 'do you' as above. *v* in *have* is pronounced /f/; to has a schwa.
5 *d* is pronounced /t/ and the *to* is weak. The words *used* and *to* are linked as if they were one word.
6 *and* is reduced to /n/ and the whole phrase sounds like a single word.
7 /pi:z/ – the /z/ sound is especially strange for students who see the spelling.
8 Say the word quickly and you'll notice *d* disappears and the word sounds like /gʊbaɪ/.
9 Similar to above, the *ll* disappears and *shall we* sounds like /ʃwɪ/.
10 *s* sounds like /z/, and the word is pronounced weakly /wəz/.

So why is all this important? For a start, teachers need to be aware of how English sounds in order to help students produce the natural pronunciation themselves. It's not really a case of being 'correct', but of sounding 'natural'. However, students can't sound natural unless they have clear models to follow.

Teaching monolingual classes, you can focus on specific problems encountered by that nationality. For example, students who have difficulties distinguishing between two different but similar sounds (minimal pairs) such as /i:/ and /ɪ/ can be given tasks where they have to hear and recognize the two sounds in various words; or/ and think of examples themselves. You do not need to 'teach' all the sounds, but focus on those which are relevant to your students and which they need help with.

Word stress

Word stress is another area which can cause difficulties. In the word *advertisement* the stress falls on the third syllable in American English (ad-ver-TISE-ment), but on the second in British English (ad-VER-tise-ment).

Task 2

Where does the main stress fall on the following words? Be careful, there are some tricks included!

1 telephone
2 cassette
3 surprising
4 conduct
5 note-book
6 address
7 worked
8 examination
9 photograph
10 photographer

Before going through this task, why is it important to focus on word stress in the classroom? It is probably less important than other aspects of pronunciation because meaning is rarely affected by mis-stressing a word. But if the pronunciation is so incorrect that it becomes almost unintelligible, then meaning would become affected.

Stress can be marked in different ways.

newspaper nˈewspaper 'newspaper Ooo NEWSpaper <u>news</u>paper

The third of these is how dictionaries normally mark stress, but most teachers, in my experience, prefer the second (with a small circle or square). The fourth example (stress bubbles) are a very visual way to represent stress, good with very low-level classes. Whatever mark you adopt, be consistent, and make sure your students know what it means. Make sure, too, that students know how to read a dictionary for word stress – this, accompanied by the phonetic transcription, gives the students a good guide to pronunciation.

Key to task 2

1 Ooo
2 oO
3 oOo
4 Oo (noun) oO (verb)
5 Oo
6 oO (British) Oo (American)
7 There is no stress because there is only one syllable, though many students will mistakenly say work-ed.
8 oooOo
9 Ooo
10 oOoo

In the classroom there are many activities you can do with word stress.

If you have been teaching vocabulary, you could have words on one side of a sheet and stress patterns on the other, and students match them (or any variation thereof). Students can listen to words and decide for themselves what the stress pattern is.

You can give two columns (e.g. oO and Oo) and a series of words which students have to categorize. As mentioned before, drill new words which will be needed to be used actively.

Sentence stress

Sentence stress can certainly affect meaning. Consider this simple sentence:

> *I gave Gaston a book.*

So, which word is stressed most?

Task 3

How does the meaning of this sentence change when the words are stressed as follows?

1 **I** gave Gaston a book.
2 I **gave** Gaston a book.
3 I gave **Gaston** a book.
4 I gave Gaston **a** book.
5 I gave Gaston a **book.**

Consider, too, the implied difference between *I'm going now* and *I am going now.* And what about *Today's Wednesday – No, it's Thursday?*

I am going now is emphatic, almost a show of determination to leave, despite efforts to make you stay. This could be correct in the right context, but the more natural pronunciation will be the contracted form, and this is what you should drill. With the 'Thursday' example, the second speaker is correcting information given by the first speaker, the stress falling on the correction – a very useful aspect of sentence stress to focus on.

Insight

Raising awareness of sentence stress is important as the stress in a sentence can affect the meaning we are trying to convey. Consider: *I'm going now. / I'm going now.* The stressed words convey the important information that the speaker wishes to express.

Key to task 3

1 It was I who gave him the book, not someone else.
2 I didn't lend him the book; I gave it to him.
3 I gave the book to Gaston, not another person.
4 I gave Gaston only one book, not more.
5 It was a book I gave him, not something else.

Such a task raises students' awareness of the importance of sentence stress and how it affects meaning. What is stressed depends in part on the important information a student wishes to convey.

We can signify sentence stress by saying the sentence ourselves, 'beating' the sentence (e.g. knocking on a table), humming it (e.g. 'da da da DA da'), clapping it, etc. But context is essential if the task is to be meaningful.

Intonation

Sentence stress goes hand in hand with intonation. Very often, someone we are speaking to may appear rude because of their intonation patterns. It is quite easy to make 'Thank you very much for your help' sound rude or sarcastic. But intonation is so hard to teach because students invariably end up exaggerating intonation patterns until they sound completely unnatural. A case in point is *question tags* (e.g. *Your name's Luc, isn't it?*). A rising intonation on the tag (*isn't it?*) implies a real question requiring an answer. But a falling intonation implies that nothing more than confirmation is required of a fact already known (*it's really cold today, isn't it?* – there is no disputing the temperature). But just try making students use tags naturally! They usually end up leaving what sounds like a huge space between the statement and the tag, and then really exaggerating the intonation of the tag.

What students can do is to listen and identify polite versus not so polite intonation patterns. The 'Thank you very much for your help' example might be said once, naturally and politely, and again, sarcastically; students must identify the difference.

A variation of this is to do the same task with a single word (e.g. *Hello*) and students must interpret the speaker's feelings (pleased to see me, not pleased to see me, surprised to see me, etc.).

Students could also mark intonation patterns on sentences (which have context) with rising, falling, and level arrows.

Pronunciation is sometimes focused on as a lesson, or part of a lesson, but most of the time, the most valuable pronunciation work takes place spontaneously as problems arise. Drilling, too, is a common feature of many teachers' classes, especially with lower-level students. Pronunciation work is generally more effective with monolingual classes because you can deal with common problems.

You will find that some course books integrate pronunciation work into their units while others keep it quite separate. Some books feature pronunciation work a lot, others much less so, just as some teachers do more pronunciation work than others.

There are lots of good books available which contain various pronunciation tasks for different levels, often with a 'fun' approach (stress bingo, phonetic crosswords, picture 'spot the difference' containing minimal pairs, etc.), and you can provide whatever pronunciation work you feel is appropriate and useful for your students. But do not neglect this part of language learning.

Summary

▶ Meaning can be affected by unclear pronunciation, whether sounds, stress, intonation, or any other feature of it.

▶ As teachers, we should expose our students to the different varieties of pronunciation and not portray one as 'better' than another.

▶ We should not ignore pronunciation work – we can have specific parts of a lesson devoted to it or deal with issues as they arise.

▶ Drilling provides students with safe, controlled practice of new language but the activity needs to be executed efficiently.

▶ Course books provide ideas for pronunciation work, as do other specialized books, but the pronunciation areas to focus on should be determined by the needs of your particular students.

▶ With monolingual classes, focus on the common problems experienced by that nationality.

▶ With all classes, focus on any problems which are affecting meaning and intelligibility.

10

···

Practice activities

In Units 4–9, we looked at various ways of focusing on language. We established that a teacher needs to cover the meaning, form, and pronunciation of new language and to do so in a way which involves the students using appropriate methodology for the level. But the missing element in this learning process is getting students to use the language they have learnt – to practise it. Without this, students are restricted to learning rules and patterns, albeit in context, without having the opportunity to operate the language they have learnt.

We saw that with **Test Teach Test** a task which could be described as 'practice' takes place right at the start, but with the purpose of being diagnostic. Normally, of course, practice tasks take place after the teacher has focused on the language itself.

We will look in this unit at some examples of practice tasks for both vocabulary and grammar, as well as looking at the teacher's role before, during and after the task.

Controlled and less controlled practice

First, let's go back to Unit 4 when we had a context of an unemployed man, Jason, going for a job interview at a bank. Jason was very casual in his appearance, too casual for a bank employing a new person. This context led us towards the sentence *You should wear a suit* which contains the language *you should* + base verb with the function here of giving strong friendly advice. We saw in this unit how we could cover the meaning, form and pronunciation. Having done all this, the teacher now needs to provide one, maybe two, practice tasks so the students can gain confidence using this language.

Task 1

Here are two possible activities, but very different in nature. Look at how each is described and consider what the main difference is in the nature of the tasks.

Activity 1

The teacher elicits from the students ideas of what a good café is like. She asks for examples of local ones and what students think of them. She also elicits examples of what would be considered unacceptable in a café. Throughout, the teacher is eliciting and personalizing, and at the same time establishing interest in the topic.

At this point, the teacher says she has a friend called Erik who owns a café. She shows them a picture of Erik in his café. The picture shows a café that is dirty, with three cats inside, and an owner who is smoking and unclean in appearance. The teacher elicits opinions from the students, as well as other ideas of what this café might be like.

All of this will take no more than three or four minutes. The teacher reminds the class that Erik is a friend of hers whose business is doing badly and she wants to advise him on how to improve his position. She elicits an example from the class in which they have to use either *should* or *shouldn't* – for example, *You shouldn't smoke*. Students then work together to say/write more examples using *should / shouldn't* based on the examples of problems given by the students earlier. They might come up with something like this:

> you shouldn't have cats in the café
> you should wear clean clothes
> you should cook good food

you should clean the café

you shouldn't make your food and drink so expensive

The teacher then gets back from the class what they have come up with and writes sentences on the board as confirmation of correct usage.

Activity 2

The teacher says she has another friend, Javier, who is Spanish. Javier is studying English in Miami but he has a problem. There is a large Spanish-speaking community in Miami and Javier finds himself speaking Spanish most of the time he is not in class. Consequently he is making very slow progress with his English. He calls you and asks for advice. The students imagine Javier is their friend and have to suggest ways in which he can improve his English and give reasons why. The teacher elicits an example – *Try to meet some American friends because they will speak English with you.* The students work together and think of more examples and then the teacher asks the class for their suggestions.

So what's the difference in the nature of these practice activities? The first *requires* the use of the target language because the teacher has set it up that way and told the class to use *you should/you shouldn't.* The second does not *require* this language to be used, but the opportunity is there for the students to use it because strong friendly advice is being given. But this time the teacher did not say 'Use *should*', she just said 'Give suggestions' and *reasons.* By asking for reasons, the teacher is getting the students to use other language, and by not insisting on *should* and *shouldn't* the teacher is allowing students to use other appropriate language in a more natural way. So, this task is much less controlled in terms of the language being used by the students.

We have, then, a task where the language being used is controlled, and a task where the language being used is guided, but not controlled. By doing the controlled task first, the teacher is giving students confidence in using the language, before asking them to be a little more varied in what they say. Remember that this class is around elementary level, perhaps pre-intermediate.

What the activities have in common, apart from the function and the related language being used, is the teacher's role. In each case she set the context, established interest, gave instructions with an example, and checked answers afterwards. More of this later.

Insight

Controlled practice will allow you to carefully target and practise the language you want to cover. Less controlled (guided) practice will mean students are using other language as well as the target language. It gives them a bit more freedom and is a little more natural.

Forms of practice activities

Practice can be spoken or written, controlled or less controlled (to varying degrees). It can also be in the form of an 'exercise' (e.g. gap-fill), or something more communicative.

Task 2

Prepositions
If we take another piece of language – prepositions of place – we can look at various types of practice. Prepositions of place include *in* the corner, *on* the table, and *under* the bed.

Try to think of five different ways in which students at pre-intermediate level could practise this language.

Prepositions are difficult for students because there are no nice, easy rules to follow, or even much logic to them. You can have prepositions of time (at 3 o'clock), prepositions of movement (go *down* the street), and prepositions of place (*under* the bed)...and that's just for starters! Students of all levels generally hate prepositions.

Here are five possible activities:

1 Students see a picture of a room and have to complete five sentences with the appropriate preposition from a given list.

Example: *The newspaper is ___ the table*– students look at
            picture and select *on* to complete the sentence.

2 Students are given two very similar pictures of a room and in
pairs they have to find differences. They cannot show each
other their pictures, but they can ask questions, and describe
their own pictures.

Example: *How many people are sitting on the sofa?*
            I have a cat sleeping under the bed.

3 Students have a picture of a room with completed sentences.
But each sentence has the wrong preposition which students
must correct. A variation of this is: students listen to a
recording of someone describing their room and look at the
accompanying picture to discover which sentences on the
recording fail to match the details in the picture.
4 Students tell each other about a room in their house/apartment
and what is there. Afterwards, the teacher asks one student to
tell the class about her partner's room.
5 The teacher provides various objects and students tell each
other where in the room to place each object.

Activities 1 and 3 are what one might describe as 'traditional
exercises'. Students usually like these more than teachers, and they
definitely have value, as long as students are doing other types of
activity as well.

Activities 2 and 4 are more communicative. 4, in particular, is
much less controlled in terms of the language being used.

3rd conditional
Let us now look at the 3rd conditional (e.g. *If I had forgotten your
birthday, you would have been angry with me*) and at typical types
of practice activity.

1 Complete the sentence with the words (in brackets) in the
correct form:
If I (win) the competition, I (be happy).
If I had won the competition, I would have been happy.

2 Find the mistake in this sentence:
If she hadn't of seen me, she would never have known.
✗ 'of' *If she hadn't seen me...*

3 Rewrite this sentence in the 3rd conditional:
I didn't study hard and I failed my exam.
If I had studied (more/harder), I would have passed/wouldn't have failed...

4 Chain sentences ... one student gives the first half of the sentence for another student to complete.

5 The teacher provides the ending of a story (e.g. a man gets dismissed from his job). Students have to write a sentence which explains this ending and which climaxes with a 3rd-conditional.
Example: *If he hadn't slept late, he wouldn't have lost his job.*

6 Students have to think of a conversation between two people. They decide on the context and the relationship between the characters. Somewhere in the conversation a 3rd conditional sentence must appear in a natural and appropriate way.

7 'Noughts and Crosses' ('Tick-Tack-Toe') – half the class are the 'noughts' and the other half are the 'crosses'. Each team selects two verbs from a given list and thinks of a 3rd conditional sentence that uses these verbs. If they produce a correct sentence, they choose in which box to place their 0 or X. A team wins when they form three noughts or crosses in a row, in the usual way. This is an example of using a classic game for language purposes. Most such games can be adapted in some way.

8 Matching sentence halves. In column **a** you have the if-clauses, and in column **b** the main clauses. Students have to match correct halves. A more interesting variation of this is to have the sentence halves on separate pieces of paper, face down on the table. One student picks up an if-clause, the other student picks up a main clause. If they match, put them to one side; if they don't, put them back face down in the same position. This activity is sometimes called 'Pairs', or 'Pelmanism' and can be used to practise many different language items.

9 Jumbled sentences.

Example: wouldn't – I – eaten – have – if – sick – less –
   had – I – felt
   If I had eaten less, I wouldn't have felt sick.

10 Students talk about their lives so far and include information
about the consequences of what they did or didn't do.

Example: *If I had worked harder, I would have gone to
   university.*

Insight

Practice activities can vary from controlled written exercises,
such as gap-fills, to less controlled role-play conversations.
Many students really enjoy more 'traditional' activities: the
important thing is to keep things varied and try to include at
least one communicative activity.

Task 3

Think of one practice activity of any type for the following which
is different from the ones given below.

1 Giving directions (elementary)
2 Comparatives (intermediate)
3 Question forms (intermediate)

For each of the above, there are numerous possible activities, and
of various types. Normally, you would want your students to do
a couple of quite different activities, as explained above (*should*).
Of the many possibilities for these three language items, here is one
example for each.

Directions

Students work in pairs and each has a diagram of a street, but each
diagram has different places shown (e.g. post office). Each student
has to ask directions to find the places not listed on her diagram.

They listen to the directions and write in the location of the place. Afterwards, students look at each other's pictures to check.

Comparatives
Students compare their country with the country they are now in, if applicable. Alternatively, use pictures to make comparisons of people and places.

Question Forms
Each student in a pair is given an incomplete text about a person. The missing information is different in each text. One student has to ask relevant questions of the other in order to complete their text.

Example: *My name is Marco and I am _____ years old.*
              'How old is Marco?'

Many of the activities described so far can be used with vocabulary as well. Let's look at some possibilities.

Imagine you have 'taught' your students words related to the following topics:

> weather (elementary)
> sport (intermediate)
> music (upper intermediate)

Certain types of activity could be used with all of these. Examples of these are **matching** (e.g. word to definition/picture) and **gap-fill** (putting the correct word into the sentence gap). But more communicative activities are also needed; some ideas for Speaking in Unit 13 are appropriate for language practice, too. A good example is **ranking**. This is when students put items in a particular order. With 'sport', this could be according to which they like watching most, or which are considered healthiest. With 'music', it could be according to which is their favourite type of music, or which instrument is the hardest to learn. With 'weather', it could be according to which is the most common type of weather in respective seasons, or favourite weather types and why. The point about ranking is that there are no right and wrong answers. It is designed to promote speaking which allows use of the vocabulary items.

For the weather vocabulary, students could have pictures of different weather types, and then write in the description. For the sport vocabulary, students could mime a sport for the others to guess. For the music vocabulary, students could discuss examples of musicians who are associated with different kinds of music, and whether they like them or not.

For review purposes, students could be given **anagrams** (words with letters jumbled up) of words previously learnt and from which they can make sentences. Or, they could be asked to find words in a **word puzzle**.

Example: frtg*football*kdrwqy

reefgvsawryhfhtedc   Your actual puzzle would

gnixobjuytedfghytg   be bigger than this!

So where do you get ideas for practice activities from?

▶ Course books and accompanying workbooks are usually excellent sources. You should adapt and supplement in the way described in Unit 21.
▶ Other resource books which give various ideas of practice activities for different language points. Make sure the activity is suitable for the level and students you are teaching.
▶ You can find a wide variety of online resources, from simple ideas or classroom tips to colour worksheets with teaching notes that you can download.
▶ Your own ideas and creativity! If you come up with a successful activity, keep it for future use.

The role of the teacher

I have already mentioned the teacher's role in the practice stages of a lesson; that role comes in four parts.

1 Before the lesson

The teacher needs to find an activity (activities) appropriate in terms of the class level, age group, composition and nature of the class, time available, and language focus (does it really provide practice of the specific language point you will have focused on earlier in the lesson?). Creating your own activity sounds a good thing to do, but don't spend two hours preparing an activity that will last five minutes!

2 Before the activity

Prepare students linguistically – are there any words you need to check they know before they begin the practice? Set the context and establish interest. Give/elicit an example of what they have to do. Arrange the class in the way you want them to work and with whom.

3 During the activity

Do not participate. Monitor to check they have understood, to give help, to keep things moving, to respond to difficulties or to quick finishers. If they are doing a speaking activity, listen and note down mistakes with the target language for correction later (see Unit 16).

4 After the activity

Go through correct answers with reasons, if applicable, or get feedback on what has been discussed. Do correction of mistakes noted, if applicable.

If you fulfil your role for these four stages, you will surely achieve your aims for this part of the lesson.

Tips for practice activities

1 Be varied in your choice of activities from lesson to lesson.
2 Do not consider 'traditional exercises' to be boring for the student – they will be only if you do nothing else; otherwise, they tend to be very popular.
3 Do not spend too much of your time preparing original material, especially if you are only going to use it one time.
4 If you are using an activity from a book, check carefully for yourself how it is going to work, what instructions you will need to give, etc.
5 If it is an activity with right and wrong answers, make sure you know what the answers are and the reasons for them.
6 Leave sufficient time for the activity to be done properly.
7 Leave sufficient time to go through answers / get feedback.
8 Do further practice another day as review – you must recycle your input and not treat pieces of language as something you 'do' in a single lesson.

Summary

▶ Covering meaning, form and pronunciation is not enough if students do not get any opportunity to use the language and practise it.

▶ Practice activities need to be carefully selected, and properly set up with instructions and examples.

- ▶ Ideally, practice will involve more than one type and include something which is communicative.

- ▶ Teachers should familiarize themselves with the activity first, and with why the answers are what they are.

- ▶ They should monitor the practice carefully and leave time to get feedback.

- ▶ They should not participate in the activity.

- ▶ Correction of mistakes made with the target language is essential.

- ▶ The language being used in the practice may be controlled, or less controlled, allowing for other language to be used.

- ▶ Practice activities should be as relevant and interesting as possible.

11

Receptive skills 1: Reading

The receptive skills of Reading and Listening (compare with the productive skills of Speaking and Writing) require an understanding of the text (*text* here referring to both reading text and recording) but also some related language work or other productive tasks before or after the text. Therefore, there will be a great deal of overlap when discussing the four skills for the very reason that they are very rarely focused on in isolation in the classroom. Even isolating them in the unit titles is misleading! However, each of these four units will have a primary focus, and this one is Reading.

Task

Here are some questions for you to think about before you read any further. Make some notes.

Why do I ask you to do this? You may think it is easier just to skip the questions and read the rest of the Unit. Well, the analogy with the classroom is that as teachers we don't just 'give a lecture' but we try to involve our students in the learning process; to make them work! In any learning process, a student is more likely to remember something in the future if they have had an active part in the learning process. That is why this book includes some tasks for you to do, just as, when you teach, you will ask your students to do a task before you go through it with them!

So, look at these ten questions:

1 Think about your own schooldays – How much did you enjoy or not enjoy Reading lessons (in any subject)? Why? What was the role of the teacher in these lessons?

2 Is reading aloud a Reading lesson?

3 Is a Reading lesson going to be boring? What can prevent potential boredom?

4 What different types of reading skill can you think of? What should we focus on in the classroom?

5 In an ESL class, what do you think a Reading lesson might consist of?

6 Should students be given tasks before or after they read the text? Why?

7 Do you think it is necessary or desirable for your students to understand all the vocabulary in a text? If not, how do you decide what they need to know?

8 Is a Reading lesson always going to have a grammar focus (refer to Unit 5)?

9 How will you find texts to use in your lessons? What factors affect the selection of texts?

10 Could one text be used at two quite different levels? If you think 'Yes', how?

One other task! Please go and find a reading text – maybe something from a newspaper or magazine, or a brochure, or a TV guide … anything at all as long as it is not too lengthy. And I will use the text below.

Schooldays

They say that schooldays are the happiest days of your life. Well, they weren't for me! I enjoyed very little of my time at school and was glad to leave. My college days, however, were much more fun and the subjects I was studying were the ones I wanted to study!

At school, I used to have a one-hour bus ride each day there and back. We started school at 9 o'clock and finished at 3.45. There were some lessons that I really hated – mostly the 'practical' classes like Woodwork because I am hopeless at that sort of thing. I was useless at Art, too. Other kids used to have fun trying to guess what it was I had drawn. No, I was good at sitting behind my desk and listening to the teacher and making notes – English, History, Geography, etc. Days when I had Woodwork, or Art, or Physical Education – those were the days I hated, the days that most other kids loved!

My teachers were a mixed bunch as well. Those that were good were very good, and those that were bad were very bad. Then there were the student teachers! The kids always gave them a really rough ride and it made you wonder why anyone would want to go into a class of 40 loud and misbehaving kids and try and teach them!

Thinking back, I'm not sure I learnt too much that was to be useful in my life. Some of it was interesting for sure, but I wish I had been taught more about the practical things in life – how to deal with interviews, filling in application forms, finance management – rather than trying to figure out what x equalled in some fancy equation.

The strange thing is, I always wanted to be a teacher myself. I had the ambition of starting off in the classroom and ending up as a school principal – of being a popular, successful, respected teacher. Well, it never happened and I don't regret it. Teachers nowadays have too much paper work to do, too many discipline issues to deal with. That's not for me. These days my ambitions are different and more realistic.

Back to the task …

1 The role of the teacher

I can only remember one approach to Reading lessons, whether in French or in English. The teacher would ask us to read a set number of pages either in silence, or taking it in turns to read aloud. This would be followed by questions, done individually, and checking of answers. The teacher's role was minimal, and more often than not he would use the time to mark homework, etc.! I did not enjoy these lessons. In particular I remember one English Literature teacher whose sole approach throughout the school year was to set us pages to read in the lesson – there weren't even any tasks to focus on, and certainly no communication between students or between students and teacher. It was thoroughly demoralizing. Talking to many trainees over the years, I discovered that a large majority had had similar experiences. Those few that had had positive experiences invariably referred to the role of the teacher in making the lesson interesting, even fun.

2 Is Reading aloud a lesson?

It may be in part, but the actual reading aloud focuses on pronunciation and not on comprehension. Unless your students are advanced, they are going to struggle with such a task, and other students may have trouble understanding. There is the possibility of some students feeling pressured – either as they are reading or as they await 'their turn'. So please don't ask students to do this if your aim concerns reading comprehension. They may (if you are very lucky) read well, but are they 'listening' to what they are saying?

3 Is a Reading lesson boring?

A loaded question! Of course, there is real potential for boredom. Maybe the topic is dull, irrelevant, or too difficult. Maybe there seems no point to the lesson. Maybe there is no communication, no interest. So, yes, such a lesson could well be very boring. But it shouldn't be, not if the teacher stages the lesson appropriately. It is the teacher's responsibility to keep interest high.

4 Different types of Reading skill

You may be rushing out of your home one day and there's a newspaper on the table and you see a headline which attracts your interest ... but you must hurry to catch your train, you have just

30 seconds. So you quickly look at the story to see what it's about, to get the **gist**. You are not concerned at this stage with detail, and you are not looking for particular information. You just want to know what the story is about. This is **skim** reading, or reading for **gist**. It implies reading quickly. It is something we do a lot.

Maybe you are looking at a train timetable. You need to know what time your train departs and where from. Or maybe you are searching for ticket prices and journey length. You have a timetable and information booklet, but it contains a huge amount of information which is of no use to you whatsoever. So, when you are reading you can – and should – disregard this information and look for what you need as quickly as possible. This is scan reading, or reading for *particular information*. This also is something we do a lot.

As you settle down to read a good book, or to study a contract you must sign, or maybe an article about a film star you like, you will not be in a hurry. Far from it, you need, or want to, read carefully ... detail is important. You need to understand what you are reading. This is intensive reading, or reading for *detail*. And yes, we do this a lot, too!

We should, therefore, provide tasks which require a combination of all these different skills, not necessarily in a single lesson, but over a period. How this can be done, we shall see next.

Insight

Skim reading is a quick reading to get the main **gist** of a text, to find out what it is about. It is not reading for particular detail or information. **Scan** reading is also quick reading, but this time to find and identify **particular** information. **Intensive** reading is careful reading for detail.

5 An approach to a Reading lesson

There are many different approaches to a Reading lesson, or part of a lesson. Here we will look at just one – a fairly standard approach, commonly used by teachers and in course books. Have the text you selected earlier handy for this, and also refer to the one above ('Schooldays' p. 112). What we will concentrate on here are **stages** and **aims of stages**, and this will further prepare us for Unit 16.

Here, then, is a possible approach:

Stage 1

Check understanding of 'essential' vocabulary (see question 7 for more on this). Don't spend too long on this!

Aim: for students to understand the meaning of words essential to the completion of set tasks.

Stage 2

Establish interest in the topic. In any lesson, but especially a skills-based lesson, this is an absolutely crucial stage. This is where the skills of the teacher are contributing to stopping this from becoming a boring 'read this' lesson. What you need to do here is to get the students interested in the topic, to make them *want to read the text*. This shouldn't take up too much of your lesson, but nor should it be a 10-second effort along the lines of 'Did you like school?' 'Yes/No' and on to the text! Looking at the text above on Schooldays, and a lesson for intermediate students, you might have your students discussing their likes and dislikes from their time at school; or describing their typical day; or remembering different subjects studied; or teachers they remember and why.

With other text-types this stage might involve *prediction* (e.g. from a newspaper headline, or from words in the text, or from a picture accompanying the text); *contextualization* (e.g. using pictures to set the scene of the topic); or *building interest* (e.g. describing an almost impossible scenario and then say 'Well, it really happened and we're going to read about it'; or sound effects from a story – this can be combined with prediction).

More often than not, this stage involves either some personalized discussion based on the topic, or prediction, but it depends on the text and the level of the class you are teaching. Using a basic text on vacations for a low-level class, you might just ask them to list as many names of countries as they can think of. But whatever you do, you are working to create interest in the text that is to follow.

Insight

Spend a little time getting students interested in the topic before reading the text you have chosen. This is a crucial stage: ask questions and get them talking so that they *want* to read it.

Look at the text you chose. How would you create interest for whatever level you think you might use it with?

Aim: to generate students' interest in the topic of the text.

The two stages so far have merely prepared your students for the Reading task. What follows will depend on a number of factors, but usually a combination of two (maybe three) different tasks based on the text will provide the main focus of the lesson.

Stage 3

If you set two different reading tasks then you should give the easier task first, to build confidence. This would be a task which requires either skim or scan reading. A task to encourage skim reading would be any that focuses on the gist, the overall theme, of the text. A task to encourage scan reading would be one that requires the students to find specific information in the text (names, numbers, places, prices, etc.) without having to read carefully or understand in detail. So, with 'Schooldays' a scan reading task might include questions such as:

Did he start school before or after 8.30 am?
Did he love or hate Woodwork, Art, and Physical Education?
When he was younger, what job did he hope to have?

None of these questions requires anything more than 'pulling out information' from the text, just as you have to 'pull out' the time of your train from a timetable. Consequently, the teacher should impose a fairly strict time limit for the completion of the task to encourage 'quick reading' (which is what scan reading involves). If the teacher allows five minutes to find the answers to those questions, then the students will read slowly and carefully, and be concerned about understanding everything they read.

Scan reading tasks could include multiple choice / true or false / matching pictures with sentences. Revising the first question above, you could ask 'He started school at (a) 8.00 (b) 8.30 (c) 9.00 (d) 9.30'. Or 'He started school at 9.00 – True or False?' Or, use four clocks showing different times – a visual multiple choice.

What scan reading tasks could you use for your selected text? Try to think of three or four different questions, and at least two different question types.

Aim: for students to have practice in scan reading skills.

Stage 4
Now you can move on to providing a task(s) that require more detailed reading. Any of the question types mentioned already could also be used here, but this time requiring *understanding* – and this could be linked to the vocabulary covered in Stage 1. To clarify this, look at these questions for 'Schooldays'.

> Was he good at Art? (No, he was *useless* at it)
> Were all his teachers of the same standard? (No, they were a *mixed bunch*)
> Did student teachers have an easy time in class? (No, they were given a *rough ride*)
> Does he still want to be a teacher? (No, interpretation of final paragraph)

These are just some possible questions. The first three demand understanding of essential vocabulary: *useless*, *mixed bunch*, to be given a *rough ride*. To answer the questions the students must understand the meanings – so these would be words to check in Stage 1. The final question requires more of a general understanding of the final paragraph. 'Why?' questions are also good for this kind of reading. And another possible *interpretation* question could be 'Do you think he liked *Metalwork* at school?' No, because he didn't like practical subjects – the answer is implied but not stated.

This kind of task, then, needs careful reading and greater understanding – but not of everything (see question 7).

It is important, though, not to just give a series of questions every time – you should vary the types of questions that you ask. The nature of the text may suggest a certain type of task. For example, matching headlines from newspapers with stories would be intensive reading. One possibility with much lower levels is matching meaning with pictures.

This stage obviously needs more time, and students should be allowed to work together and help each other – the task should be communicative, not a test.

In terms of true/false or multiple-choice type questions, however, it is very important that the teacher does not just give/elicit the answers, but asks for reasons why. Otherwise, an answer could be a guess with no understanding.

What intensive reading task could you set for your chosen text?

Aim: for students to have practice in intensive reading.

Insight
Initial reading tasks should be the easiest, to build confidence. Ask students to quickly skim or scan read the text, to get the gist of it or to find a couple of pieces of information. Then move on to more detailed questions that require careful reading.

Stage 5
This is very much an optional stage, but it is nice to finish such a lesson with something communicative. So, any of the suggestions

made for Stage 2 could be expanded and used here as a class speaking activity. Anything relating to education, schooling, teaching, or even ambitions would be an appropriate topic for a Speaking activity (see Unit 13 for more on Speaking). If you were continuing with the same class in the next lesson you might use this Reading text as a springboard for some language work (e.g. *I wish* + past perfect from the text), or for further skills work (e.g. some Listening on the same topic, or Writing). What you do will depend on time, but try to have *something* as a follow-up to your Reading activity.

What Speaking activity could you provide for your students based on the text you have selected?

Aim (for example):   for students to describe and discuss their own schooldays in a free-speaking activity.

You now have a 'sandwich effect' – the main part of the lesson (Reading skills) is sandwiched between other activities (generating interest / vocabulary and Speaking). This makes the 'heavy' part of the lesson more digestible and far less boring than the 'read this' approach which so many of us experienced at school.

Main lesson aim: for students to have practice in scan and intensive reading skills.
Secondary aim: for students to have practice describing and discussing school experiences in a free-speaking activity.

So, what would you do if you only had this class for one lesson and the Reading was taking longer than anticipated. Would you (a) skip the last part of the Reading and go on to the Speaking, or (b) continue and finish the Reading and drop the Speaking?

Faced with that choice, go for 'b'. The Reading is the main part of the lesson and teachers should try to achieve their main aims. If there is no time for the Speaking in this lesson, it doesn't matter. Failure to complete all you planned is not a sign of a failed lesson if you have still achieved your main aims. More of this in Unit 16.

Once again it needs to be stressed that this is only one of many ways to approach a Reading lesson – it is an effective and popular approach, but do not feel this is the only way!

6 Give task before or after text?

Give the tasks **before** handing out the texts. This gives the students a reason for reading – an aim. If you let them read it, before handing out the task, they will just have to read it all over again. And the first time, they will read carefully and try (and want) to understand every single word! This would not be skim or scan reading, and it would be pointless anyway with no task.

7 Which vocabulary?

We have already established the need to deal only with those words which will be needed for the completion of the tasks. In the 'Schooldays' text, three words were selected, but words such as *misbehaving*, *fancy* (equation), and *ambition* did not have to be understood in order to complete the tasks. If you check too many words, you won't have enough time for the Reading part of your lesson, and your main aims will be affected. Having said that, your Stage 5 could be Vocabulary based, maybe guessing meaning from context, possibly using multiple choice. It is good to focus on Vocabulary **after** as well as **before** a Reading / Listening task.

8 Reading and grammar

Reading texts may or may not lead in to 'grammar', as we saw in Unit 5. But there is nothing wrong in focusing primarily on skills work along with vocabulary.

9/10 Selection of texts

If you are using a course book, this will have a rich supply of texts and tasks, though you may need or want to adapt the tasks to make them appropriate for whom you are teaching. Otherwise, use authentic texts (see Unit 21) and create appropriate tasks. One text could be used for different levels – the degree of difficulty will depend on what you ask your students to do with the text. Of course, this is not to say that any text can be used with any level! But there is an element of adaptability possible to allow one text to be used with, say, two different levels. Apart from the level, your choice should be influenced by suitability (choice of topic, consideration of cultural issues, etc.), and interest (is this something which will be useful? or interesting? or maybe both?).

Insight

Course books will be an important supply of texts. Authentic texts – real newspaper, magazine or online articles – can spark particular interest as they will be very topical, but you may need to adapt them to suit your students' level.

Tips

1 Select texts which will be interesting, relevant and suitable.
2 Provide tasks which will be appropriate for the level and the students.
3 Stage the lesson so that you establish interest and give a variety of tasks.
4 If possible, conclude with a follow-up activity based on the text.
5 Remember that the main aims relate to the Reading.
6 Give the tasks before the text.
7 Give an approximate time limit which is appropriate for the task / reading skill.
8 Check answers / reasons for answers.
9 Go on to some language work from the text (optional).
10 Don't ask students to read the text aloud when the aim is comprehension.
11 Be encouraging and supportive – try to stop students worrying about what every single word means! At the start, only check the meaning of those words they really need to know.
12 Make sure your tasks match the type of Reading skill that you are focusing on.

Summary

All of this is very different from the experience I had of 'Read pages 22–42 and then I'll give you some questions to answer individually'. The approach described above is more communicative, more meaningful, more interesting, more useful. It is important to 'package' a Receptive skills lesson this way in order for this to be so. We will continue to focus on Receptive Skills in the next unit.

12

Receptive skills 2: Listening

Listening (by which I mean students listening to a recording – usually a CD, but perhaps a DVD / video – **not** listening to the teacher or each other talking) is one of the hardest activities for most students. Like Reading, it is a receptive skill, but it is usually much more difficult than Reading. Why is this? We'll come back to this question later.

Task 1

In the previous unit I described a possible approach to a Reading lesson, and we also looked at different Reading skills. Can you remember now, without looking back, what **skim** and **scan** reading skills are, and what intensive reading skills are? And can you remember the stages described?

The stages were, in broad terms, as follows:

1 Check the meaning of any vocabulary essential to the completion of the tasks. Don't spend too long on this.
2 Create interest in the topic of the text so that students actually want to read the text.
3 Set two or three different tasks which give practice of different reading skills.
4 If possible, have some follow-up activity based on the topic. Or, go on to some language work from the text.

The skills described were:

skim – quick reading for gist
scan – quick reading to pick out certain information
intensive – careful reading for detail/understanding

Task 2

1 How might you stage a Listening skills lesson?
2 What different Listening skills can you think of?

Why Listening is difficult

First, let us go back to the question of why Listening is difficult for most students.

Within the classroom environment, students become used to the voice, accent, or dialect of their regular teacher(s). Furthermore, the teacher grades her language and perhaps speaks just a little slower than is usual. The teacher constantly uses gestures, and will check understanding. A student can interrupt and ask for repetition or clarification. But with a recording, none of these factors are present.

A natural-sounding recording will usually consist of two or more speakers using ungraded language. Their voices, accents, and maybe dialects will be new to your students. These 'new' voices often come as a shock first time round. Often, too, the conversation is, or seems, fast. There is no body language and there are no gestures to help understanding. Students cannot ask the voices to slow down, or clarify... the recording starts and continues. There is no control – at least, not on the students' part. Compare this with a Reading. Students have some control over how fast or slowly they read (though they may have been given a time limit). They have to contend with new language, as they do with a recording, but they don't have the problem of accents and speed. They can quickly re-read a line that they have not understood, but they cannot rewind the recording. With a Reading, then, students have some control. With a Listening they have none. Add to this the fact that they will be trying to answer questions as they listen and the obvious result is *pressure*.

Insight

Listening is difficult because it creates a situation of pressure. Students have no control over what they are listening to: they can't slow the recording down or ask the speakers to repeat what they've said. At the same time they are trying to answer questions. You need to stage the lesson carefully to help the students as much as possible with this skill.

Staging a Listening skills lesson

As teachers, of course, we must be aware of these difficulties and try to help our students in every way we can. Just as with a Reading, we shouldn't just go in and say 'Read pages 20–25 then I'll give you some questions', so we shouldn't just go in, play a recording, and hand out questions. We have to stage the lesson. The first part of Task 2 asked you to consider how this might be done. Well, the simple answer is that a Listening lesson *could* be (but doesn't have to be) staged in a similar way to the Reading stages described in Unit 11. If we take an example of a recording about two people discussing a film they saw on TV, the lesson could go as follows:

Stages 1–5

1 Pre-teach vocabulary *essential for the completion of tasks* (as per Reading).
2 Establish interest in the topic (as per Reading) – maybe talking about films recently seen, stars they particularly like, identifying actors in photos, etc. Another possibility is *prediction*. You might, for example, show some pictures in the book from the Listening and ask students to predict what they think the recording will be about.

3 A Listening for **gist** task (e.g. 'What are they talking about?' or 'Did they like the film they saw?');
or
Listening for **specific information** (e.g. 'How many people are talking?' / 'Where did they see the film?' / 'Which actors were in it?').
Either of these tasks would provide a gentler introduction to the recording, with relatively easy questions to build confidence and get students used to the voices and speed, etc. Of course, the precise type of questions will depend on the recording and the level of your class.

4 Listening for **detail** (as Reading for detail!) – maybe asking how you know they liked or didn't like the film (requiring identification and understanding of adjectives).

5 A follow-up activity based on the topic. This could include listing and talking about the types of film that they like, favourite actors, writing a review of a recently seen film, etc. With a low-level class this could be adapted so that students give a mark out of ten for different types of film (e.g. *Western*) identified in photos;
or
using the CD to focus on a specific language point in the recording (as for a Reading text).

By staging the lesson in this way we are 'sandwiching' the Listening as we did with the Reading. In other words, we prepare the students for what is to come, and we try and create interest so that they end up wanting to listen.

Problems of 'real-life' listening

In order to genuinely improve our students' listening ability we need to focus on specific skills. However, if you are teaching in a country where English is not the first language, there is limited value in Listening lessons, given that students will only be listening to English in the classroom. That does not mean that you shouldn't do Listening, just that it is of much less value than it would be as an activity while in an English-speaking country.

So let's consider some examples of 'real-life' listening in a country where English is the first language:

- ▶ listening to announcements at a bus station / airport, etc.
- ▶ face-to-face conversation
- ▶ speaking on the telephone
- ▶ watching TV

For someone standing at a station wanting to catch a train to Edinburgh, there are different ways to seek the required information (time of train, platform number, etc.). One is to read the monitors that display the information. Another is to listen for **announcements**. Now, you don't have to be a visitor from another country to find it very difficult to understand announcements at public places! The sound is often distorted; the accent or dialect may be difficult to understand; the delivery may be fast; there is a lot of background noise, and you can't stop and ask for the person to repeat any information. On the other hand, you do usually have the visual back-up. Announcements are often repeated, and you can always ask someone for assistance.

In order to help our students improve their listening skills, we need to be aware of, and to acknowledge, the specific difficulties they might have with a certain type of listening; but we also need to direct students to the type of help they can get.

With this kind of listening the most important skill is 'listening for and extracting specific information' (times, numbers, etc.) – the equivalent of scan reading. Therefore, if we can provide an authentic-sounding recording of a station announcement, then we can provide a task which replicates real life, even if we can't replicate the exact conditions.

Face-to-face conversation has many difficulties in common with the announcements – fast delivery, different accents or dialects, background noise, having to participate in the conversation rather than 'just' listening. However, the other person's gestures and body language will help; you can ask for repetition, clarification and for the person to speak more slowly; and the context of the conversation will be established (whereas on a recording you may not have any idea what the conversation will be about until the CD is played!).

The skills are likely to be different from those needed for announcements, though. Normally, in face-to-face conversation, you are focusing on gist, or detail. Maybe the person is giving directions, or telling you what you could do over the weekend. Or maybe they are telling you their impressions of a film they saw. You *can* have 'face-to-face' Listening in the classroom – roleplays. And you can provide appropriate tasks.

Speaking on the telephone is really difficult and stressful for most students. For a start there are no gestures to help. There is the possibility of distorted sound as well as different accents and dialects. There is specific telephone language ('Please hold the line', etc.) to deal with. The problem of 'turn taking' can be difficult (when is it your 'turn' to speak?). Dealing with 'menus' can frustrate anyone ('if you want X press 4, if you want Y press 5', etc.!). Also, a student may have difficulty making himself understood. If the student is making the call, he might be able to prepare questions or check what information he needs to find, in advance. In any case, he can ask for repetition – unless he's listening to a machine. If he is, there is nothing he can do but repeat the process and listen all over again (something I have had to do more than once!). As teachers, we can help by teaching students telephone language and procedure, and by giving them a variety of tasks – including listening for gist, specific information, and detailed understanding; taking a message; making notes; and leaving a message on an answering machine. Best of all, maybe, is to give them a real task to do which involves them calling someone, maybe to get information.

Watching TV is much less pressurized, but the language tends to be fast and often colloquial. It is obviously not graded in any way, and as such can be very difficult to understand. But the visuals are a huge help. If the programme has been recorded, then students can rewind and listen again. All kinds of listening skills are required, but detail is particularly important. Thus, getting students to watch and listen to a news broadcast is very valuable, and you can provide varied tasks to help improve the students' listening ability.

Insight

If you are teaching in an English-speaking country your students will experience 'real-life' listening. This means fast delivery, different accents or dialects, colloquial language and background noise. However, gestures (conversation) and visuals (TV) are a huge help. What most students find really difficult and stressful is listening and speaking on the phone.

These examples show the importance of recognizing the factors that help and hinder students in different kinds of listening, and some of the various skills that they need to improve. Therefore, we need to select types of recordings and types of tasks which will be relevant and useful as well as interesting. These recordings will normally come from the course book you will be using, but you can add authentic ones as well. As we have already seen, texts and recordings can also be used as a springboard for language focus work.

As for the issue of different dialects (e.g. south of England vs. north of England) or different varieties (e.g. American vs. British), it is a good thing for students to be exposed to as many types as possible – though it is often very difficult for them!

By breaking the lesson into stages, choosing appropriate material and tasks, you will be decreasing the stress levels of the students. There are other things you can do as well.

Tips (to help the students)

1 Try to place the machine (i.e. CD player) as close as you can to your students (or have them move close to it).

2 Maybe play a few seconds first, to check they can hear the recording.

3 Give out the task before they listen and give them time to read it.

4 Make the first task relatively straightforward to give them confidence.

5 Reassure the students – tell them not to worry if they find it difficult at first, that you'll play it again; that they don't need to understand everything, etc.

6 Let them discuss their answers after the first play. Communication is important – it's not a test.

7 Nearly always you should play the recording a second time (occasionally three times if it is not too long).

8 Sometimes, it is appropriate to play the recording and 'pause' at crucial moments, isolating the answers. This usually helps a lot.

9 Go through the reasons for the answers.

10 Have a copy of the audio script to hand so you can clarify important dialogue in case students are unclear about something.

It is not only students that can find Listening lessons stressful, so can teachers! As with any kind of lesson using technology, things can go wrong – and they do!

Tips (to help the teacher)

1 Check there is an appropriate machine (i.e. CD player) in your room. If not, find out where you can get one.

2 Check you know how to use it!

3 Get the audio material (i.e. CD) you need well in advance of the lesson – if you leave it to the last moment and you can't find it, you will have a problem!

4 Check the correct CD is in the box – sometimes teachers put the wrong one back!

5 Listen to the recording before the lesson – check it is there and that it is audible.

6 Make sure you know which recording you are going to listen to. Check the recording number and check that you can find it. Don't leave this until the lesson has started. It adds to your stress and it gives a poor impression to the students.

7 Have a copy of the audio script just in case you need it.

8 Know what you will do if something goes horribly wrong (e.g. the CD is scratched and you can't use it) – be prepared! Don't panic.

9 Never trust any technology!

If you have access to a DVD player, then you have the possibility of extending your Listening into Listening and Watching. There are many specially made DVDs on the market which you can use. This does not mean a 'watching TV' lesson, it means staging the lesson as you would any other, having clear aims, appropriate tasks, etc. But with DVDs you have something different – variety. See Unit 24 for more on using DVDs.

Integrating the skills

So far, we have looked at Reading and Listening as almost separate entities. But we have seen that there are considerable similarities in terms of types of task, types of skill, and typical lesson staging. But if you look at typical course books, you will find that more often than not, Reading and Listening feature in a single lesson presentation. A Reading activity about someone shopping for food might be followed by a Listening activity on the same subject (or vice versa). A Listening activity about a tourist visiting New York could be followed by a Reading passage about life in this city. And so on.

We can go further than that. In the next two units we will look at the productive skills of Speaking and Writing. A truly integrated skills lesson (or, more likely, back-to-back lessons) might feature all four skills. Let's consider an elementary class doing a fully integrated skills lesson on the theme of holidays/vacations. A possible lesson frame could be:

1 Check essential vocabulary.

2 Establish interest in the topic (e.g. postcards from around the world).

3   Reading about a holiday in Australia (with a couple of tasks, maybe).
4   Listening with two people discussing a trip to Australia (again, a couple of tasks).
5   Writing – students write a postcard from one of the characters in the Listening based on the information on the recording.
6   A Speaking activity – maybe students rank favourite holiday destinations from 1 to 10.

Obviously, each of these stages needs detail – and for stages 1 to 4 you can refer back to the relevant units. For stages 5 and 6 you should refer to the next two units. The principal point is that you shouldn't always treat these skills in isolation – in fact, you should rarely do so, for the simple reason that we don't in real life! We might watch something on TV and then talk about it. We might listen to a news story and then read about it in the next day's newspaper. We might write a letter or email to a friend and then read their reply. So, *integrating* skills work is important.

In addition, as mentioned in Unit 5, skills work can lead on to (or follow on from) language focus work (other than the checking of essential vocabulary). To focus on a particular piece of language from a text or recording is useful and relevant.

Insight

Skills shouldn't be treated in isolation and two or more can easily be integrated into a lesson, especially as they may have, like Reading and Listening, some similarities in terms of task types and lesson staging.

What must be stressed, then, is that there are no prescriptive lesson types. Of course, trainers, and books such as this one, and also all course books, will suggest approaches based on experience and research. New teachers usually appreciate such guidance early on, to have lesson 'patterns' to follow. But as long as you have achievable and appropriate aims for your lesson, any lesson frame is possible. We have already seen in an earlier unit how a 'grammar' lesson might begin with free speaking. It may not fit the traditional image of a grammar lesson, but that does not matter. So, as your experience increases, have the confidence to vary your lesson patterns and approaches, to integrate more. Don't do it a particular way because 'that's how the book does it' if you do not think the 'book' way is appropriate for your class! Don't follow a suggested approach given in this book if you can think of a more suitable approach for your class. You know your students, I don't!

Summary

▶ Listening is a difficult skill for students, more so than Reading.

▶ Teachers need to stage Listening lessons in such a way as to reduce the difficulty.

▶ We should be aware of the specific problems that students might have with different types of Listening – but also of the factors that help understanding.

▶ We should provide tasks which are relevant and interesting (though their relevance will be less in a non English-speaking country).

▶ Listening can, and should, be integrated with other skills and language work.

▶ Teachers should check the audio material and machine (i.e. CD player) well in advance.

▶ It is important for students to work together on tasks in order to make the activity less pressured. Don't play the recording and then immediately ask for answers to the task!

▶ Play the recording more than once and pause it, if appropriate.

▶ Use of a DVD player, if available, also provides good practice of Listening skills.

13

Productive skills 1: Speaking

A school I worked at used to ask students on their first day to put in order what they most wanted to 'do' on their course, from a list including Grammar, Vocabulary, Reading, Listening, Speaking, Writing, and Pronunciation. I would estimate that 90% (at least) put Speaking as their number one choice. But what is Speaking? Is it talking to the teacher? Is it talking to each other about a grammar task? Is it reading aloud? Is it spoken practice of language learnt? Or is it chatting? I wonder how many of the students completing that first day questionnaire knew what was meant by Speaking. And is a Speaking lesson/stage of a lesson one of the easiest for a teacher to set up? Or one of the hardest? In short, Speaking as an activity in the classroom is much more complex than one might at first think!

Task

Think about the following questions and make some notes before reading on.

1 What's the difference between **fluency** and **accuracy** and which is more important?
2 What do you understand by Speaking in a lesson?
3 Do you think it is relatively easy for a teacher to set up a Speaking activity? Why? Why not?
4 What's the point of doing Speaking? It's not 'learning', so isn't it a waste of time?
5 What problems might occur in the execution of a student-speaking activity?

6 What do you think is the teacher's role before, during and after a Speaking activity?

7 If the students are speaking, should the teacher correct their mistakes sometimes? never? always?

8 What kinds of Speaking activities could you do in a lesson?

---

1 Fluency vs. accuracy

In simple terms, **fluency** is the ability to talk fairly freely, without too much stopping or hesitating. To 'keep going'. More than that, it also requires that the listener understands what is being said, so there must be intelligibility and meaning. With accuracy the emphasis is on 'correct English' – the right grammar, the right vocabulary.

Can you have one without the other? Yes, definitely. I have taught many students who were very fluent but not very accurate. They could talk a lot. I could understand them. But their speech was littered with errors. On the other hand, some students focus their minds so much on being accurate that they lose their fluency. Just a few weeks before writing this, I taught a student who was obsessed by accuracy. He was of an intermediate level and had a pretty good range of language, but he was simply unable – or maybe unwilling – to just talk. He would begin a sentence and ask me or himself grammatical questions about how to continue the sentence. Time and time again I said that I could not answer him because I did not know what he was trying to say. For example, he might say 'Yesterday I … what's the word?' Well, how could I know? He was so determined to construct his sentences bit by bit that the listener could rarely understand what he was trying to say. He also took an eternity to say anything, as you might imagine!

So, is one more important than the other? The easy answer is that they are equally important. But to be honest, I don't think they are. It also depends on who you are teaching. If you are teaching a high-level student who is about to take an exam to enter college, accuracy is very important indeed. However, in most ESL exams the accuracy is tested most in a 'grammar' part of the test with gap-fills, multiple choice, etc. In the speaking part of the exam the emphasis is as much on fluency as it is on accuracy. But accuracy *is* important.

If you are teaching beginners, or other very low levels, you cannot possibly expect fluency. Here, you really do have to help them build their language accuracy bit by bit until they reach the stage when they can speak more fluently.

With a reasonably high-level student who does not need to prepare for an exam, and especially if they are living in or are going to visit an English-speaking country, then I would argue that fluency is much more important. Does it really matter if they make the odd mistake when asking someone in the street for directions? Does it really matter if they use the past simple instead of the present perfect when telling an English-speaking friend about their last vacation? No, it does not – though some students think it does, as I said earlier! What is far more important is that they can make themselves understood, and can talk relatively fluently. But even if their level is not high, the ability to be understood is greater than the need for accuracy in the situations just described. For this to be possible, we as teachers need to give our students confidence when speaking and not to be obsessed with constant correction (see Unit 15 for more on correction). We need to make it clear to our students exactly why we want them to just speak for 20 minutes in a lesson. The accuracy-fixated student I described earlier thought Speaking was 'boring' – 'I want to do grammar'. Unfortunately, as accurate as his English sometimes was, he had no fluency and he drove everyone crazy as we waited for him to finish a sentence! Fluency is very important!

Insight

Fluency is the ability to talk fairly freely, without stopping or hesitating much. **Accuracy** is the ability to use the correct grammar and the right vocabulary. They are both important. However, in many situations, fluency and the ability to make oneself understood, even though this means making mistakes, is more important than the ability to speak accurately.

2 What is Speaking in a lesson?

First, let me say what Speaking is **not**. It is not reading aloud (pronunciation). It is not reading the answer to a grammar question (accuracy). It is not reading the answer to a Reading/Listening question (comprehension). In each of these cases the aims are not Speaking-related.

In a lesson, Speaking is one of two things. It could be a Speaking activity designed to give practice of language just learnt or reviewed. Here the emphasis is as much on accuracy as it is on fluency and correction at some stage will be important. This type of Speaking was covered in Unit 10. In this unit we are looking at the other type of activity – Speaking designed to promote fluency. That said, if you are teaching a low-level class then fluency is not a realistic aim, so we will look later at how you can still give low-level classes Speaking activities.

3 / 4 / 5 Practical difficulties

It sounds straightforward – just give them something to talk about. Unfortunately, at least with some classes, Speaking stages can be the most difficult to execute successfully. There are many reasons for this:

- ▶ teachers might get complacent and not plan this stage properly
- ▶ students may not see it as 'real learning' (as with the student I described before)
- ▶ the class may be very small
- ▶ the class may be very big (making 'control' a problem)
- ▶ the class may (and probably will be) all from the same country – so they will end up speaking in their own language
- ▶ they might perceive it as an 'exercise' that has to be finished as quickly as possible
- ▶ they might not have sufficient language to do what you have asked them to do

Let's look at each of these problems in turn:

Need for planning

We all do it. It's been a long day; we're tired; we don't have anything planned for the final 30 minutes, so we say 'Okay, I want you to talk about food for the rest of the lesson'. If you'll pardon the pun, that's a recipe for disaster. Speaking must be planned properly and with clear aims. See question 6 for much more on this.

'Speaking is not real learning'

No, they might not see it as 'real learning'. And, in fact, it's not *learning*; this is an important point. Learning a new language must include a high proportion of practice, of using the language. Students should not always be *learning* and teachers should not always be *teaching*. We saw in Unit 2 that the teacher has many roles to perform, and the teaching of language is only one of these. Another is to set up opportunities for students to use the language they are learning, and fluency activities is one example. New and training students often complain after such an activity 'But I didn't teach them anything', to which I would reply 'No, well done'. You must not feel that you are not doing your job if you are not constantly teaching them. If you do, there will be severe overload.

As for the reluctant students, the school questionnaire I referred to at the start of this unit (and supported by my own experience over the last twenty-five or so years) confirmed that Speaking for fluency is a very high priority for most students, so convincing them of its worth is rarely a problem – unless you do too much of it. But when you do have a student or class that needs convincing, tell them why you're asking them to do it. Tell them about accuracy vs. fluency. Tell them about the importance of using the language confidently. In other words, involve them in the teaching rationale.

Problems of large and small classes

If you teach in the UK in winter time you could well find yourself with a class of two, three or four students. This does not mean that you cannot do Speaking. It does mean that it will be harder work for you setting it up and keeping it going, and harder work for them. It may also mean that the activity may be over quicker. But this is all okay. You must not deny them the opportunity to speak because you don't think you have enough students. Similarly, if you have a very quiet class, don't give up.

In many contexts you might have classes of 20, 30 or 40 students, possibly monolingual. This is a much greater problem than the class of three. It is unrealistic to expect such a class not to use their own language for at least part of the time, and if it is a big class, you cannot properly monitor. You may even have a situation where the class becomes excessively noisy. So be realistic. If you have 30 Spanish-speaking students, they are certain to use as much Spanish as English. But remind them of the importance of using only English and encourage them to do so. Set up an activity with a clear purpose and a time limit. However, if you have your 30 Spanish students, and you are in Madrid and when class is over they have no need to speak English, the value of Speaking activities is lessened. Motivation is lower compared with students who need to use their English outside school. You may, though, find that some of your 30 Spanish students (to continue with that example) need to speak English in their jobs, or they are going to do an exam. So do not abandon the idea of doing Speaking activities, because if you do, you will not be providing the complete learning package.

Students' attitudes

Students who do not understand, or who are not convinced by, doing Speaking for fluency in the classroom, sometimes view such activities as they do a 'grammar exercise' – as a task to be finished as soon as possible. This can be infuriating for the teacher. You set up an interesting speaking activity designed for 20 minutes of conversation, and after two minutes one group proudly says 'We've finished'. It's this kind of student who will treat a 'Where did you last go on vacation?' question, with a one word answer 'Brazil', and not follow it up as anyone would in 'real' conversation with questions about Brazil. This is in sharp contrast with the class who will happily chat for half an hour and very reluctantly stop when the teacher says time is up. This is one of the big problems with this kind of lesson, it is so unpredictable. You just don't know how a class is going to respond to your Speaking activity. If you want it to last twenty minutes, and it lasts two, you have a problem. For solutions – see question 6!

If the teacher sets up a Speaking activity which is beyond the students' language ability, then the teacher has either misjudged the level of the class, or she has failed to ensure that the students have the necessary language to complete the activity. It is a planning issue. This, too, relates to question 6.

---

6 The teacher's role

Speaking is no different from any other kind of classroom activity – it needs planning and it needs proper execution. The role of the teacher is as important with Speaking as it is with teaching grammar, but the role is very different. Remember what we said before – this type of activity is not 'teaching' or 'learning'. We are focusing here on Speaking for fluency, rather than practice of specific language. With this in mind, we can consider the role of the teacher in three stages: before, during and after.

Stage 1: Before …

In the previous two units we looked at Listening and Reading skills, and described typical lesson 'patterns'. In each, it was suggested that such a lesson could finish up with what was described as a 'follow-up activity based on the topic'. For example, a lesson where the main focus was a Reading about Culture could end with a Speaking activity on the same topic. A Listening activity about Education could finish with students talking about the educational system in their countries (or, for a much lower level, ranking favourite subjects at school from 'favourite' to 'least favourite'), and so on. Typically, then, your Speaking activity will fit in to a lesson structure naturally rather than just be 'thrown in' for no apparent reason – it will be part of the lesson package. Sometimes, however, teachers will give a Speaking lesson (the entire lesson will be Speaking). Such lessons might have a less obvious aim, and be harder to sustain, but all teachers do them from time to time. Sometimes, for example, you have a class that is tired and is in the mood for just 'chatting', or it is your perception that they would benefit from a 'relaxed' lesson with no pressures of language learning or practice. This is not uncommon, but you shouldn't over-do such lessons.

Before the lesson, then, know why you want your students to speak, – what your aim is. In all likelihood, it will be part of a lesson containing other skills and/or language work and so the 'lesson fit' will be obvious not only to you but also to your students. Choose an activity (possibly from the course book) that is suitable for their level and interests, and that is appropriate in terms of the lesson fit and aims. Plan your instructions and class management. Anticipate any possible problems you might have, and that the students might have. If, for example, you would like pair work, what will you do if you get an odd number (usually two students can work as 'one')? How do you want the students sitting (if you have a choice)? Opposite each other? In a circle? Semi-circle? In other words, plan how you will set up the activity.

That is before the lesson, but you also have a role before the activity itself. You should give very clear instructions, with an example of the activity if possible. The task should be clear (the students need to know exactly what you want them to talk about and why). You need to arrange the class how you want. If the activity involves role playing, the roles should be clear as should the purpose for speaking. And give an approximate time limit. If you emphasize that you want the students talking for ten minutes ('So don't tell me after two minutes that you've finished!'), then they are more likely to speak at greater length. With much lower-level classes, give a specific task – in other words, avoid 'Talk about...' instructions which require a lot of language. Instead, give them an achievable goal (e.g. ten jobs to rank according to which they would most like to do, and with a very brief reason why).

If you say 'talk about jobs you would like to do' they won't have enough language to do so.

> ## Insight
>
> Before you start, plan how you will set up the activity. Are students in pairs or groups? Where are they sitting or standing? Give lower level students a specific task as they won't have the language to just 'talk about ...'. Always give clear instructions – and a time limit.

Stage 2: During ...

If you are teaching a class of under twenty, say, then you should remove yourself from the central position of the room. As long as you are there, the students will feel you are part of the activity and will try to keep you involved in it. By getting out of the way you are effectively saying 'get on with it'. With classes which are reasonably small (say 1–20), turning on background music (instrumental) can have a similar effect. With very small classes, the music can make it less intimidating for the students to speak. That's up to you. Some teachers like using music; others don't!

Once the activity is under way, monitor it as best you can (but it won't be easy if you have sixty in the class!) to ensure everyone has understood, is speaking, is using mostly English, and doesn't have any problems. Also, you are there to ensure one or two students in a group don't dominate the activity, and that a group doesn't finish far too quickly. You are not monitoring in order to join in, and you are not monitoring to interrupt with error correction. If you do there will not be any fluency and you will not have achieved your aim. If you have planned and set up the activity properly, it should work well, but you always face the danger of accuracy-obsessed students who don't want to speak without constant correction, and of the very shy students who are not used to such activities in the classroom. But these are problems for you to anticipate and be ready to deal with if they occur. We have discussed already the accuracy-obsessed student, but for the very shy one you could gently interrupt the group briefly and gesture for that student to say something (e.g. 'Sonoko, what do you think?'), and then walk away so as not to intimidate her. You can't, and shouldn't, do any more than this. It's all down to confidence. Very recently, I had three Korean female students who were out of their country for the first time ever. I was their teacher in a communication class – which was quite a challenge because they simply would not speak! They were shy and lacking in confidence. When learning English in Korea they just listened to the teacher giving explanations, and then did exercises. As a result, their accuracy was very good, but their fluency was non-existent. Three months later, after much gentle encouragement from the several teachers they had, you couldn't keep them quiet! Their confidence had grown, they had observed the communicative approach, and slowly had come out of their shells. So, never be discouraged by quiet students – help them, guide them, but don't put pressure on them.

Insight

Your role during the speaking activity is to move around and observe: make sure that everyone has understood, that there are no problems and that students are speaking mostly English. Give gentle encouragement to shy or quiet students. Don't join in and don't correct!

Stage 3: After ...

Try to allow enough time to get some feedback from the class. For example, one group could tell another group what they decided/discovered/discussed, and vice versa. Or you could select certain students to give some feedback. It is nice to get some kind of feedback so that you can show your interest, as well as for the students to share some of what they have talked about. This needs only to be a few minutes.

7 When to correct?

Don't interrupt the Speaking activity with correction because you will stop the flow and the students will not be able to improve their fluency. But some correction could (should?) take place *after* the activity has finished. See Unit 16 for details on this.

8 Types of Speaking activities

Of course, it depends on the level and who is in your class. Avoid culturally-sensitive topics, and avoid politics and religion at all times! As you will see more, when you read Unit 21, you should not assume an activity is 'okay' just because it is in your course book. **You** have the responsibility to decide what is appropriate in every sense. Having said that, course books do provide a multitude of ideas for Speaking, nearly always as part of a lesson 'package'. What you must do, as we saw earlier, is to set it up and make it work.

Beyond your course book, there are many Speaking resource books on the market. Again, be confident to say 'No way' if that's how you feel. Be prepared to adapt ideas to make them more suitable. But do explore whatever resources are available in your place of work. Quite often, I come up with my own, very simple, ideas. That's the beauty of Speaking stages; you don't actually need materials every time, and you can sometimes verbalize the task.

There are certain types of activity that tend to be very popular. **Ranking** has been mentioned before (putting items in a particular order). If *Sport* is your topic, students could rank sports from those they like most to those they like least; or from the most beneficial for the body to the least beneficial. If *Food* is your topic, you could again do favourite to least favourite; or most healthy to least healthy. If *Travel* is your topic, it could be most comfortable to least comfortable, and so on. The point of ranking is that there are no 'correct' answers, because it is designed to promote discussion. Higher levels can add reasons for their choices.

Sometimes, such activities may appear unrealistic or contrived, but the speaking skill involved is very real. Take the old favourite, the **Balloon Debate**. This is where students take on the identities of famous people travelling together in a hot air balloon which is overloaded. One person has to go over the side to lighten the load.

The students, in their roles, argue who it should be and why. Hardly a realistic activity, but the skill of giving opinions and justifying them is very real indeed. Incidentally, of all the many times I have done this activity with students, it has never yet failed to produce a near-riot!

Debates can be organized, though only for high-level classes. Make sure the topic has obvious points on both sides and is not too controversial.

Students can prepare and carry out **surveys/questionnaires**. This involves finding out information and reporting back. If possible, let your students go beyond your own classroom, maybe to interview other students or staff or people on the street!

Describing visuals is another good area to explore, and can be a good way to allow students with imagination and sufficient language to extend their normal classroom speaking.

Role plays can work with any levels. With lower levels, give them a realistic context (especially if in an English-speaking country) like shopping, and a realistic role (i.e. the customer, not the shop assistant).

Student talks are good for more advanced levels. Maybe, each day, one student could give a talk for about five to ten minutes on a subject of interest to them, and the other students can then ask questions. Make sure the students have had notice of this so they can prepare some notes.

Discussion on topics of interest, or maybe in the news, is a relaxed way to promote fluency, but make sure the students have something specific to talk about, and that you don't end up doing more speaking than them.

These are just a few ideas. Remember, use your course book for initial ideas, then supplementary materials. Don't expect fluency from very low-level classes – give them something much more controlled.

Tips

1 Plan the activity properly.

2 Know what you'll do if not everyone turns up and your hoped-for even numbers don't materialize.

3 Think in advance about issues of classroom management, especially if you have a very large class, rows of tables, etc.

4 You may have to 'justify' the activity to the class if you are teaching a monolingual class in a non English-speaking country.

5 Plan your instructions carefully so it is clear what the activity is, what students' 'roles' are, etc.

6 Give an idea of time so as to increase the likelihood of the activity lasting as long as you want it to! (e.g. 'You have ten minutes, so keep talking for that time!')

7 Get out of the way! If you remain the focal point in the class, they are likely to be more inhibited. With small classes, light background music can help, too. With very large classes, however, you might need to remain at the front in order to keep everything under control!

8 Make sure the activity is appropriate in terms of language required and topic choice.

9 With much lower-level classes, do not expect fluency – provide a clear task.

10 Monitor the activity as best you can, but do not interrupt. Encourage quieter individuals or groups, though.

11 Try to allow enough time afterwards for some feedback to the activity.

12 Maybe do some delayed correction work (see Unit 16).

Remember that whereas some students want to do as much speaking as possible, others can be resistant to the idea of 'just chatting' and may need convincing of the worth of doing such an activity. Don't be afraid to do this. If you are teaching adults, as this book pre-supposes, then they should be treated as adults, and that includes explaining the rationale of what you are asking them to do if they seem sceptical!

Summary

▶ Fluency and accuracy are both important, but with Speaking there is generally more emphasis on fluency – the ability to talk fairly freely without stopping or hesitating too much.

▶ The types of activities you carry out will depend on the size of the group and the level.

▶ Speaking activities need to be properly planned. Be aware of the size of your group and how this might affect your classroom management. Motivation for Speaking may be higher for students in an English-speaking country because they need to use their English outside the classroom.

▶ Speaking activities often fit naturally into the structure of a lesson, as a follow-up activity to a Reading task, for example. You might occasionally have a lesson that is exclusively Speaking, but that is harder to sustain.

▶ During a Speaking activity you should observe and monitor, and give gentle encouragement where necessary. The key is <u>not</u> to join in and <u>not</u> to correct during the activity.

▶ Always allow time after the activity for feedback and for some correction.

14

....

Productive skills 2: Writing

Maybe this unit should be subtitled 'The Forgotten Skill' since less time appears to be spent on this lesson type than any other, except in exam or literacy classes. In truth, few students seem to mind. In my experience, very few ever complain about not having done enough writing. However, it is not a skill that should be ignored. The problem for the teacher seems to be how to 'teach' it.

With the receptive skills of Reading and Listening it was apparent that there were more similarities than differences. Most things we said about Reading also applied to Listening, and vice versa. But the same is not true of the productive skills.

Task 1

Answer these questions before reading on.

1 How does Writing differ from Speaking as a productive skill?
2 What makes Writing difficult for students? And what makes it easier than Speaking?
3 Why teach Writing?

Motivation for Writing

For a start, many students need the Writing skill much less than they need any of the others, and if they are studying General English in their own country then their interest in Writing lessons may be minimal. Even if they are studying in an English-speaking country there is often limited value for them in doing Writing. If they write a postcard home, they will not be using English, for example. On the other hand, they might have to complete an application form in English. If they are working in England then they might need to do some kind of writing in their work.

If students are preparing for an exam, then Writing is much more important because they will be tested in some way. Exams usually require students to write at least two different types of answer, e.g. discursive, descriptive, analytical, letters, etc.

You might be teaching students who are now living permanently in an English-speaking country and who have no writing skills at all, not even an awareness of the script and how to form it.

So with Writing lessons more than most, the motivation is very varied. Some students will need, or will want, to do it, but for others, Writing will be seen as a waste of time.

But Writing should never be totally neglected, and if it is an important part of the course you are teaching, it should be focused on extensively. It can be difficult to get students to write in class (or at home for homework), but as with any other kind of activity, the teacher can 'sell' it. The lesson staging can be such that the students are more inclined to write with at least some enthusiasm.

Written language is often more formal than spoken language. Of course, this is not always the case. Email style tends to be very informal, even more so than conversation at times!

A student studying in an English-speaking country might have to do many different types of Writing including forms, phone messages, formal letters, and CVs or resumés. In addition, students preparing for an exam will need to write compositions, including formal and informal letters, descriptions, discursive essays, graph interpretation, narratives, etc. These different types vary in their degree of formality, and each requires specific skills and language. It is this variety which makes Writing much more difficult than Speaking.

Differences between Writing and Speaking

With Writing, the emphasis on *accuracy* is much greater than with Speaking. For a start, the written form is visible and mistakes are seen. With Speaking, students often make 'slips of the tongue' – they have said something wrong, but if they could hear a recording of what they said, they could correct the 'mistake' themselves. As we saw in the last unit, 'mistakes' when speaking are often not that important. Written tasks on the other hand often require accuracy (e.g. completing an application form) and formal language. Because they recognize this, many students feel under pressure when writing. However, with Writing, students can proof-read and self-correct. They can go more slowly and carefully than when they are speaking. It is an important skill we must teach our students – read what you have written!

Punctuation is another factor absent from Speaking. Increasingly these days, one might question the importance of correct punctuation, but whereas one can accept that the correct use of colons or semi-colons is not really so important, surely the correct use of capitalization and question marks, for example, does matter.

Spelling may also cause problems, something which mother-tongue speakers have difficulty with, never mind learners from another country! Again, people differ in their views of the importance of correct spelling, but the fact remains that, as teachers, we have to recognize what is 'correct' writing, and what is 'incorrect'. If we cannot recognize a mistake, then we cannot correct it.

With Writing, students do not have to concern themselves with aspects of pronunciation, or being fluent. Those students I mentioned in the last unit who are much more interested in accuracy than fluency, are often very good when writing. It is very common to find students who have had accuracy-based language learning, writing extremely well and accurately, but struggling to speak more than a sentence or two!

Writing tends to be more *economical* in its use of the language. There are no 'hesitators' ('mmm', 'er', 'well', etc.) that litter our conversation. Written language is direct and efficient.

Another difference between Writing and Speaking is that, when writing, students cannot express themselves visually. There is no 'body language' or gestures to aid understanding. With Writing, students rely exclusively on the language itself.

Speaking is naturally acquired and students in an English-speaking country are immersed in the language all the time. But Writing is something which has to be taught. What's more, Writing is a lonely skill – we speak to other people but we write individually. All of this makes Writing harder than Speaking.

Writing skills

What students need is to have specific writing skills developed. It's not enough for the teacher to say 'Okay, write about a country you like'. This is writing for the sake of writing, but the teacher isn't 'doing anything'. For the students' writing to improve, they need to have help in particular areas. So let's consider three different types of Writing that a student might do in the classroom – a postcard, a letter, a discursive essay. We have already said that it is rare for a student to write a postcard in English if they are sending it to their own country, but once they return home they might send postcards back to friends met when they were learning English. We will take a letter of application for a job as an example of letter writing.

As for the discursive essay, (one which argues for and against a particular topic) we will assume this is for an exam class who will need to write this kind of essay.

Writing a postcard (elementary level) requires the writer to use an informal writing style, use simple linkers (e.g. *but* rather than *on the other hand*), know how to begin and end a postcard, and, arguably, to spell correctly. The writer also needs to know the type of subjects covered in a postcard (e.g. weather) and the layout including which side the name and address are written.

Task 2

What different skills are required to successfully complete a letter of application (intermediate)?

Before looking at this task, let's consider some of the general skills required when writing. We have already mentioned punctuation, spelling, and style of language. To these we can add **correct structure**, **correct layout** (on a letter), **linking expressions** (*on the other hand, nevertheless, firstly*, etc.), **paragraphing, organizing, appropriate vocabulary, language** of **comparison and contrast** (e.g. *similarly, conversely, in conclusion*), **precis writing** (taking messages on the phone we need to summarize the main points), and **presentation** (e.g. presenting a neatly and correctly filled-in form). Obviously, the skills required will vary according to the task being set and the level being taught. We saw with the postcard-writing at elementary level that the skills required are fairly basic. This is not the case with the other types of Writing mentioned.

Key to task 2

For the **letter of application,** students will need to know how to correctly lay out the letter – where to put their address, their name, the recipient's address, etc. Layout conventions vary and change from time to time, but there are basic layouts which can be taught. Students also need to know about punctuation and capitalization. They need to know how to organize the letter, and that each paragraph should have a specific purpose. They need to know how to be economical with their language so as to keep the letter to a reasonable length. They need to know about the style of language to use (formal), and about how to use linking words and deconstructed forms (not *I'm* but *I am*).

One way of helping students to recognize an appropriate style of language for letters is to present a selection of language from two different letters – one formal and one informal. So, phrases like 'Dear Sir', 'Dear Marc', 'I'd like to have this job', 'I would like to apply for the position...' are all mixed together, and students have to separate the formal from the informal. Maybe the different examples could be from one complete letter so students can then put the letter together and have a model of a complete letter.

For the discursive essay, students will need to know spelling, punctuation, language of contrast and comparison, language of summing up, vocabulary related to the topic, how to organize, how to develop and support ideas, and how to be concise.

If we take, for example, the language of contrast and comparison (including *while*, *whereas*, *despite*, etc.), the teacher could present these expressions in sentences that are incorrect in some way, and the students try to correct them.

To practise the skill of organization, the teacher could present a complete, but jumbled up, letter and ask the students to put the paragraphs in the correct order.

By knowing which skills different writing tasks require, the teacher will be better able to help her students with their writing.

Insight

Writing tasks require a variety of skills. Students need to understand **presentation** (i.e. the layout of a letter or the organization of paragraphs in an essay), **accuracy** in terms of punctuation and spelling, and specific **language** such as linking expressions or language of comparison and contrast.

How to teach Writing

As with Speaking, we can distinguish between a lesson that *includes* Writing, and one which is *exclusively* Writing. At the time of writing this, I am teaching an exam class that will have to do a 60-minute Writing exam (one task of 150 words over 20 minutes, and one of 250 words over 40 minutes). With this class I frequently have lessons devoted to Writing skills which focus on what they will have to do in their exam. I am also teaching a General English class where Writing figures far less prominently. When it does, it is always part of a lesson containing other activities.

We saw in previous units that skills work is not usually dealt with in isolation, and when this is the case it is the role of the teacher to 'package' the lesson in a way which is appropriate for the level, the students, and the aims of the lesson. As an example of this, we shall go back to the earlier examples of writing a postcard (elementary class), and writing a letter of application for a job (intermediate level). We shall assume a lesson of about 60 minutes and look at possible lesson packages to include these writing activities.

For the 'postcard lesson' we could follow this procedure – one of many variations possible.

1 Show real postcards from different countries and students try to guess the countries.
Aim: for students to become interested in theme of lesson.
5 mins
2 Stick six completed postcards around the room (writing side on display) and give students a **Reading** task (e.g. they have a form to fill in showing the countries each writer is in, who they are writing to, and if they seem happy or unhappy in this place). Teacher then gets feedback.
Aim: for students to have practice in scan and gist reading skills. 10 mins

3 Students are given extracts of language from a letter and from a postcard (formal vs. informal) and they have to distinguish which is which. Teacher then checks.
Aim: for students to recognize appropriate style of language. 10 mins

4 Teacher elicits what types of topic are usually written about in postcards.
Aim: for students to be able to identify appropriate postcard topics. 5 mins

5 Students are each given one of the completed postcards from Stage 2 as a model of postcard-writing. They also get a blank postcard. They have to write a real postcard to someone they know who speaks English (it could be you!) and to whom they will send this postcard. This adds authenticity to the task (compare this with them writing an imaginary postcard on a piece of paper!).
Aim: for students to have practice in postcard-writing skills. 15 mins

6 Once the postcards have been written, and later sent, you could have a follow-up **Speaking** activity – maybe ranking the six countries featured in the model postcards in order of which place they would most like to visit.
Aim: for students to have practice in Speaking (putting items in order and giving reasons). 10 mins

In a lesson package such as this, Writing is just part of the lesson, but it fits in with all the other parts. The teacher has established interest, provided a model of the writing task, prepared students with the style and type of language required, established what needs to be included, and also included Reading and Speaking. All of this is suitable for an elementary class, but it remains a full lesson of language and skills. The Writing task is real-life.

Task 3

Now try and think of a lesson package for an intermediate class doing a letter of application.

Before going on, let's consider further examples of the types of Writing that can be done at these three broad levels.

At elementary level, in addition to postcards, students could do gap-fills, dialogues, informal letters, simple forms, and guided writing. By 'guided' writing I mean that students are, for example, given part of a written text already completed, and students complete the rest. 'Parallel texts' can also provide lower-level guidance – as, with the example above, students see a complete model of the type of task that they will have to do. At this level, though, the amount of writing required will be much less than at higher levels.

At intermediate level, in addition to formal letters, students could do simple report writing, simple discursive essays, guided narratives, and complex form filling.

At higher levels, in addition to discursive writing, students could do unguided narratives, note-taking, precis writing, statistical interpretation, report writing, and speculative writing.

Insight

Some lessons will include Writing as just one of a variety of activities; others will focus exclusively on Writing skills. The type of writing tasks will depend on the level of your students. As with the other skills, creating interest in the topic and preparing your students for the task is essential.

Key to task 3

Going back to the last Task, one possible lesson package for a lesson including writing a letter of application could be as follows:

1 Class discussion on types of jobs.
  Aim: for students to start thinking about basic theme of lesson. 2 mins
2 **Reading 1** – students sequence the process of getting a job (sentences on seeing a job ad., completing an application, etc.)

Aim: for students to have practice in reading for detail. 8 mins

3 Teacher shows an ad. for a job for which the students will apply. Discussion as to why they want to apply for the job and why they would be suitable.

Aim: for students to start thinking about reasons for applying for the job. 5 mins

4 **Reading 2** – students read a completed letter of application and look at a list of paragraph functions. They match paragraphs with functions.

Aim: for students to identify the purpose of paragraphs in such a letter. 5/10 mins

or

Students are given a completed letter of application which contains some inappropriately informal language. They have to identify and improve the inappropriate language.

Aim: for students to focus on appropriateness of language. 5/10 mins (if time allows, you might include both of these stages)

5 **Writing** – students write a letter of application for the job featured in Stage 3. This could be a letter already partly written (perhaps with letter layout completed).

Aim: for students to have practice in writing a letter of application. 15/20 mins

6 Students read (or are read) all the letters and choose the best applicant.

Aim: for students to have practice in evaluating qualities of job applicants. 10 mins

As with the 'postcard lesson', the above staging is only an example; there are many possible variations. But what the two examples given show is how a Writing activity can be integrated into a lesson which focuses on other areas, too. Of course, and especially with an exam class, you might instead have a lesson which is exclusively concentrated on Writing. In such a case you will almost certainly be using a course book designed for the preparation of this exam, and it will guide you as to how to approach such lessons. When teaching General English, as we said before, you will probably be using a course book as well, and this book, too, will give you ideas of how to do Writing in the classroom. Most of the time it will suggest an integrated approach, as I have in this unit. Sometimes, you might find it more appropriate to set the actual Writing task for homework – that depends on your context with your students.

One very important aspect of the teacher's role has not been mentioned yet. Given the emphasis on accuracy in Writing, the need for 'correction' is important. We will be looking at correction of both oral and written work, in the next unit. For now, it is enough to say that correction of written work does need to occur, and that there are various ways of approaching it.

Tips

1 Do not ignore the Writing skills.
2 Integrate Writing with other activities, linking and staging the different parts of the lesson.
3 Be prepared to have lessons which focus entirely on Writing when appropriate.
4 Be aware of which writing skills are required for a particular task and help develop your students' ability to use these skills.
5 Be aware of which style of writing is required for a particular activity and help develop your students' ability to write in this way.
6 With low levels especially, provide models of the activity.
7 With low levels especially, provide guided writing activities.
8 In all cases, provide writing activities which are relevant to your students' needs both inside and outside the classroom.
9 Use ideas given in course books and specialist resource books.
10 When appropriate, let students work together in the preparation of a Writing activity. This will reduce the pressure and feeling of isolation.
11 Work with the students when they are writing, help and support them, for the same reason as '10'.
12 Use varied techniques for correction (see Unit 16).

Summary

We have seen in this unit that Writing is a skill that is often neglected, partly because its relevance is not always clear, and partly because teachers don't always know the best way to approach it. The potential for boredom is great! But we have also seen that for many students, Writing is very important, either for their own lives if in an English-speaking country, or in their jobs. It can also be very important for those students preparing for an exam of which Writing will be one part. So teachers need to work on developing their students' writing skills.

▸ Teachers have to develop the specific skills required for a particular task, and make sure the students know what type of language to use.

▸ Teachers should also know how to integrate Writing into a lesson.

▸ Correction is very important because the focus on accuracy is much greater than it is with Speaking.

▸ Teachers should work on ways to reduce the pressure that students feel when doing a Writing activity:
by properly staging the lesson
by supporting students during the activity
by allowing students to help each other.

So Writing should not be ignored. However, the amount of time you spend on it compared with the other skills will be less, and will vary a lot according to who you are teaching and in which country you are teaching.

15

Spoken and written mistakes

If you are trying to use a language which you are learning, you will make mistakes. It is inevitable. Some of these mistakes are 'slips of the tongue or pen' which you can correct yourself without prompting; others are what one might call 'real' mistakes, where you do not know what the problem is and need someone to tell you. Mistakes can be spoken, or written. This unit will cover both types, and will not differentiate between *mistakes* and *errors*. As for the role of the teacher, when it comes to correction, this is by no means as straightforward as you might think, or as the student who says 'I want all my mistakes corrected' might think. **Correction**, in short, is a complex part of the teacher's role.

We will look at the following areas in this unit and the next one:

▶ Why students make mistakes
▶ Types of mistake
▶ When the correction should take place
▶ Different ways of correction
▶ Techniques of correction

Why students make mistakes

First, consider this. A child of five utters the sentence *Yesterday I went to school*. Two years later that same child says *Yesterday I goed to school*. What is your conclusion regarding this child's learning progress?

The obvious, easy answer is that the child has regressed. He has gone from correct grammar to incorrect grammar. But, in fact, the opposite is true. The initial correct utterance was probably imitation of a parent using *went* with *yesterday*. However, the second utterance suggests that the child has learnt the rule that verbs in the past end with *-ed*. What that child hasn't yet learnt is that English has many irregular verbs where this rule does not apply. But the child is trying to apply a rule he has learnt, albeit incorrectly, and this is a good thing. This is the first point that needs to be made – 'mistakes' are part of the learning process and as such should be treated positively, assuming the student can learn from his mistakes. Students need to realize that they will make mistakes because it is impossible not to if you are learning a language. What they must do is know *why* it is a mistake so as not to repeat it. Teachers have the responsibility of making the whole process of mistakes and correction a positive one that all students can benefit from.

Task 1

1 Why do students make mistakes (written and spoken)?
2 Think of as many examples of types of mistake as you can.

Stop now and do the task

As I have said before, some students are obsessed with accuracy and want every mistake corrected. When a teacher does correction work, out come their pens and they write everything down as if this is the part of the lesson when they are truly learning. You get the students who want to know which mistakes were theirs. And you get the students who insist on correcting other students' mistakes whenever they hear them! In other words, it is easy for some students to start seeing language learning as essentially learning rules and correcting errors. Fortunately, such students are in the minority because neither students nor teachers should view constant correction as desirable; indeed, it can be counter productive and become a negative experience when, as I said at the start, mistakes should be seen as a positive part of the learning process.

Key to task 1

Students, as you might expect, make mistakes for many reasons. Some of these reasons are common to speaking and writing; others are not.

1 **First language (L1) interference.** An example of this is 'false friends' (see Unit 7).
   But it is any case where a student's first language may 'get in the way'. Another example is different nationalities experiencing particular problems. Japanese learners, for example, have difficulties with using articles.
2 **Forgetfulness.** Students learn. Students forget. We cannot expect a language learner to remember everything we teach them!
3 **Lack of understanding.** Maybe the student simply hasn't understood what you have taught them. They are still trying to correctly apply a rule or form.
4 **Slip of the tongue.** As mentioned before, in an attempt to achieve fluency a student will 'trip over' and make mistakes which are not genuine ones.
5 **Unclear teaching!** Yes, for whatever reason, maybe the teacher has not taught a language point or checked it sufficiently clearly.
6 **Incorrect application of rules.** A student may try very hard to use what they have learnt, but is as yet unaware of 'exceptions' or development of this language point. For example, you cannot cover all ways of talking about the future at once, so students will only use what they have learnt. Refer, too, to the example earlier (went and 'goed').
7 **Incorrect model.** Students will hear 'incorrect' English all the time – from each other and from speakers outside the school. They will copy what they hear.
8 **Habitual.** Some students continue to make the same mistakes time after time however often they are corrected. I'm not sure there's much you can do about this!
9 **Unawareness.** If students don't know (haven't learned) something, they cannot be expected to get it right! Most of

the above can apply, too, to writing (with 'slip of the tongue' becoming 'slip of the pen'). In addition we can add the following:

10 **Alternative script.** Consider, for example, the Japanese or Arabic scripts – they are completely different from the English script and this makes writing in English especially difficult.

11 **Pressure.** As we saw in the last unit, writing is a pressurized activity and there is a strong focus on accuracy. Such pressure can induce mistakes.

12 **Style of language.** The specific styles of written language, the discourse, etc., provide specific problems and the likelihood of mistakes.

13 **Lack of practice.** Students generally get much less practice, and even less 'teaching' of Writing than practically any other classroom activity.

Insight

When learning a language it is impossible not to make a mistake. Making mistakes, whether spoken or written, is an important part of the learning process and should always be treated positively. Recognizing *why* your students make mistakes will help with the process of correction.

Types of mistake

By recognizing *why* students make mistakes with the language, teachers are in a better position to anticipate problems and to help. It also helps to be able to recognize different types of mistake. These can be very broadly categorized as follows:

▶ **Grammar.** Any mistake of structure or form.
▶ **Vocabulary.** Any vocabulary mistake, which may or may not affect meaning.
▶ **Pronunciation.** We looked at this area in Unit 9.
▶ **Appropriateness.** The utterance is technically correct, but not appropriate in the context.

Apart from pronunciation, all of these can apply equally to Writing. To this list we can add:

▶ Layout
▶ Spelling
▶ Punctuation
▶ Organization and general cohesion

Task 2

Look at the following examples of students' **spoken** mistakes. What do you think was the cause, and what type of mistake is it?

1 He writed me a letter.
2 I am seeing the television.
3 When I will see you again?
4 We need airballs for the party.
5 Will you borrow me your dictionary?
6 Teacher: 'Ask her what her name is.'
   Student: 'What your name is?'
7 He drive very slow.
8 I've watched television last night.
9 (Student in pub:) 'Give me a beer.'
10 She go home later.

Key to task 2

1 This is a further example of a student trying to apply a rule she has learnt (add -*ed* to a verb to put it in the past) without knowing that many verbs have irregular past forms. So it is a grammar mistake, but a very understandable one.
2 The student has learnt to use the present progressive to describe an action in progress at the time of speaking (e.g. *It is raining*). What she does not yet know is that some verbs are not formed with -*ing* in this way, and *see* is one such verb. In this case *watching* is the verb we would use. Another grammar mistake.

3 The student has learnt the typical sentence structure in English (subject + verb + object – *I will see you again*) but has not yet learnt the correct question form, and is unaware that we invert the auxiliary verb and subject ('When will I see you again?'). It is another example of a student making a mistake because she does not know the rule.

4 A vocabulary mistake. This student wanted to use the word *balloon* but just didn't know the word. So he invented the word *airball*, a much more descriptive word than *balloon*!

5 Some languages do not make the distinction between *borrow* and *lend*, but even after students learn the difference, they invariably have great difficulty remembering the distinction. It is a vocabulary mistake, and one I have been asked about more times than just about any other vocabulary item.

6 Here's a mistake for which the teacher must take some responsibility, and it relates to the example in 3 above as well. *What* is a question word, and the teacher has said 'Ask her *what*...' and the student has listened very carefully to the rest of the sentence – '...*what* her name is' – and has repeated this as a direct question, which it isn't!

I once observed a lesson given by a trainee teacher. He was setting up a Speaking activity based on questions. He gave examples of the 'questions to ask' by saying something like 'Ask your partner where they come from', and as he spoke he wrote on the board what he was saying. So on the board we had 'Where they come from', 'Where they are living now', 'What food they like', etc. As the Speaking activity began, sure enough, the teacher to his horror heard student A asking student B 'Where you come from?', etc. An easy mistake for the teacher to have made, but with serious consequences!

7 The student either has not learnt the distinction between an adjective and an adverb (*slowly*), or has simply forgotten to use it, as often happens. Another problem students sometimes have with adverbs is they think that they all end -*ly*, which they don't (e.g. *She drove fast, He worked hard*).

8 The present perfect tense is a complex one, and is used differently in British and American English. But one aspect is the same, you do not use a definite time reference (*last night*) *with the present perfect. In this case you would use the past simple – I watched television last night.*

9 'Give me a beer' is correct English, but if you go into a bar and use the words it might be considered rude (though this depends partly on your intonation). At the very least it would be considered unusually direct. So this is inappropriate language.

10 I *go*, you *go*, he/she *goes* – the verb adds *-s/-es* in the third person singular. However, whatever their level, students continually forget this! Forgetfulness is another consideration for the teacher. As well as treating mistakes as a positive part of the learning process, teachers should remember that students are trying to absorb so much new language and so many rules that they cannot possibly be expected to remember everything. If you are currently doing a teacher-training course, you will appreciate how hard it is to remember and put into practice everything your tutors have been telling you! And if you do anything 'wrong', it's all part of your learning experience as a new teacher!

Insight

The main types of mistakes are grammatical mistakes, incorrect vocabulary and appropriateness (i.e. too direct or informal for the context.) And sometimes students simply forget – we can't expect any learner to remember *everything*!

'Positive' mistakes

Let's look now at an authentic piece of written work done together by a group of elementary students. They wrote a supposed letter of appreciation to a departing teacher. This is what they wrote. What is your overall impression?

Dear Matt,

we want to say good buy and hand over you a little present.
We are most grateful to you for your help. You are a very good teacher.
You've got empathy and you shaped the lessons very interesting.
We think, do you like teaching.
We hope we'll meet again on the occasion of the term of autumn.
Today, we wish you many beautiful journey trought the German country.
We wish you good luck and all the best!

This is a fascinating piece of work because it illustrates so well the idea of 'positive' mistakes. At first glance you might think there are lots of mistakes and it is a poor piece of work. But consider two points. First, the meaning is clear throughout. Second, how well the students are trying to use the language. For example, 'you've got empathy and shaped the lessons very well'. 'Empathy' may not be the right word here, but it is a word they have acquired and are trying to use, and the meaning behind the sentiment is clear. As for 'you shaped the lessons very well', it may be a clumsy phrase, but it is a tremendous effort and clearly means the teacher staged the lessons well. 'On the occasion of the term of autumn' may be technically correct, but is inappropriate and unnatural. But arguably it is 'correct'!

Of course, there are examples of good and appropriate language. 'We are most grateful to you for your help' may be a little formal, but no sensitive teacher is going to do anything other than praise the sentence.

Overall, if I had been the teacher, I would have been delighted with this attempt from elementary-level students!

Summary

▶ Whether we are talking about spoken or written mistakes, teachers must recognize why mistakes might have happened (this, as we will see, can help with correction), and should treat them as a positive part of the learning process.

▶ If we perceive mistakes as a sign of poor teaching or lazy learning, we will not be helping ourselves or our students.

▶ If students are hard on themselves because their English is less than perfect – we must help them to understand they are being unrealistic and ultimately hindering their own progress. This applies equally to trainee teachers who say their lesson was a 'disaster' because a couple of parts did not go quite according to plan.

▶ We should focus as much on the 'correct' as the 'incorrect'.

▶ As teachers we must adjust our focus on accurate English according to who we are teaching.

▶ Mistakes are far more of an issue for students preparing for an exam than for those who are seeking only to improve their English. For the latter, it is more important to speak fluently and make themselves understood.

16

Correction

In the last unit we looked at some examples of spoken and written mistakes, and some reasons for them. We also discussed what the teacher's – and student's – attitude to spoken and written mistakes should be. In this unit we will look at when correction should take place, different ways of correction, and correction techniques.

Task 1

What are your views on the following questions about correction of **spoken** mistakes?

1 Should all mistakes be corrected? Should *any* mistakes be corrected?
2 If you answered 'no' to the first question, which mistakes should be corrected?
3 Should correction take place immediately, or later?
4 Who should do the correction – the teacher, the same student or another student in the class?
5 How should the correction take place?

Stop now and do this task!

The role of correction in the classroom is far from clear-cut. However, all teachers do need to know the skills of correction work, and trainee teachers on courses are assessed on their ability to recognize and correct both spoken and written mistakes.

1 Should all mistakes be corrected?

The first question is easy to answer – 'No', all mistakes should not be corrected. What's more, even if you thought they should be (as some students do), it would be impossible. Imagine a class of twenty students, all talking at different points, all making mistakes, and you trying to correct every single mistake. Impossible. Should any mistakes be corrected? Again, an easy question – 'Yes', of course. How can any person learn any new skill without having important mistakes corrected? How can a person learn to be a teacher without knowing or being told when something has gone wrong?

As we have already seen, some students will say 'I want all my mistakes corrected'. Such a student is being unrealistic, but as a teacher you might have to tell that student, or the class, why it is unrealistic as well as undesirable. I have done so many times. With a class of the right level it is no bad thing to have a discussion about learning stategies, and the rationale of what the teacher does or does not do in lessons.

2 Which mistakes should be corrected?

Now it gets more difficult! Having established that some, but not all, mistakes should be corrected, we are faced with the question of *which* mistakes should be corrected. Ultimately, of course, this is for the individual teacher to decide, based on the context of the lesson and the nature of the class. However, I think we can make some general points about what mistakes should be corrected. If students are doing a practice activity, using specific language previously 'presented', as well as other language, then mistakes involving the 'target language' should be focused on for correction (*when* and how will be discussed later). In this type of activity, the focus is more on accuracy, and therefore, at least some of the inaccuracies with the target language need to be corrected. Common mistakes are also suitable for correction. If you are teaching a monolingual class, then you are more likely to get similar mistakes being repeated, and everyone will benefit from the correction. What a teacher might determine to be a 'significant' mistake, for whatever reason, can be corrected. For example, a mistake which results in unclear meaning, or a mistake which results in the wrong meaning. If a student, for example, says 'Can I lend your dictionary', then this is a significant mistake.

If some mistakes *should* be corrected, then others should not – or do not have to be. For example, if your students have done a Reading comprehension and, in answering a question about the text, a student gives the right answer, but uses incorrect grammar, then the teacher can ignore the mistake because the aim of the task was comprehension, not accuracy. If you are chatting with students before or after the lesson, and they make mistakes when talking, ignore the mistakes as long as meaning is clear. If the students have done a practice activity and made mistakes with the target language, focus on those mistakes and worry less about any others, unless they are significant in some other way, or are very common. To correct or not, then, depends on the aim of the lesson or activity. A mistake that occurs in a controlled-practice activity might not be corrected if it occurs in a fluency activity, or a comprehension exercise.

In other words, be selective in deciding which mistakes need to be corrected, and which don't. Some teachers, myself included, might argue that from time to time higher-level students should be allowed to do a Speaking activity where the sole focus is fluency and the teacher should ignore all mistakes.

3 When to correct mistakes?

Sometimes, you might feel that a mistake should be corrected immediately. For example, pronunciation mistakes would normally be corrected straight away. If a student was answering a question concerning target language and a mistake with the target language was made in the answer, again the mistake would be corrected immediately. Sometimes, in the normal flow of a lesson, if a student is talking and a mistake or mistakes in his speech impede your understanding, you might feel that you need to correct.

Besides the many mistakes that would go uncorrected, there are also those that you would not want to correct straight away. If your students are doing any kind of Speaking activity, and especially if you want them to achieve some fluency, then to interrupt with corrections would stop the flow and possibly intimidate them.

One advantage of delayed correction is that the correction becomes less 'personal' – students will not necessarily remember whose mistake it was (though many insist on guessing!). You may wonder, though, if you do not do correction straight away, how you will remember what you hear – see question 5.

In conclusion, some mistakes will be corrected straight away, some later, and some not at all.

Insight

Some, but not all mistakes should be corrected. Sometimes these are best corrected immediately (pronunciation, for example). At other times, for example when the aim is fluency, there should be no interruption and correction should always take place at the end.

4 Who should do the correction?

There are three possibilities – **teacher** correction, **self**-correction, and **student-to-student** correction.

Task 2

What do you think are the advantages and disadvantages of each type of correction?

Stop now and do this task!

In any class, there will be a combination of all three types. In the next question we will consider techniques of correction, and also how correction can become a lesson in itself. But now let us go back to the Task.

A) Teacher correction
<u>Advantages</u>
- ▶ The correction will, or should be, quicker, more efficient, and 'accurate'.
- ▶ Student confidence – 'It is the teacher's job', 'The teacher is always right!'
- ▶ The teacher can ensure correction is handled sensitively and fairly.
- ▶ The teacher can use proper and varied techniques of correction.

<u>Disadvantages</u>
- ▶ It fails to encourage learner-independence.
- ▶ It can be intimidating for students to have 'the teacher' correcting their mistakes.
- ▶ Students might feel embarrassed, however sensitive the teacher might be.
- ▶ Too much teacher correction might be demoralizing for students.
- ▶ Other students might feel 'left out' of the lesson while a mistake is being corrected.

Despite the disadvantages expressed, the teacher should do some correction work, but must ensure it is done properly. As to how much of the correction should come from the teacher, there is no answer to that. It depends on a multitude of factors and opinions.

B) Self-correction
<u>Advantages</u>
- ▶ Students are involved in the process – this renews confidence if they can correct themselves.
- ▶ Self-corrected mistakes are more memorable and less likely to be repeated.
- ▶ It encourages learner independence.
- ▶ It gives the teacher feedback on the student's knowledge, ability and awareness.

<u>Disadvantages</u>

- ▶ Students may not be able to self-correct and consequently become demotivated.
- ▶ Students may feel pressured or embarrassed.
- ▶ Students may 'correct' what was already correct and do more harm than good.
- ▶ It is potentially more time consuming.

On balance, self-correction is definitely more positive than negative. The first three advantages listed above are really important points.

C) Student-to-student correction

<u>Advantages</u>

- ▶ Some students might find it easier being corrected by a peer (but many won't!).
- ▶ It involves other students ... gives them self confidence.
- ▶ It encourages other students to stay involved in the lesson.
- ▶ It encourages an atmosphere of cooperation.
- ▶ It helps the teacher 'assess' awareness of other students.

<u>Disadvantages</u>

- ▶ The student doing the correction may get it wrong!
- ▶ It can be slower and less effective (if student does not have correction skills).
- ▶ The student being corrected may not understand the other student (pronunciation).
- ▶ The student being corrected may not know if the correction is accurate.
- ▶ Some students may feel it is the job of the teacher to correct.

Some student-to-student correction takes place naturally, and within reason, it should be encouraged. But beware the student who constantly tries to correct other students as if they were the teacher. This can be counter-productive and irritate almost everyone in the class!

Overall, the ideal is for there to be a mixture of all three 'correctors', but the precise balance will vary according to many factors. But avoid using teacher correction because that produces a total reliance on the teacher and no encouragement of learner independence.

> **Insight**
>
> Correction can be teacher correction, self-correction or student-to-student correction. All have their advantages and disadvantages. Aim for a mixture of all three but always encourage the latter two, as these develop learner independence.

5 How to correct?

Obviously, you want to avoid 'No, that's wrong', or anything like it. That becomes negative and critical and goes against the idea of correction being part of the learning process. How you correct depends partly on who is doing the correction, the type of mistake, the context of the lesson, and the nature of the mistake. But we can make some very general points.

Tips for immediate correction

1 Indicate that a mistake has been made. How? Maybe facial gesture, verbal remark ('Again'/'Sorry?') or just a gesture for the student to stop their sentence, thus indicating a problem.

2 Locate *where* the mistake is in the sentence. How? A verbal gap-fill, perhaps. For example, if the student has said 'Everyday she go to the shops', the teacher might say 'everyday she ____ to the shops'. Use your fingers, too. With each finger representing one word, when you get to word 3 in this sentence indicate with your finger that this is the problem word. It might sound an odd thing to do, but it works! By locating the mistake the student will be able to focus on the correct part of the sentence, and not end up 'correcting' what doesn't need to be corrected!

3 Categorize the *type* of mistake. How? In this case you might say '3rd person singular?', if the students know the rule of adding *-s* or *-es* in these cases. This suggests the mistake was no more than a slip of the tongue and it will be possible to elicit self-correction, or student-to-student correction.
By indicating that a mistake has been made, where, and what type, the teacher is using her correction skills to make the correction efficient and successful, and is involving the students.

4 At this point, either the student or another student is likely to correct. If they can't, you do it.

5 Maybe get the student to repeat the whole sentence for reinforcement.

6 You could repeat the entire sentence, with mistake, with rising (questioning) intonation to make it obvious that the sentence is incorrect. Or just repeat the incorrect part in the same way.

7 Similar to point 2, repeat the sentence only up to where the mistake occurred.

8 As mentioned before, use your fingers (clearly!) to indicate, for example, that two words are the wrong way round in a sentence (e.g. 'Where you will go?'). You can use your fingers to indicate a 'swap over' of words.

9 Use word prompts to categorize. e.g. 'Tense?' 'Preposition?', etc.

10 If a student has incorrectly repeated what a previous student said, go back to the other student and ask her to repeat what she said before.

All of this might sound like a lengthy process. Normally it takes a matter of seconds for the simple reason that the student, or another, can correct easily. The process only slows down if the mistake was a real one and no-one in the class knows the problem.

Delayed correction

We saw in Unit 13 that if students are doing a fluency activity, or a Speaking activity where they are getting practice of language previously presented, then to interrupt with corrections would spoil the fluency and potentially intimidate the students. In addition, assuming they are working in groups, other students would not benefit from the correction. So how can a teacher do correction later in the lesson?

The usefulness of the 'Tips' below depends on the size of the class and the ability of the teacher to monitor. They are most valuable with a class of no more than, say, twenty, in a room where the teacher can walk around fairly freely.

Tips for delayed correction

1 Arrange the class so that it is possible for you to walk around the room, e.g. they work in groups of four in a circular-type formation.
2 Get a pen and a piece of paper.
3 Keep a 'low profile', listen to each group in turn and try to pick out mistakes.
4 Concentrate on mistakes in the target language, if appropriate, or common mistakes, or mistakes you view as important or useful to focus on.
5 Make a note, too, of particularly good sentences.
6 If you have real trouble hearing (it can be difficult!), note down mistakes which could easily be made in such an activity – a correction phase does not have to consist of genuine mistakes made by students in your class!
7 At the end of the activity, or just before, write up all your sentences on the board. Tell the students that some sentences are correct and others are not. They have to decide and correct as necessary. If there's time, let them work on this in groups. If not, go through it together. This way, everyone benefits from the correction and it is 'depersonalized'. You will almost always have someone who wants to know 'Was that my mistake?' Tell them it does not matter!
8 When going through the mistakes, locate and categorize as indicated above, and write in the correction on the board.
9 Another possibility, especially if time is short and you have lots of sentences, is to do the correction phase in the next lesson.

10 Linked to the previous point, you might 'collect' mistakes from the week and have a correction lesson as a kind of review at the end of the week. At least this way you won't have students trying to work out whose mistakes they were, because they won't remember!

The idea of including correct sentences is to emphasize that a lot of what they said was very good, but that is up to you. I sometimes do it, but not always.

My experience of working on teacher-training courses, where the new teacher's skills of correction are part of their assessment, is that there is often considerable reluctance to correct. There seems to be a number of reasons for this. One is the teacher's own lack of confidence in grammar and fear of being asked questions. Trust your instincts. You know what is right and what is wrong. Others feel that it is too negative to correct. To which I ask, how can someone learn any new skill (including teaching), if you are not made aware of what you are doing wrong? To the teacher who avoids correction I say 'you are not doing your job'. What you have to do is be sensitive and use your skills. In all my years of teaching, the one activity that students have always reacted to positively is correction, and especially 'delayed correction', as described above. I have heard students saying 'Too much grammar', 'Too much speaking', etc. I have never heard students say 'Too much correction'. Too little correction, yes, but never too much.

Correcting written work

So far we have looked primarily at spoken mistakes. Much of what has already been said can apply equally to the correction of **written** mistakes, but there are other factors, too, that need to be considered.

Most people's memories of written work at school being returned by the teacher probably include a long wait, the sight of red ink, lots of corrections and little praise. Or, they may remember pages of written work being returned with a single comment (e.g. 'Good'), making you wonder just how carefully the teacher read your work!

1 When do we correct written work?
2 How do we correct written work?

As with spoken mistakes, so with written mistakes, there is an argument for leaving some mistakes uncorrected. Look again at Unit 14 and the example of written work given and the points made about 'praiseworthy mistakes'. Consider, too, the demoralizing effect of a student getting work back which is filled with corrections.

Yes, you might argue that to leave a mistake uncorrected implies that it is not a mistake – and you would be right! But it is a question of balance and personal judgement in the context of the teaching.

If students are writing in class, you might go round during the activity giving one-to-one help and corrections. Or, you might collect in their work, correct at home, and return it – preferably – the next lesson. In other words, you again have the choice between 'immediate' or 'delayed' correction.

Symbols

Just as with spoken mistakes, teachers should try to involve the students in the correction process of written work. One way of doing this is to employ correction symbols. The teacher might underline or circle the mistake (locate it), then indicate the type of mistake (categorize) by putting in the margin the appropriate symbol (e.g. 'G' for grammar). The students have a copy of all the symbols and what they mean. They then go away and try to correct the work for themselves – though this still requires the teacher to check again afterwards, so it is a lengthier process. Symbols might include 'V' (vocabulary), 'WO' (word order), 'P' (punctuation), etc. You must be consistent in your use of symbols, and still include praise for good work.

If you use the more traditional approach to correction (and, as ever, you should aim for variety), then do not litter the work with corrections. Praise as you can, encourage, be supportive.

Class correction

Another principle of correction of spoken mistakes which can apply to written correction is the one of class correction. Take the work away and make a note of common or significant mistakes. Make a copy of this list (or write it directly on the board) for the next lesson, then have time where everybody looks at all the mistakes from the different pieces of work. This depersonalizes the correction and everybody benefits from it.

With higher levels, students can exchange their work with a partner and look for mistakes in each other's work (student-to-student correction).

Grading

As for 'grading' the work, this is up to you. Personally, I do not, unless the students are preparing for an exam, in which case I would grade according to exam standards for students to have an idea of their level in relation to the exam. Otherwise, I would always write a summary comment, as positive as possible, but no 'grade'. However, that's a personal policy!

Insight

Correction of written work can be immediate (in the classroom during the task) or delayed (take the work home and try to return it in the next lesson). Whether you correct every single written mistake is up to your personal judgement (it can be demoralizing), but always praise good work and give lots of encouragement.

Summary

▶ Correction should be part of the learning process and treated positively.

▶ It should include a variety of teacher correction, self-correction, and student-to-student correction (spoken and written).

- ▶ The teacher should indicate where the mistake is and categorize it.

- ▶ The teacher should employ facial gesture, finger work, verbal prompts, etc., to help with correction.

- ▶ With written work, the teacher should use a variety of approaches as well.

- ▶ Use of symbols for written correction should be clear and consistent.

- ▶ Not all mistakes should be corrected – focus on target language mistakes, common mistakes, or mistakes which you feel are significant for some other reason.

- ▶ If the aim is comprehension (the correct answer to a question), focus on the correct answer, not the correct grammar.

- ▶ Don't interrupt fluency work – make a note of mistakes.

- ▶ Be positive, praise good work.

- ▶ Do correct – don't avoid it!

17

Lesson planning 1: aims

If you are or are about to be a trainee teacher on a training course you will be required to submit a detailed lesson plan each time you teach. If you are a relatively new teacher, you may still be preparing less-detailed plans for your lessons. Once you have more experience, you will rarely produce an actual plan (unless you are being observed, maybe), but you will still plan what you are going to do. So in the following units we are looking at both planning in general, and producing actual lesson plans. This unit focuses on aims.

I have heard some experienced people in the profession argue against the notion of planning, suggesting that teaching and learning should be spontaneous according to the wishes and reactions of the students on a particular day. For some teachers this might work and be successful. However, I would argue that there are very few teachers, however experienced, who would be comfortable just walking into a class with no idea of what will be done in the lesson. Further, I do not believe that most students in my experience would be satisfied with such an approach to learning. But whatever the arguments, such an approach is definitely not acceptable for new or training teachers! What is true, however, is that teaching should be flexible; students must have an influence on what you teach and how you teach it, and this has an important influence on the teacher's planning.

A good lesson plan will be one which is a clear working document. In other words, another teacher would be able to teach your lesson for you by using your plan as a guide. In my experience as a trainer, I can normally predict the quality of the lesson I am about to observe from the quality of the plan which has been handed in. Obviously, the length and precise contents of your plan will depend on the length of your lesson, the type of lesson, and also the stage of the course. But all plans are likely to include at least the following:

> level of class, length of lesson, aims(s) of lesson, target language (if appropriate), personal aims, anticipated problems (for the students) and possible solutions, stages, aim of each stage, estimated timings, interaction, procedure, board layout.

We will look at most of these points in the next unit, but for now we will concentrate on aims.

Lesson aims

The **aim** of your lesson, or the aim of the stage of the lesson, is what you hope to achieve, or what you hope your students will achieve. It answers the question 'Why am I doing this?' Clear and realistic aims are essential if a lesson is going to be successful.

Some teachers phrase the aims from the teacher's perspective, others from the students' perspective. Compare these examples:

'to provide practice in scan reading skills'
'for students to have practice in scan reading skills'

Personally, I much prefer the latter. As teachers, it is more beneficial if we think of what we are doing from the students' perspective whenever possible. New teachers can get too involved in the teaching process (quite understandably!) and neglect to give sufficient importance to the students' learning. As a teacher, of any length of experience, you should think about the students as much as, and probably more than, your own teaching. When observing classes, it is good to focus on one or two students, or the class as

a whole, and observe their involvement and progress in the lesson –
how has their learning been affected by the teaching?

Formulating clear aims is not easy for the new teacher and the
result is often inappropriate or aims that are far too general. You
don't always need the rest of a plan to recognize poor aims, as the
following task will show.

Insight

The **aim** of your lesson is what you hope you and your
students will achieve. It's best to think about this from the
students' perspective: what are they learning or practising?
Above all, your aims must be *realistic*.

Task 1

Which of the following lesson aims seem inadequate? Can you
improve them?

1 'to teach the present perfect'
2 'for students to have practice in listening for gist'
3 'for students to learn new vocabulary'
4 'for students to have reading practice'
5 'to teach the positive and negative forms of the present
   progressive and to give written and spoken practice'
6 'for students to improve their pronunciation'
7 'to set up a speaking activity clearly and efficiently'
8 'Reading and Speaking'
9 'for students to learn the correct usage of selected conjunctions in
   written English and to have practice in a letter-writing task'
10 'to teach Writing'

Before looking at this task, I must emphasize the importance of a
teacher having clear aims. I said before, I can usually predict the
quality of the lesson I am about to see according to the quality
of the plan. The first section I always look at is the one marked
'Aims'. If the stated aims are clear, appropriate, and achievable
(according to the rest of the plan), then I would expect to see an

effective and successful lesson. But a plan with vague aims, or inappropriate aims (for whatever reason) is almost certainly going to result in an ineffective lesson.

Let's look now at the aims above.

Key to task 1

1 It is not uncommon in the early stages of training courses to see an aim such as this one. Personally, I am not keen on the focus on the teacher (the aim says what the teacher will do rather than what the students will achieve), but the real problem is that the aim is vague and unachievable. The present perfect tense is a complex one in any case, but all tenses (verb-forms) have a variety of forms. You have the positive (affirmative), negative, question (interrogative), and answer forms. Is this teacher going to 'teach' all four forms in one lesson? Then you have to consider the different uses of this tense (bearing in mind that the tense is used differently in British and American English). Thus, *I've been to France* refers to a past experience, whereas *I've worked here for ten years* refers to something started in the past and continuing to now. Again, it would be unrealistic to include more than one usage with, say, a pre-intermediate class. The importance, therefore, of pre-lesson **language analysis** by the teacher is essential. Equally imortant is the teacher's own **language awareness** – actually knowing and understanding the language that she is to teach. We will look at this in Unit 19.

So, this teacher probably has little understanding of what the present perfect is and what is involved in teaching it. I would expect to see a lesson which covers far too much, and done via explanations and lots of exercises.

A better aim would be 'for students to learn and have spoken practice in the positive and negative forms of the present perfect simple (indefinite past event)'. Seeing such an aim would lead me to expect a focused lesson.

2 This is a good aim. It sees the lesson from the point of view of the students, but more than that, it provides a clear and specific objective. It's not 'to have practice in listening' (too vague), but listening 'for gist'. So the teacher is aware of different types of listening skills, and has prepared a lesson which focuses on one particular skill.

3 This aim is written from the students' perspective, which is good. However, like number 1, it is far too vague. What vocabulary? How much? For what purpose? Will there be any practice? If so, what type? There's nothing wrong in having a vocabulary lesson (rather than teaching vocabulary which will be needed, say, for a later Reading task), but it needs to have focus.

An improvement would be 'for students to learn the meaning, form and pronunciation of ten words about *television* and to have practice using them in a written gap-fill and a free-speaking activity'. Better than '...to learn vocabulary'!

4 Again, it is good that it is written from the students' perspective. However, unlike number 2, it is too general. Which reading skills will be used?

Compare this with 'for students to have practice in gist reading (scanning), and reading for detail'. A teacher who plans according to the original aim is one who will probably have given little thought to the tasks being given, and is unaware of what type of reading is required of the students. This teacher might, for example, give three gist questions and allow ten minutes for the task! As we saw in an earlier unit, gist reading should be relatively quick. If it takes ten minutes it is no longer gist reading!

5 A good, clear aim – albeit written from the teacher's perspective – and a big improvement on number 1. If this aim came from the lesson plan of a trainee at the end of a course, and the first aim in the task had come from the same trainee early in the course, it would demonstrate real progress.

6 I would be pleased to see a teacher doing a lesson focusing on pronunciation, and I would be very glad not to be reading

'to teach pronunciation'! However, the aim remains far too vague. Which aspect(s) of pronunciation?

An improvement would be 'for students to have practice in recognizing and using rising and falling intonation in question tags and to recognize the different meanings implied'.

7 This aim is what the teacher personally wants to achieve; it has nothing to do with the reason for doing the activity. It is a personal aim, not a lesson aim. There is nothing wrong in having personal aims (in fact, they are very important), but they should not be confused with teaching and learning aims.

8 There is a very common confusion for new teachers on training courses – the difference between the 'What?' and the 'Why'? **Aims** are the 'Why?' ('Why am I asking my students to do this?'), stages are the 'What?' ('What will the students do?'). Both Reading and Speaking are 'What?'s. Refer back to number four for a possible improvement.

9 This is fine.

10 This is not fine. Which aspects of writing? The aim as written suggests that the teacher is going to teach the class *how* to write – and all in one lesson!

An improvement would be 'for the students to have practice in writing a letter of application, using appropriate layout, language and paragraphing'.

Sometimes a lesson may have 'main' and 'secondary' aims. For example:

Main (primary) aim: 'for students to have practice in reading for gist and for detail'.

Secondary aim: 'for students to have practice in free-speaking on topic of text'.

We saw in Unit 11 that a teacher needs to be flexible according to various factors, including her aims. We concluded that a teacher should not 'rush through' the Reading part of this lesson (or skip part of it) in order to do the Speaking. It is important to achieve the main aim properly even if the secondary aim is not achieved. Teachers, then, need to be aware themselves of what 'must be done and done properly' in a lesson, and what can be adapted or even dropped (or kept for the next lesson). We will look at this 'flexibility' issue in the next unit.

If you are observing a lesson, try to see if you can write down what you thought the the aims of the lesson were and then compare your aims with the actual ones written by the teacher. If the lesson was effective and successful, the task should be easy!

Insight

Be flexible about your aims. You might have to adapt or even drop parts of your lesson plan. If this happens, ensure that your main aim is achieved, and be flexible with other secondary aims.

Stage aims

Everything a teacher does, and everything a teacher says, should have a purpose. Well, almost everything! Aims, therefore, are not only for the lesson itself but also for each part of it. A trainee on a teaching course, submitting lesson plans, should always indicate the aim of every stage. An experienced teacher knows instinctively why they are doing or saying what they are. The word 'stage' refers to what the students will be doing – it's a kind of 'title' for the part of the lesson. Examples would be 'Reading', 'Practice', 'Boardwork'. The aim would then clarify the reason for this.

Task 2

For each of the following stages, try to give a possible aim.

Example:
Reading: 'for students to have practice in reading for gist'.

1 Writing
2 Boardwork
3 Practice
4 Context
5 Language focus
6 Drilling
7 Checking answers
8 Speaking
9 Feedback
10 Correction

Key to task 2

Of course, there are no single 'correct' answers because there are many possibilities according to the lesson being taught, but here are some suggested answers. Yours may be different but still 'correct'.

1 'for students to have practice in using narrative tenses'
2 'for students to have a record of the target language'
3 'for students to have controlled practice of the 2nd Conditional via a gap-fill'
4 'to establish student interest in the topic of the lesson (food)'
5 'to clarify the meaning, form and pronunciation of '*wish* + past perfect' (NB: each of the three points here would have separate sub-stages and sub-aims)
6 'for students to have controlled practice in repeating the new words correctly and naturally'
7 'for students to see if they have the right answers and to understand the reasons for the answers'
8 'for students to have practice in speaking fluently on the lesson topic (food), and ranking food from favourite to least favourite.'
9 'for students to tell the rest of the class what they learnt from the pair work questionnaire'
10 'for students' significant mistakes with the target language to be corrected in groups and then clarified by teacher'

Insight

The **stage** of a lesson refers to what the students are doing (writing, checking answers, etc.). You need to be clear about each stage of the lesson and each lesson stage should have its own aim.

Tips

1 Think of the lesson and its stages from the *students'* per-spective – what they will do or achieve, rather than what you will do.

2 Keep the aim as precise and clear as possible.

3 Make sure the aim is realistic (in terms of the level, the students, the time).

4 If appropriate, distinguish between main/primary and secondary aims.

5 Give priority to the achievement of the main aim.

6 Ensure that every stage of your lesson also has an aim – these aims will usually also be from the students' perspective.

7 Make sure you are clear about what the aims are as well!

Having looked at aims of the lesson and aims of each stage of the lesson, we can go one step further. An experienced teacher always knows why she is doing or saying something. What might appear to an observer to be an aimless chat could in reality be the teacher guiding the students towards thinking about a particular question. A teacher showing a class a picture of a famous star, or a hot sunny country, might be going on to a lesson on 'I wish'. A teacher briefly telling the class what she likes and dislikes about a place might just be giving an example of what she wants her students to talk about together. Such a teacher won't have to write out a plan in advance to know why she is doing what she's doing, or saying what she's saying. But until you have that experience, almost everything has to be planned in one form or another. Trainee teachers on courses will teach in one month what some teachers do in just one day, so they have the time to write a proper plan, and of course, this is expected of them. We will look in the next unit at what else, apart from aims, needs to be included in a plan, and how to approach it.

Summary

▶ Aims need to be clear, precise, achievable, and preferably stated from the point of view of students learning rather than of the teacher teaching.

▶ Teachers with vague aims in language lessons have probably not understood, or given sufficient thought to, the language being taught.

▶ The main aim of a lesson needs to be achieved, to some extent at least, even if this means being less effective in achieving the secondary aim.

▶ Every action, every word of the teacher, should have a purpose – whether this has been planned, or is instinctive.

▶ You should review the success of your lesson and to what extent you have achieved your aims.

▶ Resist the temptation to dismiss a lesson as a 'disaster'.

▶ You should think more about the students' learning than about the teaching process in isolation.

▶ Ask yourself 'what did the students do/learn/practise in my lesson?' – you might be pleasantly surprised!

▶ However, such a review might be misleading in one respect. It might give the impression that a teacher should stick, inflexibly, to her plan. Not only is this not true, but also it is a dangerous conclusion. As we will see in the next unit, a teacher must always teach with the students' needs in mind, even if this means departing from a carefully prepared plan!

18

Lesson planning 2: writing a lesson plan

This unit is specifically for those who are on training courses and who have to submit formal lesson plans for each lesson that they teach. We looked in the last unit at aims and how to formulate them, and aims are one of the items on any lesson plan. Indeed, they are the *key* item, since the aims say why the lesson is happening and what the students will get out of it. The aims of stages state the reason for each part of the lesson.

As a trainee on a course you will find lesson plans something of a chore in the sense that they take time and have to be done properly. However, they are an essential part of any training course. So, apart from the fact that you have to submit plans on such courses, what are the benefits of writing plans for teachers and students?

Most trainees on courses have never taught before and everything they are doing and hearing on the course is new. There is a lot of information, a lot of jargon, a lot of theories and techniques to digest. On many such courses the trainees have to start teaching practice right away ... a kind of 'learning by doing'. It is easy, then, to get confused and frustrated and to lose sight of the main focus of a lesson and how to teach it. Preparing a lesson plan will greatly help the teacher to think more clearly about *what* she is going to do, *why* she is doing it, and *how* she will do it. The result should be a more confident teacher, a more focused and effective lesson, and happy students. Students benefit most because they will be getting a well-thought-out lesson with clear learning objectives.

A good lesson plan ...

▶ is a clear working document for the teacher. It should be a document that a teacher can work from in the lesson, so it should be neat, clear, well-organized.
▶ has clear and appropriate and achievable aims.
▶ should include assumptions of what will help the students achieve the aims – their existing skills and knowledge as known or assumed by the teacher.
▶ should anticipate problems of any kind in the lesson and possible solutions. (See next unit.)
▶ should have clear and logical stages which link naturally. Ideally, the students as well as the teacher should see where the lesson is going and how the stages link.
▶ should include a variety of activities and interaction.
▶ should reflect how that lesson fits in with others being taught before or/and after.
▶ should be realistic in terms of what can be achieved in the time available.
▶ should not be too long and detailed (see point 1).
▶ should be flexible – a really important point which we'll come back to later.

> **Insight**
>
> Students will benefit from a good lesson plan: it means a well-thought out lesson. A good lesson plan should have clear and realistic aims, should anticipate problems, have logical stages that link together and should include a variety of activities and interaction.

Lesson plan contents (1)

Typical features of lesson plans were listed in the last unit. Here we will look at each of these features and see an example of an authentic plan written by a trainee on a training course. The example is not presented as a perfect model but as a typical plan produced by a successful candidate on a course. Aspects of the plan are unclear, but overall it is a satisfactory plan from a Pass-standard trainee.

The central feature of any plan will be the **lesson aim(s)**. This was looked at in detail in the previous unit. In our example plan the aims were stated as:

> for students to review and have practice using *like* and *don't like*
> for students to learn the use of *would like* and have practice using it

(this was a 40-minute lesson given to an elementary group of learners).

This teacher had covered *like* and *don't like* in the previous lesson. This, then, is indicated in the section **timetable fit and presumed student knowledge**.

> follows on from previous lesson (*like / don't like*)
> will continue tommorrow

This emphasizes the point that lessons should be part of an overall syllabus or structure, with links not just within a single lesson, but between different lessons. In other words, aims should apply to a series of lessons / a course, as well as to a single lesson.

Plans normally also indicate the **materials and resources** to be used:

> *Headway Elementary* (Soars – OUP) Pages 62/63
> My own visuals and word/sentence cards

Note here, in reference to Unit 20, how this trainee did not rely exclusively on the course book being used, but supplemented this with her own materials and ideas.

Good teachers – experienced as well as new – should always be working on improving their own skills and focusing on areas in which they have a weakness. On training courses, especially, there is an emphasis in assessment of *progress*; how trainees improve in areas where they have previously had problems. You should limit yourself to two or three areas in an individual lesson. The trainee in this lesson wrote ...

> to encourage students more to use the new/revised language in a communicative way.

A major part of planning is **anticipating problems** with accompanying possible solutions. This is something the next unit will focus on in more detail, but in the example plan the trainee wrote:

> students might be confused by use of 'like' and 'would like'
> solution: ask concept questions

It should be said here that this part of the plan needed to be much more detailed!

Boardwork needs to be neat, organized, and a clear 'take-away' record for students who copy from it. Particularly if a teacher is going to use the board to write up target language covered in a lesson, she should plan how to lay out her boardwork. The teacher in the example here planned two phases of boardwork. The first part was planned as follows:

like			
subject	like	*verb* + -ing	
I	*like*	*flying*	
She/He	*likes*	*flying*	= *enjoyment*
We	*like*	*flying*	

Negative:

subject	do not like	*verb* + -ing
I	*don't like*	*flying*

<table>
<tr><td colspan="3">like</td></tr>
</table>

She/He	*doesn't like*	*flying*
We	*don't like*	*flying*

For the second part of the lesson the boardwork plan was as follows:

<table>
<tr><td colspan="3">would like</td></tr>
</table>

subject	would like	infinitive	
I	*would like*	*to play tennis*	
short form:	*I'd like*	*to play tennis*	*= polite way of saying 'I want'*

Negative:
I would not (wouldn't) like to play tennis

Note that there is no reference here to question forms and answers. It would have been unrealistic to cover that as well at this level in just 40 minutes, so it was covered in a lesson the next day. The board-work is not perfect – there is no sentence stress marked, for example, but it does provide clear examples and highlighting of the form.

The remainder of the plan refers to the actual stages and procedure employed to achieve the stated aims. The five sections of the lesson itself are **stage/aim/procedure/interaction/time**.

The **stage** is effectively a title for a part of a lesson – it states *what* you will do. The **aim** refers to the aim of that specific part (stage) of the lesson; virtually everything that a teacher says or does in a lesson is said or done for a reason. It states *why* you are doing something, or why the students are doing something. The **procedure** is a description of *how* something will be done. The **interaction** concerns who is working with whom – individual work / pair work / group work / whole class. The time is the very approximate estimate of how long something is likely to take. As we shall see later, this is very flexible according to various factors.

Going back to the example plan, this is how the remainder of the plan looked:

Stage:	**introduction**
Aim:	to get students interested in the subject
Procedure:	introduce imaginary friend, Eric, and ask students what they think Eric does and doesn't like
Interaction:	teacher to class
Time:	3 mins

Stage:	**focus on form** (1)
Aim:	clarify form of *like* (revision)
Procedure:	elicit when we use *I like* meaning something we enjoy doing. Give examples and elicit more examples, including the negative.
Interaction:	teacher to class
Time:	5 mins

Stage:	**practice**
Aim:	students have practice of *like* (questions and answers)
Procedure:	divide class into two groups, give each group a set of questions and answers, students match them up / I monitor
Interaction:	groups
Time:	5 mins

Stage:	**check answers**
Aim:	clarification of answers
Procedure:	get students to give correct answers / I will confirm or correct
Interaction:	teacher to class
Time:	2 mins

Stage:	**practice 2**
Aim:	students have spoken practice of *like*
Procedure:	divide students into pairs, give each student a picture and they have to tell their partner whether they like or don't like the items. Then get each student to tell the class about their partner's likes and dislikes

| Interaction: | pairs |
| Time: | 7 mins |

Stage:	**focus on language**
Aim:	clarify meaning / form / pronunciation of *would like*
Procedure:	elicit when we use *would like* as a polite way of saying *I want*. Show form on board, including negatives. Check meaning via concept questions, and pronunciation via drilling
Interaction:	teacher to class
Time:	5 mins

Stage:	**practice 3**
Aim:	students have practice using *would like*
Procedure:	in pairs students get worksheet with sentences containing *like* and *would like* and students have to choose which to use
Interaction:	pairs
Time:	8 mins

Stage:	**check answers**
Aim:	clarification of answers
Procedure:	elicit answers from students, get others to say if they are right or wrong
Interaction:	teacher to class
Time:	5 mins

The resulting lesson, though not strong, did provide a clear focus on the target language, and practice – although this was not very varied.

Need for flexibility of timing

However important a lesson plan is for trainee teachers, and however important lesson planning is for any teacher, the key word must always be *flexibility*. A successful lesson is not defined as 'finishing the plan'; teachers have to make changes to their plan as they teach, in response to how the lesson is going and how the students are reacting to, and dealing with, what you are giving them to do. Consequently, the timings for each stage are estimated. They are very approximate guidelines for the teacher of how long each stage might take. If one stage is down as five minutes, and it takes six, seven, eight … okay. But if it takes fifteen, then the teacher either has misjudged the amount of time likely to be needed, or has allowed the activity to continue for too long. On a training course, teachers usually have very fixed time slots for their lessons, e.g. 40 minutes; they do not have the luxury of being able to carry on with their plan in another lesson, as working teachers do. So time becomes an issue, and rightly so because it forces the trainee to think about achievement of aims and the allocation of time to different stages in order to achieve the aims.

Look at this example of time allocation for stages in a 40-minute Reading lesson:

		minutes
1	Pre-teach essential vocabulary	10
2	Establish interest in topic	5
3	Reading task 1	5
4	Reading task 2	10
5	Speaking follow-up	10

Stages 1 and 2 prepare the students to complete the Reading tasks. Stages 3 and 4 are the actual reading parts of the lesson. Stage 5 is a Speaking activity related to the topic of the text. Let's imagine the main aim of the lesson is 'for students to have practice in scan reading and intensive reading skills'. As it stands, 15 minutes of the lesson is devoted to Reading, but with the necessary vocabulary input this is effectively 25 minutes. But, what if the vocabulary takes 20 minutes, and establishing interest takes 10? Suddenly, most of the lesson has gone without any Reading. It has become more of a vocabulary lesson. On a training course this is important because assessment is based in large part on achievement of aims. In a 'real' teaching situation it would not matter if the teacher was able to continue the same lesson after the break, for example. But trainee teachers need to show they can achieve aims in a given space of time. In the example above, this means making sure the students get their 15 (or 12, or 18 …) minutes of reading.

So, what if the teacher has taken longer than planned to get to the Reading? The students are nearing the end of Reading 1, but there is only ten minutes left. What do you do – continue with Reading 2 and forget the Speaking, or go on to Speaking and leave out Reading 2? Or do you do both and finish your lesson ten minutes late? Well, if it's a training course you definitely don't do both and go over time because you are expected to finish your lesson more or less on time. And in a 'real' teaching situation you probably wouldn't be able to over-run by so much either.

The answer is, scrap the Speaking and do Reading 2 because if you don't, then half of your reading aims will not have been achieved. The Speaking is a 'bonus', but does not relate to your main aims.

Insight

Timing is very important for all teachers, but particularly for trainee teachers who usually have fixed time slots for lessons. Carefully estimate the timings for each stage of your lesson plan. But be flexible: if something actually takes longer than you anticipated, take time to finish your main lesson aim and drop secondary aims.

Need for on-the-spot decisions

So, the teacher has to make on-the-spot decisions all the time if, as usually happens, activities take longer, or less time, than anticipated. Sometimes you will need to 'stretch' an activity because something before took less time than expected. Sometimes, you will need to add something to your lesson for the same reason. But whatever you do, the main requirement for you on a training course is to achieve your aims in the time given. I recently observed a lesson where the teacher spent 20 minutes 'establishing interest' but only two minutes on the main focus of the lesson – the aims were not achieved. This is why trainees need to estimate the timings of each stage, and know what part(s) of the lesson need the main focus. Experienced teachers can do this instinctively, but if you are on a training course, or if you are a very new teacher, you must estimate times according to your aims.

It is very important in any lesson to respond to what is happening in your class. If you are teaching new language and some students are finding it very difficult, you should not move on just because you have more to 'get through'! You must spend more time on this piece of language and clarify it further. You must know when to 'slow down' or 'speed up', when to quieten things down or liven them up, when to stop students working on a task even if they haven't all finished, when to abandon an activity because it is far too difficult. These are very difficult decisions for new teachers who feel safer following a plan. But as your experience and confidence grow, you will make all these on-the-spot decisions instinctively. You will 'read' your students' faces and know how to change your lesson as you teach it. Sometimes, the time of day, or week will affect how a lesson goes. Or the weather. Or what the students did the previous night. Or something in the news. So many factors can affect the mood and performance of a class, and the teacher has to know how to respond to these factors. If you don't, you are not responding to your students and their needs. All of this relates to being flexible with your plan!

Insight

Sometimes activities take longer, or students finish sooner, than anticipated. This is where you need to be flexible with regards to your lesson plan. You will have to make on-the-spot decisions, to either drop an activity or add something new, but without affecting your main lesson aims.

Tips

NB: These tips are mostly for trainee teachers doing courses where lesson plans have to be submitted

1 Don't leave the writing up of the plan to the last minute – this will result in greater stress and less confidence. The earlier you complete it, the better for you!
2 When writing it, make sure it is neat, organized and easy to follow.

3 Always think of your lesson and your aims from the point of view of your students.
4 Plan the lesson not just according to the level of the class, but also the composition of the class.
5 When teaching language, analyse that language beforehand and consider the most appropriate way to teach it.
6 Anticipate any problems students might have with the language you are teaching and with any other aspect of the lesson – and think of possible solutions.
7 Be flexible with your plan according to the reactions of your students.
8 Highlight stages that could be shortened if necessary, or dropped, and stages that must have a significant focus in relation to the achievement of stated aims.
9 In relation to point 8, be flexible with your estimated timings.
10 After the lesson, ask yourself to what extent you achieved your aims; what worked and what didn't work (and why). In other words, review your plan and the lesson in order to continue developing your skills and awareness as a teacher.

We will look now at another authentic lesson plan written by a trainee teacher.

Lesson plan contents (2)

This was a 60-minute lesson given to intermediate students.

Aim(s): for students to learn and practise modal verbs of deduction; for students to have practice in gist and intensive reading skills
Target Language: 3rd person singular affirmative and negative (*must, could, might, may*)
e.g. *He must be rich / He can't be rich* for making deductions

(Contd)

Anticipated Problems:	students will be aware of *must* for obligation and might find this use of the word confusing; opposite of *must* for deduction is *can't*, not *mustn't*; students might produce the *-ing* form (not focus of my lesson); *must* is pronounced weakly with a silent *t* (*I must go*)
Personal Aims:	not to rush instructions; clear concept checking
Boardwork:	

....

Modal verbs of deduction
....

expressing degree of certainty about the present	expressing degrees of certainty about the past
e.g. 'He must be in love'	e.g. 'He could have been in love'

certainty	possibility	certainty	possibility
must/can't	might/may/could	must have can't have	might may could ⎫ have

(NB: boardwork fails to indicate what kind of verb follows the modal in each case.)

Stage:	context
Aim:	to generate student interest in topic
Procedure:	introduce topic of family relationships, elicit types of relationship; individual students read and think about questions (1 min), then discuss in pairs and report back three pieces of information
Interaction:	teacher to class / individual / students to class
Time:	5 mins

Stage:	reading
Aim:	for students to practise gist and intensive reading skills and locate target language

Procedure:	tell students topic of text / give out worksheet / 30 secs. for gist task / 5 mins for intensive task / students compare answers / teacher checks answers / ask concept questions relating to the modal verbs in the answers
Interaction:	individual, pairs, whole class
Time:	15 mins

Stage:	**board stage**
Aim:	to provide a written record of the target language (as above)
Procedure:	elicit sentences and structures from students / further concept checking as required
Interaction:	teacher to students
Time:	10 mins

Stage:	**practice**
Aim:	grammar reinforcement / check understanding
Procedure:	worksheet –'What can you deduce from the following situations?' give example / students work in pairs
Interaction:	pairs
Time:	10 mins

Stage:	**follow-up activity (speaking)**
Aim:	authentic practice of modals of deduction
Procedure:	set the scene / students read task and I check they understand / give out clue cards / give instructions and check / students do task and guess the murderer
Interaction:	teacher to class / then groups
Time:	20 mins

What the procedure does not refer to is any reference to pronunciation work, even though the teacher referred to potential problems of pronunciation earlier in the plan. However, the resulting lesson *did* have a pronunciation focus, and it was a very successful lesson!

Summary

▶ Having established aims which are both achievable in the time available and appropriate for the particular group of students being taught, teachers must prepare stages that link naturally and lead towards these aims.

▶ Teachers need to be flexible with all aspects of their plan and should at all times teach according to the needs and reactions of the students.

▶ Plans focus the teacher's mind on what needs to be achieved and the best way of achieving it – students benefit from this planned approach.

▶ Experienced teachers can be more 'spontaneous' in their teaching, but until you reach that stage always plan carefully, not just a particular lesson, but a series of lessons – you must consider the 'timetable fit' and so avoid producing a series of 'one-off' lessons.

19

Lesson planning 3: anticipating problems

In the previous units we have looked at writing lesson plans, and formulating clear and appropriate aims. But teachers must never assume that a lesson will always, or even sometimes, go exactly as planned. They should anticipate problems, and be ready with solutions. This is an essential aspect of planning. This unit will focus on language analysis, and anticipating problems with language; the next will look at more general problems that can occur when we are teaching. Before reading further, then, do the following task.

Language analysis

Task 1

For each of the following sentences, decide what the **form** of the highlighted part of the sentence is; and what the **meaning** is in the sentence given. You need to be clear about this before we anticipate problems. Bear in mind that for these sentences there is no context, so more than one meaning might be possible.

Example: **I've been** working here for two years. (intermediate)
Form: subject + *has/have* + verb-*ing* (= present perfect continuous/progressive)
Meaning: something you started doing in the past, are still doing now, and might continue doing in the future.

1 She's **gone** to France. (pre-intermediate)
2 I'**ll have finished** by lunchtime. (intermediate)
3 It **must have been** a mistake. (intermediate)
4 You **have to pay** taxes. (elementary)
5 Can you **put me up** for the night? (pre-intermediate)
6 I'**m meeting** Zsigi for lunch tomorrow. (elementary)
7 **Could you help me** with my bags, please? (low elementary)
8 She **goes** to the gym every day. (low elementary)
9 This time next week I'**ll be lying** on the beach. (high intermediate)
10 I **used to believe** in Santa Claus. (pre-intermediate)

The form, as referred to in Unit 4, is the fixed part of the sentence, the part that does not change. Look at this simple example:

I'm going to leave
　　　　　　work
　　　　　　eat
She's going to drive
　　　　　　sing

Here we see that the fixed part is 'subject (*I*, *She*, etc.) + *going to* + base verb' If we said *I'm going to leave tomorrow*, then *tomorrow* is not part of the 'grammar' of the sentence.

If we have the verb to *depend*, the form includes the spelling, the fact that *to depend* is followed by '*on* + object', and that it is a regular verb.

The **meaning** is what this particular bit of language means in the context given. The sentence *You've lost weight* could be an expression of concern, or congratulating someone who has been on a diet and successfully lost weight.

With these points in mind, let's go back to the earlier task.

··

Insight

To anticipate possible problems in a lesson, you need to analyse the language point you are going to teach: its form and meaning. The **form** is the fixed part of the sentence: it does not change and is generally the 'grammar' part. The **meaning** is what the sentence means in the particular context.

Key to task 1

1 This is the present perfect simple. *She* is the subject and is followed by *has* or *have*, and the past participle. The past participle is the third form of the verb – *go*, *went*, **gone**; *eat*, *ate*, **eaten**; *work*, *work*, **worked**. *Work* is an example of a regular verb because its past endings are both *-ed*. The other verbs are irregular verbs because they have different and varying past endings.
  The meaning here is that the person went to France at some unspecified past point and is still there now; for how long, we don't know.

2 This is the future perfect simple. The subject is followed by '*will have* + past participle'. You are saying that whatever it is you are doing, you started at an unspecified past time, have not completed it, but definitely will at some point before lunchtime.

3 '*must have* + past participle' follows the subject. *Must* is a modal auxiliary verb, and *must have* places the time in the past. It is being used for *deduction* (informed guess) about a past event, so you think it was a mistake because there is no other likely explanation.

4 'Subject + *have to* + base verb' is used to state something which is an obligation, usually an external obligation such as a rule or law.

5 '*to put someone up* (*put* + object + *up*)' for a period of time means to give someone a place to sleep for a short period of time.

6 'Subject + *is/am/are* + verb-*ing*' (= present continuous/ progressive) here means that you and Zsigi have made an arrangement for lunch – it is a definite future arrangement.

7 '*Could you* + base verb + object' is used in this example to make a polite request.

8 The present simple in the 3rd person singular (*I go*, *you go*, *she goes*) is used here to talk about daily routine.

9 Following the time reference, we have 'subject + *will be* + verb-*ing*'. It means here that at a specified future time (*this time next week*) an action (*lying on the beach*) will be in progress, but will have begun at an unspecified time before, and will continue for a period after this time as well.

10 'Subject + *used to* + base verb' talks about a past habit or state, no longer true.

We have ten pieces of language with likely levels specified and we have established the form and the likely meaning (concept). As new teachers, you may be unsure yourselves of some of this language, but it is important to think of the problems from the students' point of view.

Anticipating problems

Task 2

For each of the ten examples, consider what specific problems students might have with the **form**, **meaning** and **pronunciation** of the language (NB: aspects of pronunciation were also dealt with in Unit 9).

Example: I've been working here for two years.

- ▶ Students might have trouble with the concept of past, present and future time.
- ▶ The name of the tense – *present* perfect progressive – may add to this problem.
- ▶ Students might confuse this with the present progressive.
- ▶ Students might be unfamilar with some past participle verb forms.
- ▶ Possible confusion with contracted form (*She's*) ... *is* or *has*?
- ▶ Confusion with other use of same tense (e.g. *I've been playing tennis* – but not now).
- ▶ *been* is pronounced /bɪn/ in natural speech.

This is not a complete list of possible problems, but it gives you an idea of the types of problems that students might encounter. In many cases we could add 'first language interference', and this certainly applies to this example. There is also a different usage of the present perfect in British and American English, though this applies more to the present perfect simple. So, go ahead now and think of problems for the ten examples. Refer to a grammar book for help!

Before looking at this task, you may wonder if it is really so important to analyse language in this way before teaching it. It is. Ninety-nine per cent of all trainee teachers that I meet tell me that they are worried about 'grammar'. That is because so few people, in my experience, studied English grammar at school, and this results in the new teacher having to teach something about which they appear to know very little. This contrasts with the typical mid- to high-level student who appears to know much more than the new teacher. They know what a conditional sentence is, what a past participle is, what a preposition is. But I said that the teacher 'appears' to know very little, and the student 'appears' to know a lot. In one respect it is true – the 'terminology', what things are, lots of rules maybe. However, the nervous new teacher, if her first language is English, has an instinctive awareness of what is right and what is wrong; what is natural and what is not; and what is appropriate and what is not. What this teacher does not have – yet – is a ready understanding of 'Why?' It is this 'Why?' question that teachers fear being asked, as well as the identification of terms.

Of course, many teachers do not have English as their first language. Many trainees that I have worked with have come from many different countries. What these teachers have, usually, is an excellent knowledge and thus greater confidence. On the other hand, their choice of language is occasionally 'artificial' – for example, they might use idiomatic language in the wrong context.

For these reasons, it is essential for the new teacher to analyse the language she is going to teach. Any teacher needs to know the form of the language, the meaning in the context being used in the lesson, the phonological aspects of the language, and the most appropriate way for students to have practice using it. This will give the teacher confidence, and in turn the students will benefit.

When planning the lesson, the teacher needs to anticipate the problems that her students might have, at their level, with the language being covered in that particular lesson. By doing this, the teacher is better prepared to deal with those problems, and will be much better prepared to cope with all aspects of what is to be taught. And the biggest fear of new teachers will be greatly reduced – 'What if someone asks me a question I can't answer?!' Again, the main beneficiaries of the teacher analysing the language and anticipating problems will be the students.

In doing the above task there was no specific group of students, no specific lesson plan. Therefore, the points we make are general ones that would not necessarily all apply to any one class; they are not exhaustive. So let's go through the task now.

Insight

The majority of trainee teachers worry about 'grammar' and about not being able to answer students' questions about the language. This is why analysing the language is so important: it will mean you are fully prepared for possible problems and tricky questions! Most of all, your students will benefit from your preparation.

Key to task 2

1 She's gone to France.

▶ The tense is called *present* perfect, but it refers to past time.
▶ Confusion with past simple (*She went to France*).
▶ Students may incorrectly add a time reference ('... *last week*').
▶ Students may confuse it with other uses of the same tense.
▶ British and American use of the present perfect is different.
▶ Students may not know the correct past participle verb forms.
▶ Students might confuse the contracted form of **has** with **is**.
▶ In the word **she's** the sound is /iːz/.

- ▶ In this sentence we have the preposition *to* and this is pronounced weakly.
- ▶ With this particular sentence, students may confuse **gone** with **been**.

The teacher, then, needs to provide a clear context which illustrates the time reference and to check understanding with concept questions / a timeline. Pronunciation needs to be worked on with the teacher providing a clear model and getting students to repeat it. Any task comparing this tense with the past simple would be valuable. Boardwork could provide a clear record of form.

These points apply to all these examples (but timelines are appropriate only for numbers 1, 2, 6, 9, 10).

2 I'll have finished by lunchtime.

- ▶ It's a complex sentence with a double contraction likely in the spoken form.
- ▶ The pronunciation of *have* will be weak.
- ▶ Students are likely to confuse this with other future forms.
- ▶ The concept of the sentence is difficult (something which will already be finished at a given time in the future).
- ▶ Students may think of this sentence as only ever applying to future time, when it may refer to something already begun.
- ▶ The preposition *by* may be confused with *at*.
- ▶ Students may have problems with past participle forms.
- ▶ With *she* and *he* students may say *has* rather than *have*.

3 It must have been a mistake.

- ▶ Students might find the concept of 'deduction' difficult.
- ▶ Students might confuse this use of *must* with its meaning of obligation (e.g. *You must do your homework*).
- ▶ Students are likely to have problems with the form (modal + *have* + past participle).
- ▶ Students will probably think this is present perfect because of the '*have* + past participle', but it's not! If it was present

perfect, for example, we would say *he has*, but here it is *he must **have** gone*.

▶ Students may be unfamiliar with some past participle forms.
▶ Students may be unclear about the time being referred to in this sentence.
▶ The degree of probability (compare with *it might have been*) may be unclear.
▶ Students will think the negative of this is *mustn't* (it's actually *can't*, as in *it can't have been a mistake*).
▶ Pronunciation of *must have* with the weak form of *have* in the contraction. With the negative, if being taught, there is the natural double contraction (*can't've*).

4 You have to pay taxes.

▶ Students may want to use *must* and be unclear of the fine difference between *must* and *have to*.
▶ The concept of 'external obligation' may be difficult.
▶ Students might confuse this use of *have* with the possessive use (*I have a pen*).
▶ The time reference may not be understood (general time in this case, but it isn't always – it can refer to future time, as in *I have to be at work early tomorrow*).
▶ The pronunciation of *have* is with an /f/ sound, not /v/, whereas with the possessive use of *have* the sound is /v/ not /f/! There is the weak form of *to* with the schwa.
▶ Students may use the incorrect form of *have* (for example, they might say *She have to…*).

5 Can you put me up for the night?

▶ Students may try to work out the meaning literally – not possible with phrasal verbs.
▶ The time reference may not be clear.
▶ The idea of providing someone with temporary accommodation could be difficult.
▶ The form is difficult. In this case the two parts of the verb are separated and the object goes in the middle. However, you can

also say *Can you put up Marek for the night?*, but you cannot say *Can you put up him for the night?*. The form of phrasal verbs is complex!

▶ Students can be overwhelmed by the number and different types of phrasal verbs, and in some cases by different meanings of the same verb!

▶ In this sentence, the weak form of *can* would be pronounced (kən).

6 I'm meeting Zsigi for lunch tomorrow.

▶ The name of the tense (*present* progressive) conflicts with the time reference (future).

▶ Students may want to use the present simple (which would be incorrect here, but correct if you meet Zsigi for lunch every, say, Tuesday).

▶ Students might want to use *will*, which they think of as the way to talk about the future.

▶ The present progressive has various uses which the students might confuse. The first they are likely to have learnt is for an action in progress at the time of speaking (e.g. *I'm watching TV right now*).

▶ The idea of a definite future arrangement, compared with intention, or other possible future function, is likely to confuse students.

▶ Spelling forms of the verb could be a problem (e.g. *meet + ing*, but not '*shine + ing*').

▶ Some verbs rarely if ever take the *-ing* form (e.g. *know, hear, like*).

▶ If students don't use the contracted form *I'm* and say *I am*, it changes the meaning somewhat and becomes more of an emphatic statement.

▶ If saying *he's* students might think they hear *his*.

▶ Similarly, *you're* may be heard as *your*, and *we're* as *were*.

▶ With *I'm meeting* the /m/ of *I'm* effectively disappears when spoken naturally.

▶ Students might be confused by the alternative negative forms (e.g. *you aren't / you're not*).

▶ Some languages have a single tense covering uses of both simple and progressive in English (first language interference might be an issue with most of these language points).

There are various other possible problems with this sentence/tense, but the above points highlight the complexity of it!

7 Could you help me with my bags, please?

▶ Students will ask about the alternative modal *can*.
▶ Idea of a polite request contrasting with other types of requests may be difficult.
▶ Weak form of *you* in pronunciation.
▶ Appropriate intonation important to convey politeness.
▶ Some students might use *to*-infinitive (*Could you to help me...?*)
▶ Students might confuse this use of *could* with others.

8 She goes to the gym every day.

▶ Concept of habitual action / routine might be difficult.
▶ Possible confusion with other uses of present simple that students might have been exposed to.
▶ Students may try to use present progressive instead, thinking of 'continuity' matching the idea of repeated action.
▶ Pronunciation of *goes* /z/ – the s can be pronounced /s/, /z/ or /ɪz/.
▶ Students may forget to add -*s* for 3rd person singular (*I go, You go, She goes*).
▶ Students may incorrectly add -*s* to plural form (*They comes*).
▶ Spelling problems (*play + -s / go + -es*, etc.).
▶ Students may try to add an auxiliary (*She does go*).
▶ Some languages have one tense covering the English simple and progressive tenses.

9 This time next week I'll be lying on the beach.

▶ The form is long and difficult.
▶ The concept is a very hard one for students (action in progress at a specified future time).

- ▶ Linked to the last point, the fact that the action will have started some time before and may continue beyond the specified time, is a difficult one to understand.
- ▶ Students will confuse this with other future forms, especially present and future progressive tenses.
- ▶ As mentioned in an earlier example, some verbs cannot usually be put into the progressive form.
- ▶ The contracted *'ll* is difficult for students to hear, and the contraction is difficult to produce.
- ▶ Students may omit the contraction and say *I will* which makes the meaning more emphatic and different from the usual contracted form.
- ▶ Spelling patterns, as mentioned before, will cause problems.

10 **I used to believe in Santa Claus.**

- ▶ Students might confuse this with the past simple (*I believed in Santa Claus*).
- ▶ The concept of past habit (*I used to smoke 20 cigarettes a day*) might be confused with past state (*I used to live in San Francisco*).
- ▶ Either or both of these concepts may be difficult for students to understand.
- ▶ Students may be further confused with other forms of used (e.g. *I'm used to + -ing / I'm getting used to + -ing*).
- ▶ The pronunciation is difficult – the *d* is pronounced /t/, and the *to* is weak and linked to the /t/.
- ▶ Students may pronounce the *s* as /z/ as in the verb (*I use a computer*).
- ▶ Students might pronounce *used* with two syllables, when there is only one.
- ▶ If the negative form is being taught, students may well incorrectly add *-d*. The correct form is *I didn't use to smoke* and **not** *I didn't used to smoke*.

Summary

▶ Analyse the language point you are going to teach. Ask yourself: what the meaning is in the context of the lesson (supplied by a text, CD, or some other means).

▶ What is the **form** of the language?

▶ What is the correct and natural **pronunciation**?

▶ Anticipate the **problems** that the students might have with this language. Which problems and how many will depend on the level and nature of your class, and on whether it is a monolingual or multilingual class.

▶ If you don't analyse the language and anticipate problems, you **will** be 'caught out'! And you will deserve to be!

▶ The longer you teach, the more you will instinctively know, and the less unsure you will be. Until you reach that point, deal with each language point as it comes up (as you have to teach it) and your language awareness will steadily increase.

▶ Don't be afraid to ask more experienced colleagues for help as well as consulting reference books.

20

Lesson planning 4:
what would you do if...?

So, you know your aims; you have planned your lesson; you have analysed any language being taught and anticipated problems students might have with it. However, there is still one more aspect involved when planning – you need to anticipate what might go wrong in your lesson, or any other lesson, and be prepared so you know what you would do. It is sometimes these unexpected problems that panic new or training teachers, especially the latter because they are being observed and assessed! If, however, you can think in advance of virtually any unexpected development in your lesson then nothing can go wrong ... well, almost nothing.

Here, then, are twenty such situations to consider ... and they have all happened to me at some time!

Unexpected problems

Task

What would you do if ...

1 you planned for an activity where students would work in pairs, but one student was absent and you had an odd number of students in your class?

2   a student arrived very late as you were teaching and had
    missed an important part of the lesson?
3   you had a student who said your lesson was 'boring'?
4   you had a student who said your lesson was 'too easy'?
5   you were doing a Listening activity and the machine chewed
    up the tape at the start?
6   you had a student who dominated the class and would never
    let anyone else speak?
7   you had left your lesson plan / materials / book at home?
8   you were asked a grammar question you could not answer?
9   you were teaching a multilingual class which included two
    students of the same nationality who continually spoke to
    each other in their language?
10 your class was very big (at least twenty students)?
11 a student(s) always finished tasks well before anyone else?
12 the students found what you are doing very difficult?
13 you had a truly mixed-ability class?
14 your planned lesson finished very early and you had to
    'fill time'?
15 the lesson time was up but you still had lots of your planned
    lesson to do?
16 you had two students in the class who clearly did not like each
    other?
17 you gave out a task and a student said 'I did this with another
    teacher'?
18 a student constantly used their dictionary in class?
19 a student's mobile phone went off in class and they took the call?
20 you explained a rule but a doubting student said 'But my other
    teacher said …'?

There does come a point in your teaching life when you have
encountered just about every possible situation (I say 'just about'
because you can never be sure!), have experienced every little or
not so little problem, and feel completely confident as you walk
in to teach. It is good to experience situations like the ones above,
because only then will you learn what to do, and your confidence
will grow so that you do not fear the same things happening again.
Well, not as much!

Let's look at these twenty situations and consider some possible solutions – though the precise solutions will depend upon the context and exact circumstances.

Insight

Some unexpected problems are truly beyond your control, i.e. a student arrives very late or your CD player breaks down. But each time you encounter a problem you will be gaining valuable experience as a teacher. You will learn how to deal with these situations and your confidence will grow.

Key to task

1 Pair work with an odd number of students

I have seen this situation panic trainee teachers far more than it should, given the relative smallness of the problem. You should not become the odd student's partner because if you do, you effectively become a student in the class and your role as a teacher is lost. You need to monitor the class, help the students as required, generally keep an eye on things – and you can't do that if you are participating in the task. So, depending on the task, two students could act as one. In your instructions you might say 'okay, you're A, you're B, you're A, you're B…Javier and Ella, you're A together, and Bruno is B'.

Another approach definitely to avoid, and I have seen it happen more than once, is to say to the odd student 'Okay, you just watch'! This is leaving the student out of the task completely and is the worst thing you could do.

2 Late arrivals

You should acknowledge this student's arrival ('Hello'), and gesture for them to sit down quickly and quietly. At this stage, do not stop your teaching to tell the latecomer what they have missed – this would annoy those students who were there on time, and effectively send the message that it is okay to arrive late.

Carry on, but when the rest of the class begin a task individually or together, go to the latecomer and fill them in on what you have done so far.

If a student is persistently late, have a quiet word to find out why. It could be a case of transport problems, but make it clear that they are losing out by missing part of your lessons on a regular basis. Above all, don't let latecomers disrupt your lesson!

3 'Your lesson is boring'

It will happen! If you have been monitoring your students and 'reading their faces' then you may have detected this student's lack of interest. It is usually easy to notice when a student appears bored, then you can do something about it before the dreaded complaint. You also need to think why this student might be bored. In all likelihood, it is because they think the lesson is too easy (see 4), or maybe they have covered this material before (see 17). In each of these situations, you can deal with the problem. But maybe they really are bored – perhaps they are reluctant students, sent by their parents. Maybe they have a low interest threshold. Or maybe, just maybe, your lesson was boring! Did you establish interest? Did you adapt the material to suit the needs and interests of your class? Were you displaying some enthusiasm and energy when teaching? Or were you just following the book and not making the lesson come alive?

Whatever the reason for the student's comment, you still need to react properly to it. Don't get angry or defensive or make an issue of the comment in front of the other students! Have a word privately with the student after class and establish the reason for the comment, then try and respond so this student will not feel bored again. However, it needs to be said that sometimes you get a student who will be bored regardless of what you do because they just don't want to be there! Try to include in your lesson topics that you know this student is interested in, maybe involve them actively in some way. Keep them busy!

4 'Your lesson is too easy'

Any of the points made in 3 could apply here. But in addition, it could be that the lessons *are* too easy. This could be because you are not pitching your lessons to the general and intended level of the class, in which case other students would probably be voicing the same complaint. Or it could be that this student should be in another class. Discuss this student with your Director of Studies and maybe it will be possible to move her to a different class. If it isn't, you will need to give this student extra and more challenging tasks to do.

5 Technology problems

There are a few things that can go wrong when you are doing a Listening activity and such problems were discussed more fully in Unit 12. If the worst happens and you cannot use your recording (your CD is scratched, the CD player won't work), and you do not have the tapescript in the book for students to refer to (thus making it a Reading stage!), then you will have to lose that part of your lesson and expand on whatever else you have planned. Most potential problems in a Listening lesson can be avoided, but if technology lets you down, there is nothing you can do!

6 Dominant students

A student may dominate the class for different reasons. They might be of a good level and know a lot and be keen to show you what they know. Or they might be naturally talkative and outgoing. And it is good to have a student in the class who participates well because a class that never speaks is a nightmare! However, you should not let a student 'take over' so that even when you ask another student to speak, the dominating student answers for them! Sometimes, such students like to play the role of the teacher and start correcting other students when you don't want them to! You must, therefore, curb the enthusiasm of this student in a way which is subtle and which does not result in him or her withdrawing from that point on. Using students' names can help (ask an open question and the dominating student (d.s.) will always answer; ask another student by name to speak and the d.s. may keep quiet!). A polite gesture to the d.s., to allow someone else to speak, can work. Or, saying something like 'Okay, thank you, but someone else'. So you are not telling the d.s. to be quiet, but encouraging others to participate more.

7 Missing materials

A nightmare scenario! But you still have to go and teach the class! There is no simple solution to this, but the longer you teach, the more materials and 'standby lessons' you will build up, and you can fall back on these in an emergency. You will also become more familiar with resource books and know where you can find a lesson at short notice. Failing that, and if the context allows it, give your class a challenging Speaking lesson to keep them busy while you think of what to do later. If the class is very low level, give them a task which revises what they have done before (e.g. write the days of the week) which again will give you a bit of time to think. Ask a colleague, or your Director of Studies for help. Best of all, check before you leave home that you have what you need!

8 Difficult questions

The moment dreaded by all new or training teachers! The last unit gave the best advice – if you have analysed the language, and anticipated problems students might have with the language, then you are much less likely to be asked a question you cannot answer.

But if you still get asked a tricky question, there are various possible reactions. If you know the answer but can't think of it right then, throw the question open to the class to see if someone else can answer. Or even throw it back to the student herself – 'Well, what do you think?!' While the class/student is trying to answer, you get a valuable minute to collect your thoughts. If this is not going to be enough time, you could set it as a homework task and then make sure you go back to it the next day. If the question is about a point irrelevant to that lesson, say you'll come back to it later but you need to move on. Or, just be honest and say you're not sure but will check. However, don't do this too often or the students will lose confidence in you!

9 Students chatting

Teachers have different views on how best to deal with this situation. Some will make a point at the start of the class to make sure – if possible – that no-one is sitting next to another student who speaks the same language (e.g. place names on seats!). Others will separate students during a class (but do it sensitively – move several students so it is not obvious that you are targeting particular people). One way to do this, if the class is not too big and it is easy for people to move around, is to say to students in turn 'you're 1, you're 2, you're 3, you're 1, you're 2, you're 3...okay, all the 1's sit here, all the 2's sit here', etc.). But if students are sitting in rows behind desks, you can't do that!

Other teachers will let students sit where they want, but strongly remind and encourage them to speak only English. Don't get too strict, make a joke out of it ('That doesn't sound like English!'). Separate them as a last resort. But don't forget, as has been said elsewhere in this book, if your class is multilingual you really must try and keep it to English only or else many students will get annoyed. If it is monolingual, all you can do is to minimize the use of first language to an acceptable level.

Insight

It's natural that students will chat to each other, particularly at the beginning of class, but this can be distracting for you and others during the lesson. Don't be too strict, use humour and encourage them to always speak in English.

10 Large classes

It's all very well planning pair and group work, and wanting to monitor students' work, etc. when you have a class of ten students and plenty of space. But if you have 20, 30 or 40 students, sitting in rows behind fixed desks, then what? Clearly you will need to re-think and adjust your expectations, particularly with regards to class management. You will find it difficult to see, or be seen by, students at the back, to move students, to monitor and evaluate progress, and maybe to keep the class in order. There, are, however, some tips to follow. You can still do pair work, it's just that each student will be restricted to working with either of the students they are sitting next to. Maybe, however, they can turn around and pair up with a student in the row behind. If this is possible, then so is group work. A resulting problem is how to get the students' attention back when you want them to stop. Some teachers might clap their hands, or raise one hand, or have some other agreed signal so the students know when they should stop working.

Certain students can help you (e.g. handing out worksheets, acting as a spokesperson for a group, etc.).

You need to project your voice well, and make sure that anything you are showing to the class (including boardwork) is big enough to be seen by everyone.

Finally, give clear ground-rules about what is and is not permitted; you have to stamp your authority on big classes so that the class knows what to do, when to do it, and how to do it.

11 Quick students

When students are working individually, in pairs, or in groups, you should monitor their work. One of the things you should look out for is a student who finishes a task very quickly, too quickly for you to be prepared to stop the others. There are various options to deal with this. You could ask this student to help another.

You could extend the task ('Think of five more examples').
You could have another task ready for quick finishers. You could,
if appropriate to the task, ask the student to review what they have
done and look for mistakes. But whatever you do, don't leave this
student idle because then she will get bored and frustrated. Keep
your students busy and challenged.

12 Materials too difficult

Maybe the student is in the wrong class and they would benefit
from a lower-level class, if one is available. Talk to your Director
of Studies and see what the possibilities are. But don't rush to
quick judgements if that student has only just joined your class.
Students need time to settle into a class and find their level within it.
They often start by thinking the class is too difficult, but are happy
enough a few days later.

It could be that the class as a whole is finding the lessons too
difficult, so maybe you are pitching the lessons at the wrong level.
Sometimes teachers need to lower or raise the level of the lessons to
adjust to the students in the class. As you will see in Unit 27, terms
such as 'elementary' are very broad and some elementary classes
are stronger than others. The teacher has to respond and adapt her
teaching accordingly.

13 Mixed ability

To some extent this point is discussed elsewhere in the book. In
Unit 27, for example, I suggest that you should avoid ending up
teaching groups separately within a single class – it is difficult, and
can lead to frustration for all concerned. However, sometimes you
might feel this is the only option if you have a student of a very
different level, and there is no other class for him to go to. In this
case, prepare separate material, tasks for this student to work on,
and spend time going over the tasks with that particular student.
But I am talking about a student who is genuinely at a different level,
not just a little weaker or stronger than others in the class, because
this happens all the time.

Another alternative – again time-consuming for the teacher when planning – is to have the same material for the whole class, but different tasks. This is another last resort, in my opinion, simply because of the extra workload for the teacher. You might have the option of letting this student use the school's self-access materials, if they exist. For example, language laboratory work, or reading/ listening to graded readers (story books graded for particular levels).

Sometimes a student will gradually adjust, maybe with the help of another student who can work with them. So pairing the student off with a sensitive stronger student might help as well.

Whatever you do don't just let this student struggle alone.

14 Filling time

However well you know your class, and however well you have planned your lesson, you can never be sure that your lesson won't finish early. You will have to fill that time because you cannot just finish early – your students have paid for a certain amount of teaching time and they must get it. My own favourite experience was when, despite having had over ten years' teaching experience, I found myself in a 60-minute lesson having 30 minutes to fill, instead of the 5 or 10 minutes you might expect! I had completely misjudged my students' capabilities with the lesson I had planned, which just goes to show that however experienced you might be, you can still get it very wrong sometimes!

Ideally, you should always have something 'up your sleeve' – an extension to what you have already done, or something quite different. This could be a quick language game, a discussion topic, a review of earlier work, or maybe a quick information exchange ('Find out what everyone had for breakfast today!'). Whatever it is, it should be something that does not require any preparation time because you are unlikely to do it anyway! But always be prepared ... just in case.

15 Not enough time

This is the opposite problem, but actually not really a problem at all. For a multitude of possible reasons, there are times when your lesson time is up and you have covered barely half of what you planned to do. This may actually reflect well on your teaching, rather than badly, if you have responded to your students in the lesson and realized that they were having more difficulty than you had anticipated and 'slowed down' as a result. Much better to do that than finish what you had planned, regardless of your students' needs. Of course, it may be that you have misjudged the level, but as long as you are aware of this and compensate for it in future lessons, no harm is done. Normally, you would be teaching the class again and can continue the 'unfinished lesson' – this has the added bonus of less preparation being needed for the next lesson.

16 Student antipathy

Sometimes a teacher can remain unaware of two students not liking each other, or one not liking the other, because they remain outwardly polite and friendly, and there is no problem. But there are tell-tale signs to watch out for in case the problem is more serious. The most obvious is when particular students do not work together when in pairs, when you have seen them working happily with others in the class. Or when a student goes out of her way to avoid sitting next to a particular student. Sometimes it is more open and obvious; sometimes – as sensitive as you might be to such situations – you have no idea until it is too late. This happened to me when I was still a fairly new teacher. I taught a class for three months and remained quite unaware that two young men in the class hated each other – until, that is, they started fighting after a class one day!

All you can do is to keep your eyes and ears open – back again to 'reading faces' – and if you sense a problem, do some tactful class management to keep the pair apart. Maybe talk to them individually if you feel this might help. However, this is a rare problem.

17 'We've already done this'

I hate this! But when students are being taught by different teachers, and there are certain materials in the school, available to any teacher, it is bound to happen to you. And at times, you will be that 'other teacher'! Usually, it is impossible to change your lesson there and then – and if this only concerns one or two students, you shouldn't anyway. You could give them different tasks to do, get them to work with students who haven't done it before, or – if possible – give them something quite different to do. If, however, it's a language point ('Oh, I've done the 2nd conditional') be honest with them and tell them that they still won't remember or know everything about it, or tell them that you will be using different material from the other teacher, and that it is important for them to review what they have done before and not think that they have ever 'done' a piece of language.

A more difficult case is when you are doing a particular skills lesson and the whole class did the same text or recording with another teacher. If you can think on your feet and come up with a different lesson on the spot, great. If not, you'll just have to repeat the lesson but make it as individual in style and approach as possible. I'm afraid this will happen to you on many an occasion! Sometimes it is good to ask other teachers beforehand if they have used a particular lesson recently with that class.

Insight

When students are being taught by different teachers it's likely that at some point, the students will already have covered the material you propose to teach – possibly even using the exact same material! Try to check with the other teachers to see what they have covered or plan to cover.

18 Over-use of dictionaries

How much you allow your students to use dictionaries, and what kind of dictionaries, is ultimately your decision. My own view is that they are a valuable learning tool as long as students know how to use them properly to get the most from them. However, the dictionary should not become a substitute for the teacher. For example, you write up a new word and immediately a student goes for her dictionary rather than listening to you. You have lost the attention of that student, she is not listening to you, and the dictionary has become a crutch for the student. Or a student checks everything you say, not quite believing you until the dictionary confirms what you have said! In these situations you need to be quite firm – and even more so with noisy electronic dictionaries, especially those that have 'voices'! Tell the students when they can and cannot use their dictionaries, and teach them how to use them. Encourage the use of English/English dictionaries, especially those produced specially for language learners. But when the situation demands it, say 'No dictionaries'.

19 Mobile phones in class

This is a particular pet hate of mine! It is just polite in any public situation to turn off the phone – whether it's in a concert hall, theatre, or classroom. But when a student not only fails to turn off the machine, but actually takes the call while your class is in progress, well I am afraid this is pure rudeness! Gesture to that student to leave the classroom to continue the conversation, but also have a sign to tell the class that all mobile phones should be switched off before the start of the lesson.

20 'But my other teacher said ...'

More often than not the student has misheard or misunderstood what that teacher actually said. It happens a lot, and when you check with the teacher concerned, you nearly always find that the teacher said nothing of the sort! Students worry when teachers appear to have contradicted each other, so always check with the other teacher so you can resolve the issue with the student. Usually this just means clarifying to them what the other teacher really did say! There will be times when you will be that 'other teacher'!

Summary

In the last four units we have seen that a great deal is involved in planning a lesson. In this unit we have looked at aspects of lessons which can cause problems at any time, mostly to do with the smooth running of classes. Most, if not all, of the problems mentioned in this unit will be experienced by you at some time in your career; and as you deal with each one in the best way according to your circumstances, so you will 'grow' as a teacher. The last four units should have left you with one obvious conclusion ... a successful lesson depends on proper planning. Be prepared!

21

Using course books and other materials

When I trained to be a teacher, I remember having to 'create' all my lesson materials (admittedly for only a total of six hours' teaching in four weeks!) because we were not using a course book. But no teacher could teach on a daily basis without access to resources, either a course book or 'in-house' materials. Yet, there seems to remain some resistance to the whole idea of using a book – usually, I find, among the least expected group – training teachers. This is understandable because we probably all had some experience at school of a teacher just setting work from the book while she proceeded to mark homework, or whatever. And this is the point. Using a course book is only the right option if it is used properly. In other words, teachers need to know *how* to teach from a book – and this is not as easy as it might sound. But if it is done properly, it is an enormous time-saver for the teacher and it benefits the students in a number of ways.

Task 1

When using a course book teachers need to **Use**, **Reject**, **Adapt**, and **Supplement**. Later in this unit we will examine what is meant by this, but for now spend a few minutes trying to understand what these words mean, and consider possible examples.

Why use a course book?

As suggested above there are advantages for the teacher and the students. From the teacher's point of view the book provides material, a syllabus structure, and consequently much less time is needed to prepare lessons. Personally, I don't see how any full-time teacher can function without a book! From the student's point of view there is a visual record of progress, easier access to material, the possibility to review work at home, and a feel of greater professionalism (compare this with lots of photocopied worksheets – environmentally unfriendly as well!). In theory, then, using a course book would seem to be highly desirable. There is certainly no shortage of books on the market, but there are numerous potential problems with their use, as we shall see.

Essentials of a 'good' course book

It is very hard to find consensus on what is a 'good' book – what one teacher thinks is good, another thinks is bad. The truth is that most books are usable. How 'good' one is depends on how the teacher uses it. However, there are some basic requirements:

It should have been written by experienced teachers and be roughly appropriate for the level intended. You can assume both. In addition, though, the book should ideally be appropriate for the country you are teaching in, and this can be a problem. Unfortunately, a great many books are British in content and culture, and if not solely British then European. It's all very well reading an article about British food when you are in London, not when you are in Tokyo or Jakarta or New York. Photographs of 'famous people' are rarely recognized by students in Britain, let alone anywhere else. However, because of the increasing awareness of this problem, more and more 'non-British' books are appearing. I was reminded of this problem just a week before writing this when a fellow teacher at a school in London, an Australian, remarked 'It's so much easier using (name of book) in London than Sydney ... at least here it means something'.

Your book, too, should be appropriate not just for the level you are teaching, but for the students you are teaching. We will develop this point later, but enough now to say that just because something is in the book doesn't mean you should use it with your students.

Ideally, the book should be visually attractive and well laid out – clear, and easy to follow. Preferably, the pages won't be too cluttered. It's nice to have a clear Contents page, and the language covered should have a logical progression (starting the book at one level, but finishing it at a higher level).

As for topics, I have to say that most experienced teachers, and a fair number of students, get a bit tired of talking about 'weather', 'food', 'holidays', 'countries' and various other standard topics that appear in most books. However, in defence of these topics, I should say that for lower levels they are 'easy' and 'safe'. Higher levels can deal with more advanced topics such as 'technology' because they have more language to talk about them. What I find difficult to accept, speaking very personally, are topics which include gruesome pictures of suffering people, or contentious issues like war and religion. Teachers, too, sometimes wonder why we are teaching students the vocabulary of, say, crime. Just how useful and relevant is this? I would argue that weather, food, holidays, etc. are in fact, more useful topics, but that much higher levels can, and should, be challenged with more thought-provoking issues.

An ideal course book should have variety and balance – language work, skills work, pronunciation, review units or sections and grammar summaries. In other words, it should be a complete package for the student.

Insight

A good course book should be attractive, clear and easy to follow. It should cover interesting topics, suitable for the level, and contain a good balance of skills and activities. Some books are very British in their content, but increasingly more 'global' or 'non-British' books are available.

Using a course book

Use, reject, adapt, supplement

The teacher's dream scenario: You look at the next unit in the book. The topic is interesting, the material is good and appropriate, the 'staging' is logical, the tasks are just right – in short, it's perfect. So, **use** it as it is. This doesn't happen often, but when it does, make the most of it! There is no need to re-invent the wheel, and new teachers, especially, sometimes feel that they have to create their own materials and do lots of cutting up and pasting. If it's not necessary – don't do it.

The teacher's nightmare scenario: You look at the next unit in the book and the topic is quite inappropriate for your students. Or the material is very dry or difficult or easy or unclear. So, **reject** it. However, having said that, if you are working in a school where you have to cover everything in the book, you will not be allowed to reject material (i.e. not use it). But if you do have flexibility, don't be afraid to say 'I can't use this with my students'. This is a nightmare because you then have to find alternative material to cover the language you need to focus on, and that takes time. Some teachers are more 'sensitive' than others, for better or for worse. I tend to **reject** quite often, but some material which I have found 'untouchable' another teacher has had no problems with, so maybe I am too topic-sensitive!

To be honest, use and reject are the least common courses of action when teaching from a book. Far more likely – indeed, most of the time – you will have material which is okay to an extent, but it needs to be changed a bit. Maybe the Listening task is too simple and you want to extend it. Maybe you don't need to use one part of a page. Maybe you would prefer to use your own practice activity rather than the one in the book. In other words, **adapt** (change certain parts as necessary), and **supplement** (use other material – your own, or from other sources). So you are still using much of what is in the book, but you are not slavishly doing everything simply because it is there! If you simply go through the book from start to finish, setting work from it, you are not demonstrating any teaching skills, you are not responding to your students' individual needs and backgrounds (go back to Units 1 and 2!) and you are not doing your job properly! Even if it's a great book, it still needs exploiting. This takes us back to the comment in the introduction to this unit – teachers, especially new or training ones, sometimes feel it is 'wrong' to use a course book for the simple reason that they had the experience of a teacher at school who simply 'followed the book'. If you do 'follow the book' then your students will indeed be bored and demotivated – and so will you!

There are other considerations, too. A course book will normally come with accompanying CDs, a Teacher's Book, and maybe a Workbook with extra practice tasks. The Teacher's Book is invaluable because it provides answers, and sometimes explanations for answers. Some will also have suggested procedure. Either this book or the Student's Book will have the tapescripts. But there is a danger in relying too much on the Teacher's Book. For a start, any book is liable to have the odd misprint or two – so although a book says the answer to a question is 'A', it might be incorrect! And even if the answer is correctly printed, as it is most of the time, that doesn't mean that it's the answer you would give! So, check the answers beforehand, and make sure you agree with them and know why the answer is what it is.

Make the course book suitable

The authors of your book have written it knowing the approximate level it is intended for. But only you know your students. You have to make the book suitable for the people you are teaching.

There are many books available these days, but the chances are that you will be assigned a book to use. You may be lucky and be given some choice; you may be very unlucky and not have a book at all. But whatever book you hopefully have, be critical in a positive sense. Don't, as many new or training teachers do, have a quick look at it and say it's no good. I have heard many excellent books dismissed in this way on training courses, partly because of the feeling that 'it's not fun'. Similarly, new teachers are sometimes tempted to describe almost any practice activity as a 'game'. This should most definitely be avoided, assuming you are teaching adults. For many students 'game' = 'not learning'. But even if your students do like the occasional game, (and there's nothing wrong with games in the classroom from time to time) it doesn't mean that you have to keep using the word because you don't like what's in the book! You'll be surprised at what students like. In my experience, the so-called 'conventional grammar exercise' is actually very popular, as long as it is balanced with more communicative work. And if it is done in pairs or groups, or if students have the opportunity to discuss and compare their answers afterwards, so much the better. In other words, don't be too quick to assume that something is 'boring'. You need to set the activity up in an interesting way, prepare the students for it, etc., but do not ignore lots of good material in the book because it's not 'fun'! The important thing is for learning to be interesting and challenging.

The other general point I would make is about the level. The levels we use ('elementary', 'intermediate', etc.) are very broad and you will always have a mixed-level class to some extent. A common complaint among training teachers is 'They're not all the same level'. Well, what do you expect? How is every student in the class going to be of the same level in all aspects of the language? Of course, there are occasions when, for various reasons, you will have someone of the wrong level in the class, but that is different from having a range of intermediate students in one class. The book, therefore, is for this very general level. Consequently, you will need to adapt, supplement and reject material in order to make it right for the precise level of your class.

Insight

All students and all groups are different: their backgrounds, their interests and their level. You will **use** a lot of course book material, but you will also need to **adapt** it to make it suitable and **supplement** it with other material, your own or other resources.

Tips

1 Critically evaluate the material in the book in relation to who you are teaching.
2 Reject the unsuitable and use the ideal. Otherwise, adapt and supplement the material.
3 Use the book if there is one (you may have to anyway) – the students expect it. Besides, you'd be crazy not to!
4 Check answers to exercises, and make sure you can justify them if necessary.
5 Make real use of the material, don't just say 'Okay, do exercise 3 on page 40'. You must use your skills – establish interest, prepare them, clear instructions, etc.
6 Don't skip about in the book (Unit 3, then 6, then 14, then 2…) – the units are in an order for a reason. You can't just pick the parts you like the best!
7 Make sure that the way you use the material in the book is appropriate in every way to the students in your class.
8 Teach your students how to get the most out of the book in their free time (assuming they have their own copy). For example, books normally have separate grammar summaries, vocabulary summaries, pronunciation guides, and maybe tapescripts.
9 Make it clear to them why you are not using everything in the book (assuming you are allowed not to cover everything), and why you are using other material. They are adults and you can involve them in the teaching rationale. Work not done in class can always be done at home.
10 Make full use of the material – new teachers tend to cover in a week what an experienced teacher would cover in a month!

Using other materials

The point has already been made several times that teachers need to supplement the material in the course book with other material. Fortunately, there is a very good range and variety of resource books on the market – look at what your school has – as well as online resources. You also have the 'home-grown' material for those who are creative and have some time to do it! But it doesn't have to be anything special – maybe just some questions of your own to accompany a Listening task. Or, very commonly, an idea of your own to get the students speaking together.

Also, teachers should make good use of **authentic** material.

What is authentic material?

This is real-life material not specially published or adapted for classroom use. Examples include brochures, posters, newspapers (real or online), magazines, leaflets, signs, notices, songs, radio, TV. It is best to use something reasonably up-to-date, at least as far as reading matter is concerned (so, today's or yesterday's news, not last month's). It is good to use authentic material simply because it is *real* and something your students might be exposed to on any day. However, the value of such material may be more limited when teaching in a country where English is not the first language because the students *won't* find some of this material quite as easily in English (books, brochures, leaflets, etc.). However, online material is easily accessible for most and students can be encouraged to read online newspapers or magazines or listen to radio online. In fact, it is important in non-English-speaking countries to direct your students to material of all sorts which is available in English (magazines, books, English-speaking radio and TV).

> ### Insight
> **Authentic material** is material not specially published or adapted for classroom use. It is good to use because it is real and, often, very current and topical (i.e. newspapers). The internet means you and your students can access English-speaking material (online newspapers, radio and TV) wherever you are.

Exploiting it
Units 11–14 cover approaches to skills work so you should read those units for ways to use material for purely skills focus.

However, you may want to use the material, at least in part, to focus on language. What we covered in Unit 5 is particularly appropriate for this.

In general, having chosen appropriate material, devise tasks which are graded for the level being taught (and the students in your class), making these as practical, useful and interesting as possible. Decide, too, which aspects of the material you want to focus on. This will be partly determined by the level of the class – what you want an elementary class to do with a newspaper article will be different from what an upper-intermediate class will do with the same article. The level will dictate the nature of the tasks.

Newspaper articles are an especially good source of authentic material. Here are eight ways to use newspapers in the classroom.

1 You can focus on one article/story for Reading, Speaking or Vocabulary.
2 You can focus on one article for specific language.
3 You can compare how different papers cover the same story.
4 You can focus on the use of headlines (e.g. prediction of the story to follow).
5 You can focus on the different parts of a paper.
6 You can use the articles as a springboard for debate with higher-level classes.
7 You can give students a headline and they write an article; then they compare their article with the original.
8 If you have the facilities, you can compare the TV news report of a story with the newspaper one.

Task 2

Think of six different ways to use a holiday brochure in the classroom (say, a brochure advertising vacations in Mexico). I'll give you some suggestions below.

Key to task 2

Here are just a few possibilities.

As with the newspaper articles, you can use brochures to focus on specific language, or as a Reading comprehension. You could also focus on the specific vocabulary featured in brochures (e.g. *discount*, *package tour*, etc.), or on the style of language used – for example, what 'not far from the beach', and 'cosy room' really mean!

Speaking possibilities are many: students could choose their favourite trip from a selection of brochures and role-play a conversation asking for more information or booking the trip. You might also get the students to imagine that they *did* go on the trip and to discuss what the reality was. As a Writing activity, students could prepare a brochure advertising their home town or a place that they have visited. Maybe you could use your brochure on, for example, Mexico as an introduction to a text or recording you have on the country, or as a follow-up to the text or recording.

Summary

▶ Course books are there to be used and they should be used critically by the teacher. You should make full use of the material, and follow the guidelines of **Use, Reject, Adapt, Supplement**. You need to make the material suitable for the students in your class.

▶ But don't be too dismissive of a book or some of its contents. And don't just 'pick out' the parts you like!

▶ Books save preparation time, provide a structure, give ideas and material, language notes and guidance, a visual record, and a daily reference.

- British-based books are less appropriate in other countries, but seek out any books which might have been published in the country you are teaching in.

- Check the contents of a book, including the Teacher's Book, to make sure you know how something is supposed to work, that you agree with the answers, and can justify the answers.

- Yes, a book may be boring, especially if you just go from one page to the next. So make it interesting and stimulating.

- Authentic material provides exposure to real English and it can be used in many different ways. It also provides variety.

- There is plenty of other material, such as resource books or online material that you can use for alternative ideas. Again, by using other resources you add variety to your lessons.

22

Testing students

Your first thoughts on seeing the title of this unit will probably be 'exams', or 'tests'. These are indeed, part of what is referred to here as 'testing students', but only a part. Teachers test students all the time because testing means to find out what students know and remember. Five examples of classroom testing are:

- ▶ concept questions; test if students understand meaning
- ▶ eliciting; tests what students know and remember
- ▶ language exercises; test what students know
- ▶ comprehension tasks; test what students understand
- ▶ drilling; tests students' pronunciation

However, beyond normal classroom practice, students may take the following types of tests:

- ▶ placement
- ▶ diagnostic
- ▶ progress
- ▶ achievement

We will look at these types of testing and at the difference between subjective and objective assessment.

First, though, a test for you!

Task 1

Complete the following:

1 Tests are motivating for students.
Students _____ (rewrite first sentence)   *1 mark*

2 The Cambridge FCE, CAE and CPE exams are: (choose one)
(a) placement tests (b) diagnostic tests   *1 mark*
(c) progress tests (d) achievement tests

3 We test students informally in class all the time. True or
False?   *2 marks*

4 The marking system should be _____ (rely)   *1 mark*

5 The reliability of the marking system is affected by the
_____ given to each section.   *5 marks*

6 When I was at school I _____ tests   *1 mark*

7 be-interesting-do-to-tests-format-and-in-varied-should
(rewrite using all words)   *8 marks*

8 One of the biggest disadvantages of testing is _____ *10 marks*

9 Objective assessment is _____
Subjective assessment is _____   *1 mark*

10 Which word is spelt correctly? (no dictionaries)
accomodation – benefitted – neccesary – reciept – business
                                                          1 mark

Progress tests are what teachers will give their students from time
to time. At some schools they are a requirement; at others, they
are strongly encouraged. Typically, they take place once a week /
every two weeks and their aim is usually seen as testing what
students can remember of what they have recently learnt. This
undoubtedly is one aim of such tests, but I also like to present them
to my students as an important opportunity for them to review
what they have done in class, and to clarify what they are still
having difficulty with. Sometimes, I will even let students work
together on such tests, but with one important proviso – they
cannot refer back to notes or books. Why? Because if they can
make themselves remember without such help, they are more
likely to remember more easily in the future.

Such tests do not have to be in test format, like the above example (which we go back to shortly). They can be done as quizzes, for example, with students in teams answering questions. You could also get your students to make up the questions for a quiz, telling each team which language points they need to think of questions about. Or, students could prepare posters which display important points learnt in the recent lessons.

In other words, be *varied* in how you conduct progress tests. That said, there is nothing wrong from time to time in giving students an authentic progress test. Many students welcome it, seeing it as a 'proper' part of learning. But you need to give them notice that they are going to be tested soon (tell them when), and what they are going to be tested on. Some course books will have ready-made 'tests' after every few units, or you can prepare your own.

Let's go back to the task above to make some more points about testing.

Insight

Any kind of progress test (in test format, or as a quiz) is an opportunity for your students to review what they have done in class and to find out what they might be having difficulty with. Progress tests should never be just about seeing how much students remember.

Key to task 1

1 The correct answer is *Students are motivated by tests.*

Yes, students are usually motivated by tests, but the great danger, of course, is that they might do badly and be discouraged. This is why I personally prefer students to help each other when doing such tests, because for me the aim is for them to review what they have learnt, rather than to be examined on what they can remember.

As for this question, you were required to write a passive sentence, and using a different tense from the first. Not an easy task ... but only one mark awarded!

2 The correct answer is *achievement*.

An achievement test can take two forms. It can be an *internal* test given by you at the end of the course, usually done in exam format. And it can be an *external* exam written and marked by an outside body. The examples given in the question are all UCLES exams – First Certificate in English, Certificate of Advanced English, and Certificate of Proficiency in English. You are unlikely to be asked to teach an exam class until you have a lot of experience, so this unit will not focus on the exams themselves. However, you may need to administer an internal achievement test. If you do find yourself having to teach an exam class, without much experience (it happened to me!), you will work from an exam course book which will tell you most of what you need to know. Beyond this, seek help from your Director of Studies. There is a huge range of public (external) examinations that students can take around the world at all levels. Some are a passport to universities, jobs, promotion, etc. The TOEFL exam, now available to be done entirely on computer with an immediate result, is primarily for entry into universities in the United States. It is, as you would expect, all in American English.

Internal achievement tests, like progress tests, are generally welcomed by students because it gives them what they perceive to be a measure of their progress. If I sound less than convinced by my own words it is because I think 'exams' are limited in their ability to prove to students what they know and understand. Students have to know how to do an exam, how to prepare for it, how to tackle it. Exams have an important place in learning, but maybe not as important as some students believe. How many times have students and teachers been very surprised at someone's result?! But, of course, it is a wonderful feeling for both parties when a student does very well in an achievement test.

3 *True* – a point discussed at the start. Note that two marks were on offer here for a true/false question, compared to only one for the first question which required grammatical knowledge.

4 *Reliable* (and logical). The marking system for this test is hardly that! If you are setting a test, award marks (if you are going to award any at all – you don't have to) that reflect the difficulty of the question, and the type of answer required.

5 *Weight.* If a test is divided up into different sections (e.g. Reading, Vocabulary, Grammar), does each section carry equal weight? Should it? Do your students know how they are being marked? They should. Five marks on offer for this! (See 4.)

6 This asks for an opinion, it does not test anything and you cannot assess opinions! As far as the question itself is concerned, most students have negative memories of tests – rows and rows of desks, silence, conditions, invigilators, stress. Should it be like this? Maybe exams have to be, but not internal tests.

7 This should read *tests should be varied in format and interesting to do* (and hardly deserves eight marks!).

If you are devising a test, vary the types of question because this will make it a little more interesting. For example, you could include multiple choice, true/false, correction of mistakes, writing sentences, sentence transformation, etc. Make the test as varied and unpredictable as you can.

8 Well, there are several! The point is that you cannot mark an answer to such a question when there is no obvious answer. How will you award the ten marks? Only to students whose opinion is the same as yours? This type of question has no place in a test.

9 **Objective tests** are those which have right and wrong answers, with no ambiguity. Example: The capital city of Scotland is (a) Glasgow (b) Aberdeen (c) Edinburgh. The TOEFL test is a classic example of objectivity as it is entirely multiple choice, as above. Marking is unaffected by the marker, consistent, accuracy based, and easy to assess.

Subjective tests are those which require the marker to assign marks according to a marking scheme. Obvious examples are composition (essay) writing, and exam 'interviews' (Speaking exams). With such testing, it is imperative that students know what the marking criteria are. Marking is affected by the interpretation of the marker and is therefore less consistent and harder to assess.

Many tests are a combination of these two types, and this is probably ideal.

In terms of establishing proper and fair criteria for marking, and conditions for testing, you should consider the following points:

▶ Does it test what you want it to test?
▶ Is the test reliable/long enough to allow students to complete the test successfully?
▶ Is the marking system reliable and fair, and known to the students?
▶ Is it culturally fair?
▶ Is the format varied and interesting?
▶ Is the 'test' going to be carried out in an atmosphere which is not unnecessarily stressful?

Make sure you go over all the answers and reasons with the class.

10 The answer is that *none* of them is spelt correctly! It is a trick question – hardly fair. For the record, the correct spellings are: accommodation – benefited – necessary – receipt – business.

We have looked at progress and achievement tests so far – now for two other types.

Placement tests are carried out by a school when students first arrive. They are designed to find out the approximate level of the student in order to place her in the right class. These tests tend to involve grammar (often multiple-choice questions), and speaking (a brief chat with a teacher). Sometimes they are more involved, but when a school has thirty students to test and place in two hours, it is not possible to have a full and proper test. Sometimes, as a result, students need to be moved to a more appropriate class after a day or two. Most placement tests are standard and are used each time there are new arrivals.

Diagnostic tests include placement tests, but also include other types. Teachers give diagnostic tests or tasks on a frequent basis when teaching (as in the 'Test Teach Test' method described in Unit 6). In fact, any time the teacher gives the students something to do with the aim of finding out how much they already know, this is diagnostic testing.

Insight

Progress tests monitor what students have recently learnt and take place throughout the course. **Achievement tests** are *internal*, usually at the end of a course or *external*, written and marked by an outside body. **Placement tests** assess a new student's level. **Diagnostic tests** aim to find out how much students already know.

Task 2

Already we have looked at various types of testing that take place in the classroom when we are teaching. For each of the below, think of two examples of tasks we might give our students, and whether the 'assessment' is subjective or objective.

1 Grammar   **2** Vocabulary   **3** Reading   **4** Listening
5 Speaking   **6** Writing

Suggested answers will come later!

Every school I have ever worked at has used placement tests and progress tests. The progress tests are usually left to the teacher to administer because the teacher is in the best position to know what kind of test to give, and what needs to be included.

Some schools I have worked at have had an internal achievement test – a standard one based on the syllabus followed for that particular level. Such a test is sometimes also used to allow a student to go up to the next level. (I'm not keen on this because in my experience a student is allowed to move up regardless of their result, so what's the point?) It is also common for students to be issued with an internal certificate and teacher's report on their progress when they leave. This rounds off the course of study nicely and does give the student a sense of achievement with or without an actual test.

Continuous assessment is a type of testing not normally found in EFL/ESL except in the form described above, where teachers write a report for the student on the basis of their work and progress on the course, and also when teachers consider whether a student could move up (or down) a level based on their work in class. External assessment, however, is nearly always done on the basis of exams.

Back to the task...

Key to task 2

1 Grammar
transformation exercises (see Q1 in the 'test' at the start of this unit) – objective
open-ended sentence completion (more than one answer possible) – subjective and objective since one answer might be considered to be 'better' than another.

2 Vocabulary
matching – objective   use of vocabulary in essays – subjective

3 Reading
true/false – objective   questions requiring interpretation – subjective

4 Listening
multiple choice – objective   note taking (e.g. main points) – subjective

5 Speaking
repetition – objective   description of pictures – subjective

6 Writing
gap-filling – objective   essays (compositions) – subjective

Summary

▶ Testing is an integral part of teaching – teachers do it all the time in their lessons. Most tasks we give, most eliciting we do, most questions we ask have the aim of 'testing' our students in some way.

▶ Beyond normal classroom practice, students take placement tests and progress tests, and sometimes achievement tests (internal and/or external).

▶ Teachers most have to concern themselves with progress tests. They should know how to administer tests which are fair, varied, and interesting and which have clear testing objectives and criteria, and which are familiar to the students.

▶ Question types may require either objective or subjective assessment, or a combination of the two.

▶ Teachers should vary the types of test they give, and allow interaction between students if they feel this is appropriate.

▶ Testing should always be seen as part of the learning process and should be done in as pleasant an atmosphere as is possible in the circumstances.

23

Teaching one-to-one

This book is almost entirely a general introduction to classroom teaching. This unit, however, does look at one specific class type – teaching one-to-one. The reason for this is that I have yet to meet an experienced teacher who has not done this kind of teaching, but training courses rarely prepare teachers for it. As you might imagine, it requires a very different role for the teacher – and for the student. I have done a great deal of one-to-one teaching and I enjoy it; but I know other teachers who avoid it if at all possible. But it seems to me that more and more students want to learn this way, and more and more schools are offering specialized one-to-one courses, so it is a type of teaching that cannot be ignored here.

There are different one-to-one contexts. For most teachers, it is a way to supplement their salary; their one-to-one classes are out of school hours and privately arranged; or offered directly by the school the teacher is working at.

For others, one-to-one classes are offered by the school in normal school hours and the teacher is required to teach them.

A minority specialize in one-to-one as their main teaching income, usually supplemented by income from elsewhere. Increasingly common are 'Homestay' courses where the student lives in the teacher's home. The teacher not only gives lessons, but also goes out with the student, cooks for him, etc. It is 'total immersion' on both sides!

If you are a teacher working in a country which is not your own, it is essential that you find out first if you are permitted to teach one-to-one classes. You should check your contract and, if in doubt, ask your employer, because if you are not supposed to teach one-to-one classes, and you do, you may find yourself on a plane home. Even in your own country, there may be something in your contract to this effect, the reason being that you may take potential business away from the school. Schools sometimes prefer to arrange private classes themselves on behalf of teachers, but the problem with this arrangement is that a substantial part of the student's fees goes to the school and not to the teacher.

For my own part, I have taught one-to-one classes arranged by my school, arranged privately, and for a company which sent teachers out to companies to teach members of its staff. From a financially selfish point of view, I prefer privately-arranged classes because then the whole fee goes to me. It is very frustrating to learn how much schools often charge for this arrangement, and how little of it goes to the teacher.

Insight

Most teachers teach one-to-one lessons, though training courses won't prepare you specifically for this. These lessons are often privately arranged and can also be part of your contract hours at a language school.

Task

There are many issues to consider, especially with privately-arranged one-to-one lessons, and not only regarding the actual teaching. But let's begin with the teaching and learning considerations. Consider the following questions.

1 Why do some students choose to learn this way rather than going into a regular class?
2 What are the learning advantages and disadvantages for the student?

3 How can a teacher prepare for a one-to-one course with a student when that student has approached that teacher and asked for, say, a month's worth of lessons, four hours a week?

4 What are the main differences involved for the teacher when teaching one-to-one rather than a regular class?

5 What do you think are the rewards and headaches of this kind of teaching?

Before looking at these points, it is important to approach a series of one-to-one lessons in a way which is both professional, and which protects your and your student's rights. If you are making a purely private arrangement with a student, follow these points:

Tips

1 Agree on a price either for each lesson, or for the series of lessons. Make sure the price is neither significantly higher nor significantly lower than the 'going rate'.

2 If you have to travel, travel costs should be included.

3 Agree on procedure if lessons are cancelled by either side. This might mean that if the student cancels less than 24 hours before the lesson, they still pay you all or most of the fees. Or if you cancel, the lesson is offered at a later date. Whatever is decided, make sure both sides discuss and agree the terms.

4 Agree, also, on when and how you will be paid.

5 If the student later asks if a friend can also participate, it is no longer private tuition, so you cannot charge double the price!

6 Make sure that the lessons will take place in an appropriate setting.

7 If you are being paid for, say, 60 minutes' tuition, that means 60 minutes, not 55. Lessons should be uninterrupted (e.g. don't stop to take a phone call).

8 If you are teaching a student who is also a friend, make it clear when the lesson itself begins and when it ends.

9 Do not arrange very long lessons because one-to-one is tiring for both parties. For most teachers and students, one hour is long enough.

10 Plan as thoroughly as you would for any other class; do not treat one-to-one classes casually.

Back to the task ...

1 Reasons for students wanting one-to-one

From my own experience, I would say that there are many reasons for students doing one-to-one classes.

▶ Schools usually give total beginners one-to-one teaching when they first arrive until their English is good enough to go into a class.
▶ Students preparing for an exam sometimes feel they need more intensive practice.
▶ Students sometimes feel that they want to have as much tuition as possible to improve their English quickly.
▶ Students often need to improve their English for their jobs.
▶ Students wanting to work in an English-speaking environment will need to bring their level of English up before applying.
▶ Some students just prefer one-to-one tuition over classes.

Whatever the student's reason for wanting one-to-one, you need to know what it is if you are to provide for that student's needs.

2 Advantages and disadvantages

The advantages are obvious enough – the student does not have to 'share' you with other students. Their learning is more intensive and more geared to their own needs, they can ask as many questions as they want, ask you to teach them skills that they need or want, and have lessons pitched at their precise level and desired pace. They will normally cover much more material and language than they would in a regular class. As such, progress is normally faster, and more visible to both parties.

But the disadvantages are equally obvious. Of course, the student cannot work with other students in the class; so there is no pair or group work, or even just someone to talk to. This restricts teacher/students interaction which makes learning hard work for the student, with considerable concentration and attention required at all times. Some students feel the need for interaction and company, while others much prefer the intensive nature of one-to-one learning. For those students with limited time available, and a definite goal, one-to-one can be advantageous. But for students on holiday, only wanting to improve their skills, one-to-one makes little sense.

Insight

The advantage of one-to-one teaching is that it can be tailored to suit the individual student and progress is usually faster. However, the dynamic is different: the focus is on teacher / pupil and requires considerable concentration and attention on both sides.

3 How can a teacher prepare?

If a student approaches you and asks you to give them private tuition, the temptation can be to think it is a soft option which will bring in more money. But the correct way to react to such a request, if interested, is to discuss with the student exactly why they want one-to-one and what their needs are. If it is a student you already know, it is easier. But if it is not, then there is much you need to find out before commencing. The best way to approach this is via a *needs analysis*. Students pay for one-to-one lessons because they want a teacher who will meet their needs and accommodate their learning style – and they usually want some control over what goes on in the lessons. Consequently, it is crucial to evaluate the needs, level and expectations of that student.

You need to find out three things:

▶ The student's current *level*. You could use a grammar review test from a course book of the approximate level you think your student is. But you need to supplement this with an informal 'interview' to gauge the spoken ability of that student in terms of both accuracy and fluency. If possible, give them some reading, listening and writing, too.

▶ The student's *needs*. How much input does she want? Does she want to follow a set syllabus? Which skills are important for her to study? In what context(s) will she be needing to use her English? Is she preparing for an exam? Does she require English for her job? Find out as much as you can about what your student wants from you (this could be done in discussion and the 'interview' could form part of your level analysis). You must also be fair to yourself and the student if they ask you for a specialized course which you are not equipped to teach. For example, if you are asked to teach medical English and you have no knowledge of this, nor access to relevant materials, tell the student that you cannot teach him/her.

▶ The student's *previous language learning experience*. This will help you teach the student in the way which is best for him/her.

Having done the above, together you can agree on a specific study course with clear aims. Once the course is under way, be very flexible and adjust the content and approach of lessons as you see fit, or as the student requires.

Beware of students who only want 'speaking'. It sounds an easy option, but it is a vague request and it is hard work for the teacher to maintain nothing but conversation for a whole hour, maybe several times a week!

There is one other aspect which you need to think about before agreeing to teach the student. Do you think the two of you will 'get on'? It is important to have a good rapport with the student you are teaching, and this is another reason for meeting them beforehand.

4 Differences between one-to-one and regular classes

You obviously can't do pair or group work, and doing Reading lessons seems inappropriate because they can do reading at home.

The student is paying for tuition, not to be given work to do individually which they could do outside the lesson.

But virtually everything else mentioned in this book applies equally to one-to-one teaching; it's just that it will be very teacher-centred.

▸ You will need to prepare more because material is covered quicker. The material itself can be selected, at least in part, by the student. Have at least 50% more material than you think you need because it is much harder to 'fill time' with one-to-one. Any unused material can be used next time.
▸ You will need to be very flexible.
▸ You will have to concentrate hard throughout.
▸ You should fit in with the student's needs and go at their desired pace.
▸ You can be less concerned with time because there are no other students to teach.
▸ It might be appropriate to use more of the student's own language if you know it.
▸ It is easy to monitor progress.
▸ It is potentially more rewarding because of the last point.

Insight

You'll cover material much more quickly in one-to-one lessons and therefore you'll need to prepare much more material, probably at least 50% more.

5 Rewards and headaches

Most of the rewards and headaches have been mentioned. For me, the toughest aspect of this kind of teaching is the demanding nature of it; you get no opportunity to 'relax' (e.g. when you ask students to work in groups in a regular class). The most rewarding aspect for me is building a unique relationship with the student and giving them what they need, and then seeing their progress if all goes well.

I have had many rewarding one-to-one classes, but let me describe one such class. I was teaching in a school where one of my new students was a near beginner called Zsigmond Sipos, from Hungary. Zsigmond could only come to classes twice a week for three hours a time but he wanted to improve his English quickly in order to take the Cambridge First Certificate exam ten months later. He asked me if I would teach him privately for the remainder of the year and prepare him for the exam. To have gone from his then level to the level required to pass the exam in such a short space of time would have been beyond most students. But Zsigmond knew exactly what he wanted and needed, and he played his part fully in influencing the direction and nature of the lessons. He was the ideal one-to-one student because he had very clear goals and a determination to succeed which was admirable. He worked incredibly hard, asked many questions, did lots of homework, and used English outside our lessons whenever possible. The lessons were intense, but at the same time they were very easy for me because the requirements were so clear, and the student so motivated. By December he was ready to take the exam, and he passed it with an 'A' grade. The credit for this lay almost entirely with Zsigmond, not with me, because he approached one-to-one learning in exactly the right way. But when he called me to tell me of his result, I was very pleased and proud. And that is the principal reward of one-to-one teaching!

However, as I mentioned before, some teachers do not like the intensity of this type of teaching, preferring the interaction of a regular class. But sometimes you will have to do one-to-one teaching even if you would prefer not to, if only to get some extra money!

Tips

1 Keep a record of all work done; particularly important given the flexible nature of the lessons.
2 Maybe provide the student with the record, or encourage her to keep her own, to make review of work done easier.
3 Keep notes on points that come up as you teach to come back to later. It is too easy to forget otherwise.

4 When doing speaking practice, you could record the conversation and then replay the tape for correction work.

5 Focus more on pronunciation as it is easier to do so one-to-one.

6 Still elicit and encourage learner independence. If you don't, it will be too easy for the student to rely on you entirely and take no responsibility for her own learning.

7 Spend time training the student how best to use reference books, such as dictionaries and grammar books.

8 Review work previously covered. This is always important, but with one-to-one you cover so much more that it is especially important to review progress.

9 If you are using a course book, you will need to adapt a lot of the tasks as they are mostly designed for pair and group work.

10 The student won't mind you finishing late, but you should never finish early.

Summary

The most important points to take from this unit refer to 'being professional'.

▶ The demand for one-to-one learning is growing, but for the student it is expensive. In return for paying high hourly fees, students rightly expect value for money.

▶ Students usually have clear and specific requirements, for which the teacher needs to prepare by doing a needs analysis.

▶ The teacher should not commit herself to a course she is not equipped to teach.

▶ The teacher must also plan thoroughly for each lesson, and be extra flexible in her teaching.

▶ There should be an agreement between parties regarding time, location and fees for lessons as well as travel and photocopying costs, and arrangements if lessons have to be cancelled by either side.

▶ Lessons should begin punctually and not finish early. Nor should they be interrupted by the teacher because of phone calls, etc.

24

DVDs and other resources

When the possibility exists to move your lesson away from the traditional classroom format, you have the chance to add variety to your course; to do something different. Such possibilities might include:

▶ **Computers**

'C.A.L.L.' is 'Computer Assisted Language Learning and is obviously a hugely popular option in these times. Students have many options for both independent and guided learning and practice, and schools realize the importance of C.A.L.L. Complete learning courses on the internet with no face-to-face teacher access will surely become popular with students who are unable for any reason to attend a school. The TOEFL examination can now be done exclusively on computer, and as this is probably the most-taken EFL exam in the world, the need for computer access in schools becomes even more necessary.

▶ **Language laboratory**

Perhaps considered old-fashioned by some, the language lab. remains popular with many students. Many types of activity are possible, ranging from 'Readers' (graded stories in print and on CD), to exam practice. Students can work at their own pace, and choose the type of task they wish to do. It is a good way to improve listening skills.

▶ **Excursions**

Going out with your class to places of interest, and linking the trip to set tasks (before, during or after) is an excellent way to make learning authentic and interesting. You need to ensure that you are allowed to make such trips if they are to be in normal lesson hours.

▶ **Self-access**

Schools often have some kind of self-access centre where students can work independently outside lesson times. Typically, self-access material includes reading and listening materials at different levels. Computer facilities may be part of the self-access centre or may be housed separately. Teachers should not only encourage students to use the self-access centre, but also make sure that the students know how best to use it effectively.

Access to DVDs

Access to DVDs brings with it many advantages and potential problems for the teacher, but the range of activities you can do is considerable. There are many specialized DVD courses available, some linked to a course book. These courses cover all levels from beginner to advanced and give the possibility of regular DVD use featuring the same characters. Ready-made material comes as part of the package (which, as with a course book, you will need to adapt and supplement for your particular students). The tasks may focus on skills work, grammar, functional language, or a combination.

You can also do 'one-off' DVD lessons with recorded broadcasts (but you must check copyright requirements ... all suggestions made here assume that this has been done). TV news or other programmes can be an excellent source of material for lessons which may be independent of others you have taught on the course, or linked in some way. For example, if you have been doing a lesson(s) on newspapers and news coverage, it is logical to focus on TV presentation of news. If you have been doing 'humour' as a topic, then extracts from comedy shows (with tasks) would tie in well.

The third way of using DVDs is the one that students would probably prefer, but which is usually the least appropriate, and that is 'just watching' something, with no tasks. It is a pleasantly easy option for the teacher (and I, in common with most teachers I'm sure, have chosen this easy option from time to time!) but one which has no aims. It is an option which is probably best suited for an end-of-course 'reward', but otherwise some students may wonder what the point is.

As with any lesson, the teacher must plan and stage what she is to do. The lesson should have clear aims, whether language or skills-based. And the students need to be prepared for the lesson (necessary vocabulary, interest established). For students who question the validity of watching a DVD, you will need to stress what the point of the lesson is.

Insight
A DVD lesson should not be an 'easy' option. You need to plan your lesson, with clear aims and stages, just as with any other lesson.

Ways to use DVDs

You can do all of the activities below with DVDs, but they will not all be appropriate. Your choice of activity will depend on the usual factors – level of class, composition of class, nature of class, aims of lesson, age group, and time available.

1 Silent viewing
The students watch the picture with the sound turned down and predict what they think is being said. They then re-view with sound to check. The extract may be just half a minute or so, perhaps, longer. This can be done at any level – with beginners, for example, it can be as simple as 'Good morning, how are you?'

2 Sound only

The reverse of 1, the students turn away from the screen and only listen. They can predict the context ('where are they?' 'who are they?', etc.).

3 What happens next?

This prediction exercise is perfect for story-DVDs. One way of doing this, given the right DVD, is to have students predict how they think the story will end. It is also good when something unusual or unexpected is about to happen. It doesn't have to be restricted to action – students can also predict what someone is going to say. I remember using one DVD where two people met, one wearing a hat. As they greeted each other one person raised his hat and the students had to predict what the other person was saying. They all came up with variations of 'Pleased to see you' only to discover the actual words 'You've lost all your hair!'

4 Description

Students work in pairs – one watching the next part of the DVD with sound off, and describing the action to their partner, who is looking away. This gives practice of descriptive language, interpretation of action, gestures and context, and – for the 'listener' – listening for detail. Only for higher levels!

5 Picture freeze

Students see a still from the DVD which is 'paused'. They can do any kind of prediction task described above. A variation would be to use adjectives to describe how the person might be feeling, what they might be thinking, and what they look like. Beyond this, students could also predict the context, maybe even the time of year, etc.

6 Comprehension

Students view the DVD or part of it and complete a comprehension task. This is a 'visual listening' comprehension lesson following all the guidelines given in Unit 12.

7 Making a review

As a follow-up, students can be critics and write a review of what they have seen. Alternatively, this can be done as a speaking activity.

When watching the DVD, therefore, students make notes which will be used for the review. You would need to elicit possible 'headings' for this review before viewing.

8 Quiz questions

Students watch an extract from the DVD and, working in teams, they have to write, say, two questions to ask the other teams about the extract. They could both be comprehension, or one might be an observation question (e.g. 'how many chairs were there in the room?'). At the end, each team asks their questions to the others. Finally, you replay the extract to confirm all the answers.

9 Observation task

Play part of the DVD and ask your question(s) **after** viewing. This could be an observation question (as in 8). Make sure your students know what type of question they are going to be asked, to make sure they concentrate hard on the action.

10 What happened before?

You show a later part of a DVD (maybe the ending) and students have to predict what happened before to lead to this.

Whatever 'follow up' you might do after the DVD itself (and a couple of suggestions were given above) might take place in the next lesson, or the next day, since DVD lessons tend to be quite long and demanding for all concerned!

Task 1

What are the advantages and disadvantages of DVD use for both students and teacher?

Think about this before reading on.

Tips for using the equipment

Let's deal straight away with the disadvantage of using DVDS, which can be the machine itself. If you are very lucky, there will be a DVD player and monitor in your classroom. Otherwise, there may be a DVD 'room' which you have to reserve in advance, or a DVD player /monitor which you will have to book and transport to your classroom. If reserving is required, make sure you double-check your time and day so that you don't find at the appointed time that you have made a mistake and cannot use the equipment.

Having made sure of this, check beforehand that you definitely know how to operate the machine – how to fast forward and rewind, the volume and pause buttons, etc. If there is a remote control, all the better, but again, you must be familiar with its controls. You may also need to 'install' the machine and know which cables plug in where. This is my personal nightmare!

Finally, you have to 'know your DVD'. Watch it beforehand and become familiar with it. Know where you need to pause and where answers are to tasks featured. And know how long the recording lasts! This last point is important because you could get a 60-minute lesson out of a 5-minute recording. So if the recording lasts 30 minutes and your lesson lasts 40, considerable adapting will be needed; or you could continue on another day if this is possible.

In short, know your equipment. Don't avoid using the DVD because of fears of what might go wrong. That said, be prepared just in case there is a catastrophe and you cannot use the DVD!

Insight

Not all DVD players are the same, so make sure you know how to use the one that is available to you, the controls, how to plug it in, etc. Always watch the material beforehand and check how to find particular scenes or episodes.

Key to Task 1

Advantages

1 Using a DVD gives your lessons *variety*. This is very important for maintaining interest and motivation, especially when you are teaching a group for a long period. Do not, therefore,

overuse this type of lesson. Once every few weeks is probably sufficient.

2 Partly because of the above, students' *interest* is usually high. But this is also because of the fact that 'television' is worldwide, and something students want to understand and enjoy outside class.

3 The visuals and sound make the language more *memorable*; context is clear.

4 DVDs can increase awareness of *culture*; especially useful if the students are not studying in their own country.

5 DVDs can be used in a number of ways. They can be used to focus on specific language and skills, as well as providing a link with earlier or later lessons.

Disadvantages

1 The concerns about using the equipment, as discussed earlier.

2 Students may not see it as 'real learning' – so tell them what the purpose is.

3 You may have to prepare your own material and tasks.

4 Students sometimes get frustrated by the 'stop start' nature of the lesson.

5 With very big classes not everyone may be able to see the screen properly, and some of the techniques described above become very difficult.

Insight

Using DVDs adds variety, creates interest, is usually memorable and has a useful cultural element. Be aware, however, that you will usually have to prepare your own material and tasks and that DVD lessons are not often workable with large classes.

Task 2

Imagine you are going to use a 5-minute TV news broadcast with a group of upper intermediate students in a 50-minute lesson. What might you do, and with what aims? And what might you have done/might do after this lesson?

Using a video camera

Before we look at a possible response to this task, there is one other option available to the teacher. If your school has one, you can use a video camera to make your own 'film'. This adds another list of technical concerns because you have to know how to operate the camera properly, as well as how to replay the recording afterwards! (Unless of course you have one yourself, and you are willing to use it for this purpose!) But if you have this facility, and are not discouraged by the things that could go wrong, it adds another dimension to your teaching – with the right class.

There are a number of ways to use this piece of equipment. Here are five possibilities:

▶ role play (e.g. in a shop)
▶ debates
▶ mini talks (a student prepares and gives a talk on a subject of interest)
▶ surveys (e.g. interviewing staff, students, or outsiders on a given topic)
▶ plays (with each student taking on a role)

When viewing what you have recorded, supply a task for students to do while they watch. You can note down significant mistakes for later correction. Be aware, though, that some students do not like being filmed. My view is, even if only one student is uncomfortable, don't do it.

Key to task 2

An earlier lesson could have featured:

▶ style of language featured in news broadcasts
▶ a discussion about news coverage in students' country/ countries
▶ vocabulary for news topics

- ▶ a look at how newspapers cover news, and contrast this with TV
- ▶ a discussion of recent news items

For the lesson itself, interest could be consolidated by getting students to predict from headlines what news stories might be about. They could also predict which would be the main item. This could also be done from the attached pictures shown to accompany the headlines.

When watching the broadcast, gist listening could be focused on ('What are the stories about?'); and more detailed listening ('Make a note of the most important points of each story'). Alternatively, comprehension questions could be provided.

You might focus on all the stories, a selection, or only one. You could also extract specific language to focus on. Maybe, for example, students have to listen out for selected words and deduce the meaning from context.

As a follow-up, any of the speaking topics mentioned in the pre-viewing stage could be used. Or, students could write a newspaper report of a story in the typical style of a newspaper.

Summary

Using DVDs is one of a number of ways in which the teacher can do a lesson away from the normal classroom setting. Using DVDs brings special challenges for the teacher in terms of using equipment, but this concern should not stop the teacher from making use of this resource.

- ▶ You can use DVDs for any level, and use a whole range of techniques to make the most of it. But you should not over-use the DVD.

▶ DVD lessons, like any other, must be carefully planned with clear aims and stages.

▶ If the facility exists, you can also record your students doing work and view later with tasks and correction.

▶ Teachers should also encourage students to use other out-of-class resources such as self-access, computers, and language laboratories.

25

Professional awareness and development

There are a great many people who 'train' to be teachers on short
courses, often of about four weeks full time. Some, of course,
undertake much longer training courses; others have no training – they
learn 'on the job' (not recommended!). When I trained to be a teacher,
back in 1984, I enrolled on a recognized four-week training course.
This involved a combination of teaching practice (a total of six hours,
teaching two different levels), written work, input from trainers, and
observations of classes given by experienced and qualified teachers.
I have worked on such courses as a trainer for many years, and many
thousands of prospective teachers enrol on such courses each year.
Often, trainees on such courses think, hope, even expect, that at the
end of the four weeks they will be 'teachers'. Employers sometimes
wonder how someone can become a teacher in such a short space of
time. The answer is, you can't. There is sometimes a misunderstanding
about what such courses set out to do, and what can realistically be
achieved in such a time. Professional development continues, and has
to continue, throughout a teacher's career.

Sometimes, too, it can be forgotten that a good teacher doesn't
necessarily make a good employee, and vice versa. The expectations
placed on a teacher are more than only knowing how to teach.
Professional awareness in any workplace is an essential expectation
that any employer will have of an employee.

This unit looks at these two key areas of a teacher's profession.

Professional awareness

Task

Consider what expectations different groups have of a teacher. Think about **students, staff, employers**. It might help to think about your own experiences of 'good' teachers (not just the ability to teach well); and of your experiences in the workplace, either as a fellow employee or as an employer.

Stop reading now and make a list of points.

Expectations of students

Students are fee-paying clients of a school or other educational establishment. Yes, they want a good teacher, but they want much more besides from the school, and also from the teacher.

1 **They expect a teacher to know the subject she is teaching and how to teach it.**
   This was covered in the first two units and is an obvious expectation.

2 **They expect a teacher to be reliable and punctual.**
   If a lesson is scheduled to begin at 9 a.m. then the teacher should be in the classroom at that time – ideally, a few minutes earlier to prepare the classroom and welcome the arriving students. The teacher shouldn't wait for everyone to arrive before starting the lesson; then late-comers know that they can continue to arrive late without missing out on anything, and the punctual arrivers become understandably upset at the 'dead time'. There is no excuse for teachers sitting in the staffroom chatting when they should be in the classroom.

3 **They expect the teacher to be more than a teacher to them.**
   A teacher should not see her relationship with the students as only going in, teaching, and leaving again. The teacher should

show an interest in the students, chat to them outside class, be available – all points made in the first units.

4 They expect the teacher to be understanding of their particular set of circumstances.
So, find out something about the students you are teaching.

5 They expect the teacher to be professional, fair and polite – and consistent in their behaviour both to the group and to the individuals within it.

6 In some circumstances, they expect the teacher to be dressed in a way which is appropriate to the culture of the country they are in.

Insight

As a teacher you will be expected to be professional: to be punctual, reliable, polite and fair. How you teach is important, but how you behave outside the lessons is important too. Friendly and approachable teachers are highly valued.

I have witnessed situations where a good teacher was unpopular with the students and commanded little respect simply because they were not friendly or approachable outside lesson time, or even during lesson time. I have heard students describe someone as an 'average' teacher, but as well-liked because of the way they acted towards students. It is professional to give more than your teaching skills to those that you teach; it is the same that you would expect of someone teaching you.

Expectations of staff

Teaching is a stressful occupation and one which involves far more than 'just' teaching 25 hours a week, or whatever. It involves planning, marking, attending staff meetings, going to workshops or conferences, maybe participating in social activities, definitely being available to students outside class time. It requires you to have a lesson to teach at the appointed time – knowing what you are going to do and what you need for the lesson, as well as always having following lessons at the back of your mind. To the students you need to be unfailingly polite and friendly, whatever you may think of them personally.

All of this can result, at times, in high degrees of stress and frustration, and sometimes the staff-room is the place where this frustration is expressed. What you shouldn't do is add to this stress level.

1 **Respect other people's space.**
   For example, if you and a colleague share a desk, don't put your books, etc. in the space of your colleague!

2 **Offer support and encouragement.**
   The staff-room tends to be the place where teachers express frustrations, so offer a sympathetic ear.

3 **Choose the right moment to seek help and encouragement, or to ask questions.**
   If a colleague is hurrying to a lesson, or appears stressed themselves for some reason, don't pester them with something that can wait until later. You have to respect their mood!

4 **Put things back in the right place!**
   Few things irritate teachers more than being unable to find a DVD or book, etc. because it has not been returned to the right place, or has simply not been returned.

5 **Don't hog the photocopier or other resources.**
   If you have access to a photocopier, don't spend too long using it if someone else wants to copy. So, don't start looking for the right page while you're at the machine; do it before. If you're not in a hurry and there are others waiting behind you, give way. If the paper runs out while you are using the photocopier, or if the machine jams, don't just leave it for the next person to deal with.

6 **Share ideas and experiences.**
   It is good on both a personal and a professional level to share your successes and 'failures' in the classroom. If a teacher, for

example, is searching for a practice activity for the present perfect, and you know where there is a good one, tell them.

7 Maintain the records required.
If a teacher has to take your class at short notice but you haven't filled in your record of work done, you won't be very popular! (See the next unit for more on this.)

8 Clean your board before leaving the classroom.
You should leave the room how you would hope to find it if you were about to teach there. So, a clean board and a reasonably neat and organized room. And if another class is coming into your room, vacate the room on time – don't over-run.

9 Don't take something out of another teacher's room without asking.
What has happened to me many times is a teacher 'borrowing' my room's CD player without asking me first, because they don't have one! If you have asked first and borrowed something, return it – don't expect the other teacher to have to come and collect it.

10 Don't complain too much.
Don't continually moan and complain as if you are the only person working there with niggles. Don't bring such levels of stress into work that it rubs off on everybody else.

I have experienced many types of staff-room – most, very friendly and mutually supportive, and 'student-friendly'. I have been in others, where staff barely spoke to each other and students knocking on the door were sent away because the teachers were on a break. Fortunately, the majority of experiences have been excellent and teachers are a very mutually supportive group. But I do remember certain individuals – one who hogged the photocopier all the time, another who was a full-time complainer, another who just wouldn't cooperate with anyone. As in any workplace, you meet a variety of different characters. But the overall point is that teaching is a stressful (but very enjoyable) job, and you need to respect the people you work with – their characters, backgrounds, interests, etc. – just as you need to respect the students. If you do not, your employment is unlikely to be long term!

Insight

Teaching is a stressful job, so good working relations and a good staffroom atmosphere is important. You are sharing equipment and materials with other teachers, so be careful how you do this: it can be a cause of real irritation.

Expectations of employers

Some time ago, I gave a questionnaire to three employers of teachers about teacher behaviour, and their answers are included here.

1 Punctuality and reliability.
Teaching is not one of those jobs where you can arrive ten minutes late and just catch up on the work. The students will be there expecting to be taught. Of course, sometimes it can't be helped, but if you make a habit of it then you will earn yourself a reputation for being unreliable and this may reduce your chances of further work at that school.

2 Record keeping.
As already mentioned.

3 Neat dress.
Some schools will have a dress code; others may be relaxed. In any case, find out what is appropriate and acceptable to wear, especially with regard to the local culture.

4 Professional behaviour.
This is an overall heading for everything mentioned in this unit, but in particular your behaviour towards students and fellow staff.

5 Don't criticize the school or staff when talking to students.
Whatever your feelings, it is not professional to express them to the students.

6 Read your contract.
Find out what you are and are not permitted to do, and what you are obliged to do.

7 Attend staff meetings and in-service training sessions.
This may be compulsory, anyway!

8 Be willing to be observed and to observe others.
See the section on **Professional development** (below).

The directors I spoke to mentioned their common complaints about teachers:

'teachers losing registers (rolls)'
'teachers not returning materials'
'teachers being constantly late'
'teachers who don't have a positive attitude towards students'

....
Insight
Employers expect many similar things of you as your students, plus a positive and professional attitude towards the students and the school itself.
....

Professional development

At the beginning of this unit, the point was made that some trainee teachers, and some employers, may expect too much from a short training course. Also, some employers can be very doubtful about the value of such courses, wondering how anyone can 'become' a teacher so quickly. Well, you can't. Four-week training courses, validated by different bodies, are popular worldwide – and there are courses which last longer but involve the same amount of work. But participants and employers need to be clear about the typical content of such courses (mentioned at the beginning of this unit), and the aims.

These courses typically involve participants teaching for a total of about six hours at two different levels. That's it. Six hours. Many teachers do that in a single day. Participants, then, should be realistic. Don't get upset or disappointed if your observing tutor still gives you 'points to work on' in your final lesson! Don't imagine or expect that after six hours of carefully controlled teaching that you are ready to deal with all types of class and student. What such courses do is to provide you with essential teaching skills – the methodology – as well as some theory behind it. But even the methodology is limited in its scope, as it is in this book, because you can only 'learn' so much in the time available. What you have to do to pass the teaching component of these courses is show convincingly and consistently that you can do what is asked of you (the assessment criteria for teaching practice). If you pass, then you are equipped to begin teaching, with support and supervision – you have shown that you can teach reasonably successfully and have demonstrated an appropriate degree of self-awareness which will allow you to continue to develop your skills. In a sense, the real training starts once you begin your first teaching assignment. It is then that you have to begin teaching different levels, age groups, types of student, types of class; and then that you have the sole responsibility for your own teaching. It is at this point that your **development** begins.

Insight

Your real training and development as a teacher begins once you begin your first teaching job. From this moment onwards you need to think about how to expand your knowledge and experience, and keep up-to-date with the EFL / ESL world.

Most experienced teachers, myself included, would say that it took them a good two years of teaching before they felt reasonably confident and able in most teaching contexts. Also, it takes this long to gain full confidence about the language itself that you are teaching. If new teachers accept these facts, and do not expect the impossible from the short training courses, then they will have more realistic expectations of themselves. The short training courses described are excellent and invaluable, but only as a starting point.

Employers need to recognize the limits of these courses, too. They need to offer support and guidance to new teachers, whilst at the same time recognizing that no training course providers are suggesting that they are providing you with the 'finished article'. As we all know, you can be teaching for many many years but still learning and developing – or you should be!

If we can accept these points, then we can think about how this 'post-training' development can happen; or, in the case of teachers teaching with no prior training, how 'on-the-spot' training and development might occur.

Tips

1 Seek the opportunity from time to time to observe other teachers' lessons.
2 Ask your Director of Studies or an experienced teacher to observe you teaching at regular intervals and to give you feedback.
3 Continue to self-assess your own teaching (as you would have done on any training course you did/are doing) and to develop your strengths and work on your weaknesses.
4 If available, watch DVDs your school might have of lessons.
5 Attend in-service sessions at your school or nearby (staff development).
6 Attend workshops and conferences if you get the chance. In particular, the annual conferences held by IATEFL and TESOL (see below).
7 Read new publications and periodicals about the profession, usually available at your place of work.
8 Talk to more experienced teachers and learn from them.
9 Try out new ideas you have read or heard about – don't just continue churning out the same old lessons in the same old way!
10 When you're ready, do further teaching qualifications (e.g. an MA related to the profession, such as Applied Linguistics; or a Diploma course). Normally this would require an absolute minimum two years' experience first. Your place of work can advise you of the options available.

11 Show an interest and desire to be involved in other aspects of school life, perhaps helping with administration, or social activities, or materials design.

12 Join professional organizations such as TESOL or IATEFL if you are working freelance. If you are not, your school is likely to have institutional membership.

13 With more experience, write articles for ESL publications and give talks or run sessions at workshops.

14 Eventually move into other areas as well as teaching; such as writing, training, examining.

15 Recognize that the profession itself develops and moves in new directions. Keep in touch and move with it, maybe even influence its direction in some small way!

16 Keep in touch on the web! There are many useful sites – just do an ESL or EFL search and you'll be given many addresses to explore.

TESOL – Teachers of English to Speakers of Other Languages. Has over 20,000 members worldwide. Website: http://www.tesol.org

> TESOL Central Office
> 700 South Washington Street
> Suite 200
> Alexandria
> Virginia 22314
> USA

IATEFL – International Association of Teachers of English as a Foreign Language. Has over thirty branches worldwide and over 1,000 delegates attend its annual conference. Website: http//www.iatefl.org

> IATEFL
> Darwin College
> University of Kent
> Canterbury
> Kent
> CT2 7NY
> England

Summary

▶ Teachers and employers need to be realistic about what can be achieved on a short training course.

▶ These courses provide the essential basics of teaching and theory.

▶ New teachers need to always maintain their development beyond any training. This development can take place in a variety of ways, as described.

▶ Teachers with no training need to find ways to learn the basics on the job.

▶ Teachers, like all employees anywhere, need to have professional awareness.

▶ Students, colleagues and employers all have expectations of how you should 'behave'.

▶ In short, good teachers need to be more than good teachers; they need to be good colleagues and employees, and they need to remember that they are working in a very responsible profession which aims to maintain high standards.

26

Career prospects and job hunting

People go into this profession for different reasons. Many only want to spend a few years travelling and see teaching as the ideal way to earn some money along the way. Others have expectations of making it their long-term career. Sometimes, experienced teachers from the state sector decide that they want to try a different kind of teaching. Many want a career change, to leave their current employment in order to do something completely different. Then there are people like me, who fall into none of the above categories! Having finished university I still wasn't sure what I wanted to do, until one day I saw an advertisement for an EFL training course and thought I would send away for the information. That eventually resulted in my doing the course and starting my first job the Monday after it finished. The rest, as they say ...

This unit looks at two main areas – finding work, and developing career prospects. It is not intended to 'sell' the profession and make it seem more glamorous than it actually is. My honest opinion, shared by virtually every colleague I have worked with, is that it is a mixture of good and bad, like most jobs. The 'good' includes the opportunity to travel; meeting people from all over the world; working with many different colleagues; having a good degree of independence once you're inside your classroom; not being in a traditional '9 to 5' job; variety; usually longer holidays than other jobs; and working with young people – a fact appreciated more as you get older!

On the negative side – and I am speaking personally here, not everyone would agree with me – the money is generally not good. In fact, given that most teachers have graduate status, the salaries paid by some schools is scandalous, especially when you compare salaries with other graduate professions. Actual career prospects are also comparatively limited. In addition, too many teachers in certain countries have little security, having work only as long as there are enough students to teach.

Insight

Like all professions, teaching English as a foreign language has its positives and negatives. It is a varied and interesting profession, with the opportunity to travel and to meet all kinds of people. But the pay and conditions can be disappointing.

I am not here to make personal recommendations, but the one institute I will mention is now closed, so I feel I can talk about it without being accused of trying to influence readers. But I once had a truly rewarding time working at a teacher-training centre which also had ESL classes, where going to work every day was a pleasure. English International in San Francisco, owned and run by Jeff Mohamed and Deanne Manwaring, was a model of how this profession should be. Conditions were very comfortable. Resources were excellent and frequently upgraded. Staff were very well looked after; students were extremely happy, and everyone was treated with respect. It was the only occasion when I woke up in the morning happy to go to work. *I would like to think that there are many other institutes like this one in the world – and I have experienced other good schools, too – but I have worked in other places where conditions and resources were poor, prospects limited, and staff treated with little respect. The profession is improving, but still has some way to go before it can compare favourably with many other graduate professions, and I make no apologies for saying so. Still, the positive points are considerable, which is why I am still in the profession, seventeen years after starting my first job.

*There is now a website for English International which provides an excellent source of information for those in the profession, or entering it (see Unit 30).

The Cambridge ESOL CELTA course alone sees around 10,000 new teachers trained every year. Add to that figure those training on other courses, those without qualifications looking for work, and experienced teachers looking for work, and you will see that there is a lot of competition for jobs. It is extremely important, therefore, to make any job application as professional as possible, and to know what to expect at any interview.

Finding a job

Increasingly, people look for work on the internet (see Unit 30). Others will go through Recruitment Agencies (Unit 30), and others will see jobs advertised in newspapers – in the UK the Tuesday *Guardian* and Friday's *Times Educational Supplement* remain the best bets.

Many people will find their first work with chain schools – those with 'branches' in many different countries. Perhaps the most famous of these is International House. There are definite advantages to trying to find work at such a chain because any central application can lead you to one of many different 'branches', unless you are seeking work in one particular area. Normally, you apply to the central office. Some of these chains also run training courses (International House, for example, runs CELTA), and training with the chain can be advantageous when applying for work with them! Recruitment agencies will allow you to be considered for different schools in different countries, rather than one particular organization. Again, there is a 'central' office where you go through the application procedure, and many employers will seek staff through such agencies. Requirements and conditions will vary widely, but the agency can advise you on this.

The British Council is one of the largest employers in the profession, with schools in over fifty countries. They will usually, however, ask for some experience, but you can contact them directly and find out their up-to-date requirements (Unit 30 again).

Some teachers start out working for voluntary organizations. The Peace Corps in the United States and Voluntary Services Overseas in the UK are two examples, and their addresses are also in Unit 30. VSO places nearly 2,000 volunteers a year in more than fifty different countries. Volunteers receive a local salary, as well as flights, accommodation and insurance. The Peace Corps has placements in around seventy countries and they have a toll-free number in the United States to contact.

There are some restricting factors, however, which you need to be aware of before applying. If you are a European Union citizen applying for work outside the EU you may, depending on the country, require a university degree (usually in any subject), and need to gain a work permit and visa – not necessarily a formality. The same applies to United States citizens applying for work outside the United States. In addition, some schools have a policy of, or at least a preference for, employing teachers whose first language is English.

Applying for a job

Whichever of the above paths you choose, you will need to submit an application. This will involve having a résumé (CV), a covering letter if you are applying by post, and probably your educational and training certificates. You will then need to have an interview.

Your **résumé** needs to be professional in appearance, not handwritten, not too long, and containing only relevant information.

Tips

- ▶ Be honest!
- ▶ Don't over-sell yourself.
- ▶ Make the résumé easy to handle and to refer to.
- ▶ Include full contact details.
- ▶ Make sure all time-periods are covered.
- ▶ List your time in chronological order.

- ▶ Include all relevant qualifications and experience.
- ▶ Highlight any teaching experience you have.
- ▶ Specify which training course you did or are doing.
- ▶ Do not include irrelevant details.
- ▶ Mention any skills you possess, especially knowledge of foreign languages.
- ▶ Include names of referees – at least one of whom should be a professional referee.

Rightly or wrongly, many employers will insist on a photograph! Others will also want to know your age. If you do have to submit a photo, make sure it is a recent one and you look casually smart. I was once shown an application from a young man who had submitted a photo of himself wearing only a pair of shorts! That is not the way to present a professional image!

A **covering letter** should accompany your résumé. Schools and agencies receive many applications and I'm afraid that some applicants do not appear to put much effort into them judging by some of the ones I have seen.

Tips

- ▶ Make sure you **do** include a covering letter.
- ▶ Keep it brief.
- ▶ State clearly what job you are applying for and where you saw it advertised.
- ▶ If you have to hand-write, write neatly.
- ▶ Use proper paper, not something torn out of a notebook.
- ▶ Say why you want the job and why you should be considered for it, but don't over-do it!
- ▶ Proof-read your letter for spellings, etc.

Insight

It's worth spending time perfecting your CV / résumé and writing a neat covering letter specifically tailored to the job you are applying for. Always check and double check your application, especially for spellings.

The interview

All being well, you will be invited for an interview, either at the institute itself, or at a central office which handles all applications. I have interviewed many people over the years, and it has been interesting to see the different approaches adopted by interviewees – from the very formal, well-prepared candidate to the very casual, take-it-as-it-comes candidate. Neither is necessarily better than the other, but it is advisable to 'play safe' and follow certain guidelines.

Tips

▶ Arrive on time! It creates a bad first impression if you don't.
▶ Dress appropriately! At least look as if you have made an effort.
▶ Don't make it seem as if you are doing the employer a favour by coming to the interview – over confidence, or even arrogance, do not go down well.
▶ Answer questions fully and honestly.
▶ Come ready with questions of your own (see later).
▶ Know something about the institute you are applying to.
▶ Be relaxed and friendly in your manner; try to let your personality show through.
▶ Talk about your previous experience when asked; if you do not have any, talk about your training course and what it included and what your teaching experience was like.
▶ Show enthusiasm; make it seem as if you really *do* want the job!

Another important part of any interview is knowing what sorts of questions you might be asked, and what information you need to gain from the interviewer. Yes, you are the one who is looking for a job and being interviewed, but that doesn't mean that you should accept a job offer without knowing sufficient details about the job and the context.

Here are some typical questions that you should expect to be asked:

> *What types of class have you taught?* – including levels, sizes, age groups. If you have no experience, talk about the classes you taught on your training course, if you have done one.

> *What materials did you use?* – including course books and supplementary materials.

> *What did you think of the course book(s) you used?* – give a fair evaluation and avoid 'it was fantastic' or 'it was terrible' because all books have their pros and cons.

> *What level(s) do you prefer teaching and why?* – it is perfectly okay to have preferred levels (most teachers do), as long as you make it clear that you would be prepared to teach any level.

> *What different nationalities have you taught?* – be prepared to discuss the particular problems they encountered and how you helped them to deal with these problems. Avoid making any sweeping general statements about a particular nationality.

> *Why did you become a teacher?* – it's the obvious question to expect if you are applying for your first job, so be prepared with a good answer!

> *Why have you applied for this job?* – another obvious question to expect, so know something about the institute you have applied to and show an interest in the organization (a few questions of your own about its history would go down well!).

> *What are your future plans?* – the only answer to avoid here is something like 'Well, I only want this job for a few months because I want to get a better job once I have more experience!'

Why do you want to work in this particular country? / Do you speak the language? / What languages do you speak? – if you do not speak the language of the country you want to work in, show an interest in learning it.

What do you know about this school? – as mentioned earlier ... do your homework!

Do you have any questions? – have some ... but not too many!

So what questions should you ask? Well, a good interviewer should cover all the essential points, if they haven't been dealt with in any literature sent out to you before the interview. However, you shouldn't leave the interview without knowing the answers to the following questions – but if you need to ask all of these, then it suggests the interviewer didn't do a very good job!

- ▶ How many hours a week will I have to teach? (25 is a standard 'maximum')
- ▶ How will these hours be split? (maybe a 'block' or a 'split shift')
- ▶ Will I have to work evenings or weekends?
- ▶ Will all my teaching be in one building or will I have to travel?
- ▶ If travelling is involved, how much?
- ▶ What levels will I have to teach?
- ▶ What age group(s) will I have to teach? (this might mean teaching children)
- ▶ Do I have to be in the school even when I am not teaching?
- ▶ Am I paid for this 'non-contact' time?
- ▶ How much will I be paid?
- ▶ Will I be paid weekly or monthly?
- ▶ How will I be paid?
- ▶ Are national holidays paid?
- ▶ What holiday or vacation allowance do I get?
- ▶ When can I take my holiday/vacation?
- ▶ Is it paid or unpaid?
- ▶ Do I get sick pay?

- What's the cost of living? (what seems like a high or low salary might in real terms be different depending on the cost of living – in some countries a little money goes a long way, but in others a lot of money goes not very far at all)
- What taxes do I have to pay?
- What length of contract do I get and what notice is required on either side?
- Are my flights paid for?
- Does the school provide or give help finding accommodation?
- If the school provides it, who will I share with, and how far is the accommodation from the school?
- Does the school arrange or give help getting work permits, etc.?
- How well equipped is the school in terms of facilities and resources?
- How many other teachers are there?
- What in-service professional development does the school provide?

Do not sign any contract without reading it carefully and checking anything you are not sure about. Make sure you have a copy of that contract. If you do not feel comfortable with any aspect of the job or conditions, don't take it.

Insight

During your interview you should learn all about the job, the pay and conditions. Your interviewer will provide much of this information, but will also expect you to ask some pertinent questions, so be prepared.

But this is a two-way process, and many employers or agencies will tell you of teachers who have agreed to everything, then called at the last minute to say they have taken another job (or not called at all). This is highly unprofessional.

Once in a job, seek help and guidance from your Director of Studies as well as more experienced colleagues.

Prospects

For those who decide that they do want to make this their career, if only for a few years, there are ways to improve your pay and conditions and to do things other than only teaching. But there is more to it than that. You need to develop your own skills and professional awareness (see Unit 25) so that you keep in touch with developments in the profession, and new teaching ideas and theories. As well as following the tips mentioned in Unit 25, you need also to have an idea of possible career development opportunities.

The majority of teachers start out by doing a 'Certificate' course (e.g. Cambridge ESOL CELTA, or a Trinity College Certficate), but others will do a similar, less-recognized course. Some will find a teaching job despite having had no training! After a minimum of two years (maybe less with Trinity) of actual teaching experience, there is the option in most countries of doing a 'Diploma' course. This includes practical and written exams as well as observed and assessed teaching practice. Many centres will expect you to have the Certificate as well. In the United States the common 'next stage' is an MA in TESOL. The Diploma has little recognition in the US. MAs are becoming increasingly popular in Europe, too, as the demand for permanent posts increases.

By doing a 'post-Certificate' course and gaining an extra qualification, you are improving your prospects of work outside the classroom, as well as of a permanent contract in your own country. In the UK, for example, it is virtually impossible to get a long-term contract without the Diploma.

So what are the possibilities? Some teachers, like myself, move into teacher-training. To become a CELTA trainer, for example, you need several years of varied teaching experience, and then complete a trainer-training course. The training courses are thorough and carefully monitored but if you are successful you become an approved trainer.

Another possibility is writing! This does not necessarily mean writing books, but maybe articles for specialized ESL publications.

Presenting papers at conferences/conventions (e.g. the annual TESOL or IATEFL conferences/conventions) is a good experience to have, if you don't mind addressing an audience of a hundred people!

Teaching Business or other English for Special Purposes (ESP) classes can be more financially rewarding, as well as broadening your experience.

Administrative positions within a school are what many people eventually seek. Acting as an 'ADOS' (Assistant Director of Studies) leaves you equipped to become a 'DOS' (Director of Studies), in charge of the academic direction of the school and its academic staff.

Others, who start teaching adults (16+), choose to move into the field of teaching Young Learners; some go in the opposite direction.

A good move after you have some experience is to become an examiner. This will not earn you a lot of extra money, but it will give you good experience.

For the very ambitious (and brave!) your target might be to one day set up your own school … good luck!

Summary

In this unit we have seen some of the ways to find work; how best to apply for work; the essentials of an interview, including questions you will be asked and should ask yourself; the considerations before agreeing to take a job; and what prospects exist after you have some experience. Prospects and conditions are not fantastic, but the job itself often is – the actual experience of teaching students from all over the world, and the possibilities of travelling all over the world. As was emphasized in the last unit as well, there is a great need for professional behaviour from you, and a recognition of the need for professional development. There is also the hope that you yourself will be treated with professional respect, and rewarded in a way which your qualifications and background merit.

27

A guide to levels

A common question asked by new teachers is 'What does 'Intermediate' mean?' (or any other such term). And a common complaint is 'I have a mixed-level class.'

Labels to describe levels of students, such as 'intermediate' and 'elementary' are very broad and a class described as, say, 'elementary' could well include students who seem to be of different levels. It is important, then, to remember that such labels are more guides to the general and approximate level of students in a class, and that students may be better at one aspect of the language (e.g. speaking) than another (e.g. 'grammar'). You do need to pitch your classes to the general level of your class, adapting material as required, bearing in mind that one intermediate group of students may be 'stronger' than another.

Insight

Labels to identify different levels are very general and broad. They are a useful guide but all your groups will vary. Also, some students within a particular level may be stronger in certain areas, such as reading or grammar, and weaker in others, such as speaking or pronunciation.

A class which is in some way mixed-ability – and the bigger the class the more likely this is – will always be more difficult to teach. What you should avoid, if possible, is effectively teaching separate groups within the class, with different tasks, etc. If you do this, you will no longer be teaching and managing 'a class' but separate groups. This is both difficult and ultimately counter-productive. You should give extra support and guidance to the weaker students in the class (for example, when others are working together), but do not pitch the lessons to the needs of the lowest-level students within the class, because if you do that you will frustrate and handicap those whose level is generally higher and who are in the majority in the class.

Insight

Mixed-ability is a common issue in groups, especially large groups. It makes teaching more difficult and you may feel you are teaching different groups within the class. This requires more thought and preparation – and more flexibility.

Do not hesitate, for example, to stop group work even if some people have not finished a task. Students who have already finished something do not want to have to wait every time for all the others to finish. You have to allow a reasonable amount of time for a task, but to be prepared to say 'Okay, stop there' and then go through answers together as a class.

Be aware, too, that in some schools a system of 'continuous enrolment' operates. This means that new students can join an established class at any time (often this means any Monday). So the composition of your class will fluctuate as students leave and others arrive even though you are teaching a fixed course. You will find, as a result, that the overall level of a class can change to varying extents on a fairly regular basis. It is not ideal, but as teachers we have to adjust our lessons and plans accordingly. Have a look at Unit 20 for more on this.

The following guide should give you some idea of what a 'typical' student at a given level should be able to do at the end of his or her course. Six labels are defined here, but some schools may have further levels.

(NB: This is an adapted guide courtesy of SKOLA Schools, London.)

Beginner

A student finishing a Beginner's course should be able to do or know the following:

▶ the alphabet
▶ tell the time
▶ give simple information about himself/herself
▶ ask other people for simple information about himself/herself
▶ communicate in simple terms in everyday places
  e.g. ask for directions
      order a meal
      make suggestions
      buy items in a shop/store
▶ listen to and understand simple, natural speech and conversation, and complete simple tasks
▶ read some authentic texts such as timetables or brochures and find the information they need
▶ do simple writing tasks such as taking or leaving a message

Elementary

A student finishing an Elementary course should be able to do or know the following:

▶ talk about past time
▶ make future plans or arrangements
▶ describe people using simple adjectives
▶ describe places using simple adjectives
▶ express his / her hopes or intentions
▶ ask people to do something for them
▶ cope in simple social situations
  e.g. talk about the weather
      describe simple physical problems
      give advice

- listen to natural speech and conversation, and understand the gist of what is being said
- use authentic newspapers and find specific information required
- write simple letters and be able to link ideas together

Pre-Intermediate

A student finishing a Pre-Intermediate course should be able to do or know the following:

- talk about more abstract ideas
- participate in discussions and be able to interrupt politely, and take turns in communicating
- give a logical argument to support a view
- converse with relative ease in everyday social situations
- use formal and informal English in appropriate social situations
- help people with problems by making suggestions and giving advice
- listen to natural speech and conversation and begin to understand nuances and subtleties
- read most authentic texts and books for pleasure
- write letters, both formal and informal

Intermediate

A student finishing an Intermediate course should be able to do or know the following:

- express her or his opinion
- agree or disagree with other people's opinions
- express how he or she is feeling and their general emotions
- use conventional social language in greeting and welcoming people

- talk about hypothetical situations in the past and present
- talk about past habits
- speculate about the present and future
- listen to natural speech and conversation, and understand detail
- read authentic texts such as newspapers and magazines and understand the general meaning
- write letters to friends

Upper Intermediate

A student finishing an Upper Intermediate course should be able to do or know the following:

- use all the main structures and tenses in English with a high degree of accuracy
- begin to express sarcasm and irony
- use appropriate speech in a wide range of social situations
- understand and express humour
- argue an opinion with confidence
- follow lectures and other monologues and be able to take notes
- read most authentic texts and be able to understand them with relative ease
- write letters, compositions, reports, summaries

Advanced

A student completing an Advanced course should be able to do or know the following:

- express himself/herself easily
- integrate well with people whose first language is English
- vary stress and intonation to affect meaning
- follow and understand most forms of entertainment
- use a vocabulary of about 3,000 words
- study for a high-level qualification in English

28

Language glossary

This unit is designed to give you as simply as possible a guide to just some language terminology that you will need to recognize and use as you start out teaching. But do treat it as no more than a guide ... for more details, consult your grammar book.

Verb forms and tenses

Here are five examples of verbs, each with four forms.

	a	b	c	d	e
1	to go	to eat	to read	to work	to listen
2	went	ate	read	worked	listened
3	gone	eaten	read	worked	listened
4	going	eating	reading	working	listening

Form 1 = the infinitive
Form 2 = the past simple
Form 3 = the past participle
Form 4 = the present participle

Look first at examples **d** and **e**. You will see that forms 2 and 3 are identical; the verb ends *-ed* both times. Such verbs are called regular verbs, and they are very straightforward, except for some irregular spellings. For example, a verb such as *cry* in form 2 and 3 would become *cried*.

Examples **a**, **b** and **c** are different because the 2nd and 3rd forms do not follow this pattern, or even have a separate consistent pattern. These are **irregular verbs** and students hate them! There are many irregular verbs and each has its own pattern. Some have no variation at all (e.g. *to hit, hit, hit*), while the example above in **c** has the same form for 2 and 3, but different pronunciation!

You may wonder what the difference is between the past simple and past participle. The past participle (form 3, or 'verb 3') is used in conjunction with the auxiliary verb *has/have/had*. For example *I have* **eaten**, *She has* **gone**, whereas the past simple form would be *I* **ate** (*a sandwich earlier*), and *She* **went** (*home yesterday*).

With regular verbs there is no apparent difference – *I* **worked** (*yesterday*) and *I have* **worked** a lot recently. But the first case is form 2, and the second is form 3!

The infinitive presents its own problems to students. Consider these two sentences:

  I like **to watch** *TV.*   and   *I may* **watch** *TV later.*

The first sentence has the full *to*-infinitive form, the second does not (in this case because it follows a modal verb – *may*). Teachers and grammar books vary in how they label this second example. Some call it the 'infinitive without **to**'; others call it the 'bare infinitive'; while others call it the 'base verb'. Just be consistent in whatever terms you use.

Finally, students (and some teachers!) confuse the present participle with a gerund. Both have the *-ing* form, but the present participle (form 4 above) is a verb, while a gerund is a noun. Look at these two sentences:

  I'm eating my lunch.   I like swimming.

In the first case, the *-ing* form is a verb; it says what you are doing. In the second, it is a noun and *like* is the verb, just as in *I like books, I like music,* etc.

Higher-level students are usually very familiar with all these terms, but lower-level ones may not be, and you may not want to burden them with such terminology until their level of English is much better. You will find that some students will refer to verb 3, for example, maybe asking you 'What's verb 3 of sleep?' Now you know what they mean!

You need to know such terms when identifying **tenses**, and you also need to be aware of the difference between **tense** and **time**.

Task 1

Look at the following sentences and use a grammar book to help you. For each one, identify the **tense** and the **time** it refers to. Unit 19 will also help!

Example: *I left* the country last week – *past simple, referring to finished past action.*

1 I work every Saturday.
2 She leaves on Saturday.
3 I'm writing this sentence.
4 I'm meeting Matt later.
5 I was watching TV last night.
6 There was a good film on TV last night but **I had seen it before**.
7 I've been to Canada.
8 I've worked here for a year.
9 I'm sorry I'm so dirty, **I've been working on the car**.
10 That's the phone ... **I'll get it**.
11 I'll have finished by lunchtime.
12 I'll be leaving tomorrow.

Doing this task you should quickly become aware that very often in English the name of a tense does not relate to the time it refers to. This causes many problems as, for example, when a teacher asks 'What's the tense?' and a student replies 'Future' when she means the sentence is talking about the future. As far as future time is concerned, low-level students will often use *will* for any future reference believing that this is the future tense. Here, too, you must be careful. We do not have a single 'future tense' even though we refer, for example, to the 'future simple' tense. There are many different ways to express future time (and present time, and past time) in English and they do not all require the use of tenses. Consider *I used to smoke* and *I may leave later*. One refers to past time and one to future time, but neither is a tense.

That said, tenses are very important, and teachers who refuse to use terms such as 'future simple' are not really helping their students when most course books and grammar books recognize such labels. But you must always be clear when teaching to convey the time reference of any piece of language.

Back to the task ...

Key to task 1

1 present simple, referring to habitual action – so 'general time'
2 present simple, referring to future time
3 present progressive (also known as 'continuous'), referring to action in progress at the time of speaking – so present time.
4 present progressive, referring to future time
5 past progressive, referring to past time
6 past perfect simple, referring to earlier of two past events – so past time
7 present perfect simple, referring to (indefinite) past time
8 present perfect simple, referring to unfinished past state – so past and present time
9 present perfect progressive, referring to recent past time

10 future simple (or '*will* future'), referring to spontaneous decision (present time) about something you will immediately do (future time)

11 future perfect simple, referring to future time

12 future progressive, referring to future time

These are merely examples to demonstrate how, sometimes, the name of the tense does not necessarily refer to the time being described.

Tense forms

Present simple is the first form of the verb

Past simple is the second form of the verb

Past progressive is the verb *to be* in the past (*was/were*) + verb *-ing*

Past perfect simple is *had* + past participle

Past perfect progressive is *had been* + verb *-ing*

Present progressive is the verb *to be* in the present (*is/are/am*) + verb *-ing*

Present perfect simple is *have/has* + past participle

Present perfect progressive is *have/has* + been + verb *-ing*

Future simple is *will* + base verb

Future progressive is *will be* + verb *-ing*

Future perfect simple is *will have* + past participle

Future perfect progressive is *will have been* + verb *-ing*

In each case, of course, there is a subject at the start!

1st/2nd/3rd person

You also need to be aware of the rule regarding verbs in the 3rd person singular.

1st person	the person/people who is/are speaking (*I/We*)
2nd person	the person/people you are speaking to (*You/You*)
3rd person	the person/people you are speaking about (*He, She, It, They*)

With 3rd person singular (*He/She/It*) the verb takes *-s* or *-es*:

I work / You work / She works   I go / You go / He goes

Students at all levels have trouble remembering this rule.

Language terminology

Now let's look at a few other selected examples of language terminology.

Articles – *a/an* (indefinite), *the* (definite)

Adjectives – usually modify a noun: *big, expensive, blue, loud*

Adverbs – usually modify a verb: *quickly, efficiently, hard, well, successfully* (but *hard* can be an adverb or an adjective)

Auxiliary verbs – *be, do, have*

Clause – part of a sentence containing a subject and a verb

Common nouns – those that do not begin with a capital letter: *table, chair, pen*

Compound noun – a noun made up of two words: *address book, ashtray, door-handle*

Conditional sentences – (see below)

Conjunctions – joining words: *although, but, however*

Contraction – *I am = I'm   They are = They're*

Countable noun – a noun that can be counted: *pen(s), book(s), car(s)*

Functions – the 'reason' for speaking: *invitation, suggestion, apology*

Modal auxiliary verbs ('Modals') – *may, can, should, might, would* (see below)

Phrasal verb – verbs with more than one part which do not have a literal meaning: *to look up (a word in the dictionary)*

Possessive adjectives – *my, your, their*, etc.

Prepositions – e.g. *by, on, under, across, through, beside, in, out*, etc.

Pronouns – *I, we, You* are examples of subject pronouns
me, us, you are examples of object pronouns
mine, yours, hers are examples of possessive pronouns

Proper nouns – 'names': *Spain, Thomas, Everest*

Question Tags – e.g. *It's cold, **isn't it**? She's late, **isn't she**?*

Conditional sentences

Conditional sentences feature in all course books from around elementary level. There are, in fact, a great many types of conditional sentence and not just the three or four presented in most books. But given that you will have to teach the basic types at some stage, here is a simplistic guide to **conditionals 1, 2, 3** ... but bear in mind that this merely scratches the surface of this bit of language!

'Look at that sky. If it rains, we'll go back inside.'

The sky threatens rain, so the possibility of this is quite high. We are referring to a possible future happening. The definite consequence of rain would be the speakers going back inside. The first part of the sentence is '*If* + subject + present simple', and the second is 'subject + *will* + base verb'. This grammar with this use is the standard and simple type of **1st conditional sentence**.

'If I won the lottery this week, I'd quit my job.'

We are again referring to future time, but on this occasion, the possibility of the *if*-clause being met is remote, though still possible. Compared with the chance of rain in the first example, the contrast is clear. We have past simple in the first clause, and 'the modal verb (*would*) + base verb, in the second. This 'low possibility'/ hypothetical future is one type of **2nd conditional sentence**. Again, this is a simplistic and incomplete definition, but it's a start!

'If I hadn't eaten that undercooked meat, I wouldn't have become sick.'

... but I **did** eat the meat and I **did** become sick. So this sentence is set in the past and you cannot change what has happened. The *if* clause has the past perfect, and the main clause has 'a modal (*would*) + *have* + past participle'. This is a standard **3rd conditional sentence**.

You need to know this because students often ask about conditionals and, as I said, course books are very fond of these three conditionals, so you will teach them on a regular basis. Once you start teaching higher levels, you and your students will be exposed to the numerous variations of conditional which we use in our everyday spoken language.

Modal verbs

Finally, a further look at modal verbs. There are so many functions attached to modals, which again underlines the importance of illustrating meaning properly, and checking understanding. When students ask 'what does *must* mean?' there is no answer, as the following task should demonstrate.

Task 2

Look at the modals in these sentences and say what you think the function might be.

Example: 'You **must** do your homework' (teacher to student) – obligation

1 'Who's that?' 'It **must** be the delivery boy.'
2 '**Can** I go now?'
3 'I **can** speak five languages.'
4 'You **can't** smoke in this school.'
5 '**Could** you help me?'
6 'I **could** play squash for an hour when I was younger.'
7 'You **may** leave if you want.'
8 'It may rain later.'
9 'You **may** not go out tonight.' (parent to child)
10 '**May** it always be so!'

This task serves as a taster of the complexity of modals in terms of their various meanings and different shades of meaning. Which functions you teach will depend in part on the level of the class, but virtually all levels of course books feature uses of modal verbs.

Insight

Conditional sentences and modal verbs feature regularly in all course books and you will become very familiar with them. With higher levels you will begin to touch on the more complex conditional types and the wide variety of functions of modal verbs.

Back to the task...

Key to task 2

1 This is making a **deduction** – you ordered a pizza, there's someone at the door, so in all likelihood it is the pizza boy.
2 **Asking permission** to leave.
3 Talking about present **ability**.
4 **Prohibition.**
5 Making a **request.**
6 Talking about **past ability.**
7 **Giving permission.**
8 Expressing **possibility.**
9 **Prohibition / refusing a request.**
10 Expressing a **wish** (a rather specialized use of this modal).

Summary

In this unit we have defined just a few common language terms. Obviously, you should refer to a grammar book and the grammar guides in any course book for more detailed and contextualized information. But you do need to know terminology, especially when teaching higher-level students, as they are familiar with such terms. In other words, you need to have the *knowledge* before you can begin the planning of how to *teach* language. This is a gradual learning process. It is often this 'terminology' that most worries new teachers – all you can do is to learn it yourself as you go along. It's almost like learning a second language!.

29

A glossary of terms

Here is a list of selected terms that you will encounter in the profession, most of which have featured elsewhere in this book. Please note, however, that I could have listed 400 if I had wanted to, so this list is far from exhaustive!

aims Top alphabetically, and top in importance. Your aims are your goals, what you want to achieve and what you want your students to achieve, both in the lesson as a whole and in each part (stage) of a lesson. You can have main aims, and secondary aims. Try to think of your aims from the point of view of what students will do/learn, rather than what the teacher will do/teach.

appropriateness This covers a number of points. In terms of *language*, what we **say** may be technically correct, but not appropriate to the context. It may be too formal, for example. In terms of *material*, what we ask our students to do/read/listen to, etc. must be appropriate according to the culture and background of the group, as well as their age, sex, general interests, the course and the lesson aims.

authentic Authentic material is real-life material, such as a newspaper or brochure. It has not been altered for classroom use, but the accompanying tasks will make it appropriate for the level and needs of the class. Authentic language is real, unscripted and ungraded language, such as a news broadcast from the radio.

clarification This is when you want to check that students have understood meaning (see **concept questions** and **timelines**), or when you need to go over something which has not been understood. It is also the checking of instructions and tasks. Avoid questions like 'Do you understand?' because this is not an effective way to clarify.

closed pairs This is when students work in pairs with someone sitting directly next to them (c/f open pairs)

concept questions One of the best ways to clarify/check that students have understood an item of language is to ask concept questions. These are short questions or prompts, usually requiring very short and simple answers. They check understanding of the concept (meaning) of language. When checking understanding of structures within a sentence, avoid using the structure in your concept questions.

contractions When the subject and auxiliary verb are 'joined', e.g. *She's* (*She is*).

controlled practice When students do a practice activity where the nature of the activity means there is a tight control over the language that they use. The teacher restricts the students' language so that the target language is used a lot. Written gap-fills are a good example.

context The context is the situation, and the situation provides meaning. Context could be in a text, a recording, pictures, spoken scenario from the teacher, etc. Language must have context because language must have meaning.

diagnostic A diagnostic test is to find out the level of a student; how much she knows. Within a lesson, a diagnostic task (test teach test) is to see how much students already know about a piece of language being focused on in your lesson.

....

drilling This is when students repeat a piece of language with the aim of pronouncing it correctly and naturally. They do this having first heard a model to copy. *Choral* drilling is when they all say it together (confidence-building), and *individual* drilling is when they say it by themselves. There are different types of drill, but the basic repetition drill is probably the most common type used by teachers. (See also front chaining.)

....

eliciting Try to get the students to tell you as much as possible, rather than you telling them everything. Ask them questions, find out what they already know, involve them. It relates to keeping the students actively involved in the lesson and participating fully.

....

feedback (plenary) If students have done a task together, get some reaction afterwards as a class. For example, if they have been discussing preferred holiday destinations, find out afterwards what some of them decided. If students have been working on an exercise together, you have to go through the answers with the class afterwards and clarify as required. 'Plenary' is 'whole class feedback'.

....

front chaining/back chaining When drilling a long or otherwise difficult sentence, it can help students if you 'break it down' from the *front* or the *back*. For example: 'I'm getting used to driving on the left' becomes 'on the left'... 'to driving on the left'... 'getting used to driving on the left' ... 'I'm getting used to driving on the left' (*back chaining*). Each part is drilled in turn with the whole sentence being repeated at the end.

....

function There is always a reason for saying something – all speech has a *function*. Examples of functions are invitation, suggestion, apology, refusal, criticism, praise, complaint, deduction, request, offer, giving permission and order. Functions can be illustrated via context.

gist When reading a text or listening to a recording, students can be asked to listen for the *gist* – what the text or recording is about; the general sense or meaning of it.

illustrating meaning Rather than *explaining* what something means, teachers should illustrate meaning in some way – via context, visuals, mime, realia, etc. In other words, the teacher should show meaning, not explain it. This is also known as conveying meaning.

L1 The student's first language or 'mother tongue'.

language grading The language teachers use in the classroom must be of a level which will be understood by the students, without it becoming overly simple. Obviously, the lower the level of the students, the more graded the teacher's language has to be. Speaking more slowly is not sufficient if the language being used is too difficult to understand.

lexis Another word for *vocabulary*.

mingling When students get up and move around (as with a 'Find someone who ...' exercise). With very large classes, and especially when they are sitting behind desks, mingling is not a realistic option.

model sentence This is a sentence in context which includes a stucture which the teacher wishes to focus on. It allows the structure to be looked at within a meaningful sentence rather than in isolation. For example: *I'm leaving tomorrow morning on the first flight* contains 'subject + *to be* + verb-*ing*' (present progressive). It is sometimes also known as a marker sentence.

monitoring When students are working together, the teacher should go round as best she can and observe their work and provide help and support. Monitoring also involves 'keeping an eye' on the class, looking to see if someone has finished a task, for example. Even when the class and teacher are working together, the teacher should maintain eye contact with the students and observe reactions and problems. Watching and reacting is a key teaching skill.

monolingual classes Classes where all the students are of the same nationality. Unless you are teaching in an English-speaking country, most classes you teach will be of this type.

MPF The *meaning*, *pronunciation* and *form* of a piece of language.

multilingual classes Classes with more than one nationality.

open pairs If one student interacts with another student in the room, but not one sitting next to them, this is *open pairs*. This might occur, for example, when one student is asked by the teacher to ask a question of another student in the room.

productive skills Speaking and Writing – where the students must *produce*.

receptive skills Listening and Reading – where students *receive* and comprehend.

rapport Teachers need to build a good relationship with their students, but also foster good relations between the students. This is rapport. A good classroom atmosphere and good relations between all in the class is essential.

schwa The only sound in the language with its own name, the schwa / ə / is the most common sound in English.

situational presentation Typically, this is when the teacher provides a situation (**context**) in order to focus on an item of language contained within a model sentence. It is a relatively teacher-centred means of introducing language, but students are involved through the teacher eliciting from them in order to build the context.

scan reading Reading in order to find specific information without needing to focus on or understand other parts of the text.

skim reading Reading for overall gist.

stage A stage in a lesson is a separate part of it. Each stage should have its own aim (objective).

STT Student Talking Time.

structure Some sentences will have a fixed grammatical structure (invariable) which may be a tense (*I'll have gone* by 3pm contains 'subject + *will have* + past participle' = future perfect simple); or maybe not (*I used to smoke* contains 'subject + *used to* + base verb'. When asking concept questions to check understanding, avoid using the structure in the question.

target language This is the language being focused on in a lesson.

test teach test This is a way of focusing on language in a lesson which first involves some diagnostic task; then the teacher clarifies meaning; then the students do practice tasks.

timelines The visual representation of time; very useful with tenses.

TTT Teacher Talk Time – which shouldn't be unnecessarily high!

warmers Short activities used at the start of a lesson which are not necessarily **related** to what is to follow. They are useful to wake a class up, give latecomers more time to arrive, etc.

Such activities could also be used as fillers when you have time on your hands at the end of your lesson, or during a lesson to vary the pace. Activities can include simple tasks like 'Think of ten adjectives beginning with c'; or 'Find out what everyone in the room had for dinner last night.'

....

weak forms Typically these are vowel sounds in unstressed syllables. In 'Can you help me?', the word can is pronounced /kən/.

....

30

Some useful addresses

These are just a few selected addresses you might find useful now,
or later.

United Kingdom

Cambridge ESOL
1 Hills Road
Cambridge
CB1 2EU
England
tel: 01223 553311

IATEFL (International Association of Teachers of English as a
Darwin College
University of Kent
Canterbury
Kent
CT2 7NY
tel: 01227 276528
website: http://www.iatefl.org

KELTIC Bookshop
154 Southampton Row
London
London WCIB 5JX
England
tel: 020 7229 8560

Trinity College
London External Exam Board
16 Park Crescent
London
W1N 4AH
England
tel: 020 7323 2328

Saxoncourt Recruitment (Shane Schools)
59 South Moulton Street
London
W1Y 1HH
England
tel: 020 7499 8533

English Worldwide
The Italian Building
Dockhead
London
SE1 2BS
England
tel: 020 7252 1402

VSO (Voluntary Services Overseas)
317 Putney Bridge Road
London
SW15 2PN
England
tel: 020 8780 7527

ARELS (Association of Recognised English Language Services)
2 Pontypool Place
Valentine Place
London
SE1 8QF
England
tel: 020 7242 3136

British Council
10 Spring Gardens
London
SW1A 2BN
England
website: http://www.britishcouncil.org/jobs

EL Gazette / EL Prospects
Dilke House
1 Malet Street
London
WC1E 7JA
England
tel: 020 7255 1969

United States

JET (Japan Exchange and Teaching) Program
Japanese Embassy
2520 Massachusetts Ave NW
Washington, DC 20008
USA
tel: 202 939 6722

Peace Corps
Room 8500
1990 K St NW
PO Box 941
Washington, DC 20526
USA
tel: 202 606 3780

TESOL (Teaching of English to Speakers of Other Languages)
700 South Washington Street
Suite 200
Alexandria
Virginia 22314
USA

tel: 703 836 0774
website: http://www.tesol.org

American Language Academy
1401 Rockville
MD 20852 A080
USA

TESOL Placement Agency
address as above

ECIS (European Council of International Schools) – North
America
105 Tuxford Terrace
Basking Ridge
New Jersey 07920
USA
tel: 1 908 903 0552

AASA (Association of American Schools in South America)
14750 NW 77 Court
Suite 210
Miami Lakes
Florida 33016
USA

Internet sites

Please note that I have been unable to check each of these addresses
personally, but each has come recommended! Otherwise, do a
search for 'efl' / 'esl' / 'tefl' / 'tesol' and you are sure to get a huge
selection of sites!

www.english-international.com (especially recommended to
check out)
www.eslcafe.com

www.aaaefl.co.uk
www.jobs.edunet.com
www.globalesl.net
www.britishcouncil.org/jobs
www.ihworld.com
www.tefl.net
www.tefl.com
www.jobs.tes.co.uk
www.educationunlimited.co.uk/tefl
www.saxoncourt.com
www.dictionary.com

Index

Note: references are to units followed by their sections or tasks (e.g. 13:1).

Credits